A joy to read, this book has a pra[ ] the world's biggest challenges — wate[ ] decide if you need to read more.

M000233164

The Environment Institute
The University of Adelaide, Australia

Disruptive and provocative, Zetland is the Ben Franklin of water. He hurls common sense against professional aristocrats to ensure our priceless liquid asset belongs, democratically, to 7 billion amateurs like you and me.

James Workman, Author
Heart of Dryness

Incentives matter. Zetland provides engaging narratives on the interaction of rules, institutions and people that communicate economics ideas far better than mass media and popular culture do.

Jay Wetmore, P.E., past President
American Society of Civil Engineers (MN)

With economics at the centre of present-day international water diplomacy of national governments, this book could hardly be more timely. David Zetland touches upon the current issues of water resources management and puts them in an economic context that sheds light beyond the obvious and well-trodden pathways towards sustainable development.

Michael van der Valk, Hydrologist and Scientific Secretary
The Netherlands National Committee IHP-HWRP (UNESCO & WMO)

Bold, provocative and refreshing — Zetland brings common sense to the water scarcity discussion.

Spreck Rosekrans, Senior Analyst
Environmental Defense Fund

With his straight-forward writing style and mastery of the subject, Dr. Zetland delivers an accessible interpretation of how economics can (or should) impact water policy.

Richard Rauschmeier, Financial Examiner
Division of Ratepayer Advocates, Water Branch
California Public Utilities Commission

Incentives matter. David Zetland explains why in his plain-speaking tutorial book on water. It informed me, and I thought I knew all this stuff already. If you want to understand how water should be managed, read *The End of Abundance*.

John F. Raffensperger, Senior Lecturer
Management Science, University of Canterbury

This book is impressive! Zetland has been able to capture the complexity of water without confusing the reader. This is a clear cogent "reveal" of a very difficult economic topic and yet simultaneously quite easy to enjoy as a book.

Robert O'Donnell, General Manager
AquaNexus

Water is the most precious commodity there is, and yet, most of us don't think much about it. Its availability in seemingly unlimited quantities, and at almost no cost, just by turning on the tap. But the age of water abundance is coming to an end, as David Zetland explains. Unlike many authors in this genre, Zetland does not try to terrify us with apocalyptic scenarios of water wars and mass starvation. Rather, writing in an engaging and informal style, he gives us a realistic assessment of the impending age of water scarcity and how we will need to change our ways to deal with it. Read this book — you'll never think the same way about water again!

John Quiggin, Australian Research Council Federation Fellow
University of Queensland

David Zetland has written a very informative, accessible and necessary book which explains the reality of water scarcity and the imperative of applying sound economics and local control to what was previously the exclusive preserve of engineers and politicians. In fact, it is a book that every water engineer and local politician should read to their benefit and that of their customers and citizens.

G. Tracy Mehan, III, former Assistant Administrator for Water
US Environmental Protection Agency

One of the biggest challenges faced by the water industry is simply poor public understanding of the issues we face, and a paucity of effective public education vehicles regarding water availability and consumption. If more people better understood the actual challenges and issues of global water resource management, we would have fewer problems. David Zetland's book should be a significant contribution towards meeting this need — by carefully assessing, through the lens of economic theory, the water choices and actions that we all participate in every day.

Steve Maxwell, Managing Director
TechKNOWLEDGEy Strategic Group
Author of *The Future of Water*
Publisher of the annual *Water Market Review*

At a time of growing concerns about the availability of fresh water world wide, markets can play an important role in more effective allocation and management of this scarce and valuable resource. David Zetland's *End of Abundance* introduces economics into everyday decision making about water in an original and engaging way. The material is valuable not only for policy makers, but for each of us in better understanding the challenges and potential solutions to a growing water crisis.

Gary D. Libecap, Donald Bren Distinguished Professor
Donald Bren School of Environmental Science & Management
Professor of Economics, University of California, Santa Barbara
Pitt Professor, Economics Faculty, Cambridge University
Research Associate, National Bureau of Economic Research
Sherm and Marge Telleen Research Fellow, Hoover Institution
Senior Fellow, Property and Environment Research Center

A primer for talking about the fundamental elements of water management: scarcity, allocation, value.

Paul W. Lander, PhD, LEED AP
Lecturer, Geography & Sustainable Practices Program, University of Colorado
Chair, ASLA Water Conservation Network & AWWA WaterWiser Committees

David Zetland understands and explains that efforts at sustainable water management are well-served by a no-nonsense economic analysis of overuse and pollution. Amid the commentary it is incentives that matter most.

Piet Klop, Senior Fellow
World Resources Institute

Zetland writes with a lively, engaging style that conveys the urgency of thinking differently about water policies, and communicates both the efficiency and the humanity of market-based water policies and the innovations that such policies would encourage.

Lynne Kiesling, Distinguished Senior Lecturer
Northwestern University and Knowledge Problem

There are plenty of articles and books on water scarcity but few offer the insight and economical framework that are necessary to understand and address this scarcity. *The End of Abundance* is a significant contribution to the contemporary discourse on water management and is a must read by anyone who cares about water or wants to learn about the issues. The book is refreshing in its candor and irrespective of whether you agree with all of its prescriptions, it is informative, factual and a delight to read.

Shahram Javey, Ph.D
Founder and CEO of Aquacue, Inc.

The End of Abundance is an enthralling and witty account of a serious warning for all of us. Either we accept paying more for the water we consume, or else we let politicians do the daunting of job of allocating scarce water resources. Blogger and economist Zetland poses the right choices and suggests how to turn wishful thinking into viable outcomes.

Alberto Garrido, Director and Professor
Research Centre for the Management of Agricultural and Environmental Risks
Department of Agricultural Economics and Social Sciences
Universidad Politécnica de Madrid

The book is full of interesting new considerations, sharp writing and innovative thinking. Although I do not agree with everything David says, I appreciate his straightforwardness in the debate on sustainable water use. Well worth reading to get David's perspective on the water world.

Carlo C. Galli, Technical & Strategic Adviser
Water Resources, Nestlé

There is no scarcity of books describing the challenges the United States and nations across the globe face in managing water to meet today's needs and future demands. The good news is that effective solutions exist. The better news is that David Zetland has written a book that presents solutions to these water challenges that protect public health, ensure ecological vitality, and support economic growth. He delivers the rational way forward in a style and language that the public as well as public officials — and if we are lucky, politicians! — can understand and act on.

Michael Deane, Executive Director
National Association of Water Companies

I've been in water since 1993 and have looked hard for an economist who really understands water and its markets. David Zetland is the find, and I'm so thankful that he continues his blog and his writing. We MUST move to smart market based management of our water or we will continue to have shortages. We now have solid real models that show that markets work and politics — so far as water management — do not.

Ric Davidge, MPA, Chairman
AQUEOUS International, Inc.

David helped me understand the importance of applying market-based pricing to address water scarcity. Not an easy task, but he does so convincingly, and places it in the context of today's complex social and political realities. An engaging read for anyone interested in water.

Terry A. Clark, AICP, PMP, Senior Consultant
Cardno ENTRIX

The most thoroughly researched treatise on water economics I've ever read. *The End of Abundance* sets a precedent and creates a water/road map for world water managers. David manages to maintain a wry sense of humor inside a sobering exploration of population growth, waste ignorance, unbridled water withdrawal, pure greed, entitlement and blatant disregard for the very substance that makes up 80 percent of our bodies. Demand exceeds supply in many parts of the world, and it will here also unless we embrace aguanomics to intelligently use of our most precious resource. I'm making this mandatory reading for my staff... they need to get this.

Michael Christian, CEO and President
American Hydroponics

An economist with a sense of humor examines the dark clouds of California's pending hydrological apocalypse and finds a silver lining.

Lloyd Carter, President
California Save Our Streams Council
Award-winning journalist/blogger
who has written about California water issues since 1969

If David Zetland's *End of Abundance* is like his aguanomics blog — witty, intelligent, iconoclastic, unrepentant, and provocative — then it's going to be quite a ride.

Michael E. Campana, Professor and President
Hydrogeology and Water Resources, Oregon State University
American Water Resources Association

This is not a text for those seeking a rehash of the standard "water wars" catechism. Zetland outlines a fresh, creative approach to allocating a valuable resource in regions with competing demands. Importantly, his vision does not entail an expensive and sluggish command-and-control bureaucracy coddling whatever class of water users happen to enjoy momentary political favor. Protecting our environment, growing our food, and supplying our cities has always required the ingenuity of a free people. It is time we realized that in managing our water.

Philip Bowles, President
Bowles Farming Company

Seldom in my experience has any politician ever stood up and said "There is a principle here, and that principle is worth losing an election over." *The End of Abundance* offers principles on how to balance supply and demand in the provision of water to the world and suggests that voters will accept them. Now all we need are some brave politicians.

Max Borchardt, Australia Editor
Global Water Intelligence

The End of Abundance is a unique and exemplary book. It's a treasure chest of economic insights on water scarcity — a vitally important policy problem where economic wisdom is sorely needed. Economics is all about choices that people make under conditions of scarcity. This book is highly readable and well-informed, provides many real-world examples, suggests solutions, and clearly explains key concepts to non-economists. Policymakers, managers, engineers and concerned citizens should read it!

Eran Binenbaum, Lecturer and Technology Transfer Economist
University of Adelaide

The End of Abundance is a healthily provocative wake up-call. The book challenges the status quo and the most entrenched preconceived ideas to lead us to the realization that water managers facing scarcity can no longer solely focus on ensuring water supply and system management but must create the dynamic leading to the actual management of water itself. David suggests a profound shift of perspective that brings a new dimension to the water world: economics.

Laurent Auguste, President and CEO
Veolia Water Americas

The End
of
Abundance

economic solutions to water scarcity

David Zetland

Aguanomics Press
Amsterdam ~ Mission Viejo

2011

Cover design by Nicholas Newton (nic_newton@yahoo.co.uk) $\sim$ photo of
Death Valley, California (© 2008 David Zetland) $\sim$ photo of author (© 2009
Hugh Zetland) $\sim$ interior typeset in Helvetica with LATEX $\sim$ copy-edited by
Sheri Gordon (shegordon@gmail.com). Version 1.2 (Oct 2011).

ATTN: Quantity discounts are available for orders of 20 or more copies. For
information, please contact the author at dzetland@gmail.com.

Visit www.endofabundance.com for commentary, resources and updates.

Publisher's Cataloging in Publication
Zetland, David

The end of abundance: economic solutions to water scarcity / David Zetland
— 1st ed.
p.   cm.
Summary: "An analysis of how management institutions may fail to cope
with freshwater scarcity and how to reform them."—Provided by publisher.
Includes index.

ISBN-13: 978-0615469737   LCCN: 2011905833

1. Water resources development — Economic aspects 2. Water resources
development — Government policy I. Title
HD1691.Z48 2011

Contents

II Social water choices   133

7 Managers and politicians   139

Managers and bureaucrats may make decisions and policies affecting collective goods for their own benefit — not the benefit of constituents. Community oversight and/or benchmarking outcomes can reduce abuses.

8 Dams, pipes and pumps   157

Water infrastructure users like to shift costs to others. Misplaced and mispriced infrastructure can encourage wasteful water use and distort development for a long time. Fights over infrastructure increase with scarcity.

9 Water and the environment   175

Environmental water flows are increasingly valuable. Special interests support policies that ignore values, waste water, and harm the environment. Technology will not save a misvalued environment.

10 Weather and climate change   189

Human adaptation can reduce harm from bad weather and climate change. Markets and prices make it easier to implement robust, decentralized systems of protection.

List of Tables

List of Figures

Prologue

Marlowe leaned against the Packard and looked at his watch.[1]

Christ. She's taking her time.

He lit another cigarette. The smoke blew downtown. They had to get moving.

She ran up, out of breath.

"I got it! Frank won't notice it's gone for a few hours."

"That's not what worries me, babe. We've got to get to San Pedro before the *Esmeralda* leaves for Shanghai."

They drove away, taking side streets and ignoring most stop signs. The freeway wasn't far.

"Philip — Do you think we'll make it?"

"Marlowe, sugar. Only my mother calls me Philip...San Pedro usually takes 15 minutes."

Marlowe hit the gas as they approached the freeway, but something was wrong.

Cars everywhere — front and back, stretching in every direction.

"Heavens! Where did these cars come from? How are we going to make it?"

"You got me kid. I've never seen anything like it."

"Where are these people going? We're in a hurry! Can't we get around them?"

"I doubt it. Even the cops are stuck. They never planned on having so many cars on the road at once. Remember the billboards? They promised abundant roads for driving freedom."

"But we're going to miss the boat...and my sister's in trouble!"

"Sweetheart, the End of Abundance is gonna put a lot of people in a world of hurt."

---

[1] With apologies to Mr. Chandler.

2

The beginning of the end

Water shortages are caused by water management institutions that ignore scarcity. Economic tools can efficiently and fairly manage scarce water. Demand for water depends on technologies, tastes and prices.

In the drought year of 2009, San Diego faced a water shortage. Local water managers needed total demand to fall by 20 percent, so they ordered each household to cut its consumption by 20 percent below historic levels. This solution sounded good on paper, but it failed to consider that some people had been conserving water for years. The proposed rule would penalize water misers for consuming volumes that water wasters could use without facing penalties.

The public outcry surprised managers and politicians. They replaced the 20 percent plan with a regulation on lawn watering and used more water from storage. Crisis was averted, but the result failed to deliver reliability, efficiency, or fairness. San Diego's water managers claimed that they did their best in extreme conditions, but San Diego has struggled with water scarcity since 1946. They were saved in 1977 and 1992. They were saved in 2009. Will they always be saved?

These struggles are showing up more often in more places. They are not the result of incompetent water managers. They are the result of managers and their political overseers using outdated or inappropriate institutions (customs, rules and laws) that assume demands must be met, abundant supplies can always be found, and a functional and efficient system needs only strong pipes and breakeven revenues. Those institutions may not consider how the value of water varies with use, reconcile historic rights with current notions of fairness or efficiency, or appreciate the social and environmental costs of ad-hoc rationing in shortage.

This book uses economic tools to tackle the end of abundance and manage the scarcity that results from demand exceeding supply. These tools vary from the familiar (markets and prices) to the subtle (behavioral cues, property rights, and community associations). In all cases, they are meant to decentralize decisions, expand choices for individuals, and improve the way our societies manage water. The tools use economics because scarcity lies at the heart of economic thought and economists have a long history of managing scarcity to produce happy individuals and successful nations.[2]

We'll start by looking at how poor economics ended the abundance that good engineering gave us.

Scarcity to abundance to scarcity

When the well's dry, we know the worth of water.
—Benjamin Franklin, *The Way to Wealth* (1758)

Nothing is more useful than water: but it will purchase scarce any thing; scarce any thing can be had in exchange for it. A diamond, on the contrary, has scarce any value in use; but a very great quantity of other goods may frequently be had in exchange for it.
—Adam Smith, *The Wealth of Nations* (1776)

Water, water, everywhere,
Nor any drop to drink.
—Samuel Taylor Coleridge, *Rime of the Ancient Mariner* (1798)

Coleridge may have been talking about seawater, but freshwater in the late 18th century was often just as unsafe to drink. Franklin spoke from a different perspective; he worried about running out of limited clean water. Smith confounded the two ideas in his observation that clean water had a high intrinsic value but little value in comparison with diamonds. But Smith lived in Scotland, a place that's still known for its voluminous freshwater supply — and the whiskies that are made with it.

Smith's Diamond-Water Paradox (diamonds with no intrinsic value are valuable in exchange but useful water is not) can be unraveled by adding the dimension of scarcity. Diamonds are valuable because they are scarce; water is not when it is abundant. Coleridge and Franklin spoke of the value of scarce clean water, but Smith was more familiar with abundant clean water.

---

[2]Economists are not alone. Lawyers, anthropologists, sociologists, psychologists, political scientists and others have useful opinions, and I'll try to include them.

The battle to replace unreliable, unsanitary supplies with abundant, clean water began with 19th century networks for distributing drinking water and removing wastewater. Boston (Franklin's birthplace) had piped water in 1796 and sanitary sewers in 1833. London's campaign for clean drinking water and sewage disposal began soon after the cholera outbreak of 1854 and Great Stink of 1858. Napoleon launched a campaign against filthy open drains and dwindling drinking water supplies. Fifty years later, Paris enjoyed modern drinking water and sewage networks.

The end of the 19th century gave two answers to the Diamond-Water Paradox. Economists had gone through the "marginal revolution" of understanding how people gave high values to a few units of a good but lower values to additional units of that good. These values "on the margin" reflect the simple idea that we value the first sip of water more than the fifth liter. But even as economists "solved" the paradox, engineers revived it. Their successes delivered abundant clean water at affordable prices. In the 20th century, we had so much of this useful fluid that we found new ways to use it. Our notions of "enough" changed from enough to drink to enough to fill a pool, from enough to grow food to enough for the lawn, from enough for a bath to enough for a fishery. Until enough wasn't enough. In other words, the engineering triumph of increased supply was not accompanied by an economic triumph in restraining demand. When demand exceeded supply, scarcity replaced our hard-won abundance. The diamond-water paradox returned in a different form: we couldn't use prices or markets to manage scarce water because our existing institutions took abundant water for granted.

Managing water scarcity with different tools

The end of abundance cannot be blamed on any individual or group. It results from good intentions, changing circumstances, and outdated practices. It begins when water managers are told to bring abundant water to all who demand it. They usually succeed in building systems that deliver water and prosperity to urban, agricultural and industrial customers.

But then something goes wrong and supplies grow tight. Lawns dry out, farmland goes bare and schools close. Water systems designed for physical interruptions, broken pipes or drought cannot ration scarce water among competing demands. Scarcity turns to shortage as customers clamor for the water they *need*. The typical responses (emergency deliveries from local or imported sources) only make the next crisis more likely.

Can shortages be blamed on droughts? No. They result when demand exceeds supply for longer than water managers' talents and resources. Shortages can be ended much more quickly by a change of incentives than supply-side actions to build a desalination plant or transfer water from neighbors who probably can't spare a drop.

As I write (in early 2011), California is experiencing its heaviest precipitation in years, Australian reservoirs are spilling excesses, and the Mississippi river is flooding nearby farmlands. Does that mean that Californians, Australians and other people in water-stressed areas can ignore this book? No. First, drought will probably return to California, as it has in the past. The tools for managing scarcity will be useful when that happens. Second, tools that handle droughts can also work with floods. Robust institutions can allocate dry land just as well as they allocate scarce water.

The end of abundance means the supply side/cost recovery model of water management no longer delivers the results we want, but that model still dominates the business — from California to China, Florida to Fiji — and it will cause trouble until we change the way we manage water. Economics offers an alternative focus on balancing supply and demand — whether there's too much supply or too much demand. This book explains how to gain and maintain that balance using economic tools to allocate scarce water in a way that minimizes costs, maximizes value and reflects local values.

These changes do not require new skills of water managers or other technocrats who are efficient at running systems. They require changes in the underpinnings of the system, so that economic incentives are integrated into the management of scarce water. Those changes need to be implemented with the leadership and cooperation of political and social leaders. Factions that benefit from the status quo will oppose changes, but they can be neutralized by going deeper than rules, to change institutions that affect all of us.

Local institutions manage local water

An "institution" is a set of informal norms and formal rules that are as intuitive to insiders as they are complex to outsiders. The institution of marriage, for example, varies by location and culture. Organizations and institutions are not the same: Harvard University is an organization providing education according to many institutional rules and norms.

Most institutions are difficult to describe, highly adapted to local conditions, and effective in balancing competing interests. For the same reasons, institutions can block change or the adoption of ideas from other places.

Institutions can be classified in four layers. The deepest layer includes culture and other informal norms of behavior that evolve over centuries. The next layer includes basic rules such as constitutions that are fixed for decades or change very slowly. The third layer contains rules and regulations that may last for years but are often the subject of political and regulatory modification. The fourth layer is barely fixed; it consists of our choices of how to allocate resources in markets or organizations.

Institutions can reduce transaction costs (the time and expense involved in finding, negotiating and enforcing exchanges in markets) by providing grounds for agreement. Dutch water boards (*waterschappen*), for example, have been managing water quality, quantity and infrastructure since the 13th century. In Spain, irrigators in some regions use *tribunals de las aguas* (water courts) that date from the Moorish era to manage disputes among irrigators over water supplies. The tribunals' public hearings created a useful tradition of fair dealing; their oral nature incorporates changing ideals while respecting the wisdom of the past.

But institutions can also raise transaction costs and lower productivity. A market for trading water in an area without restrictions on groundwater use, for example, will stress groundwater resources if sellers increase groundwater extractions to replace exported surface waters.

As a rule, institutions for managing water are better at dealing with risk if they are decentralized, voluntary and frequently updated, but it's difficult to convince people to discard known institutions for promises of greater efficiency or fairness. Institutions create valuable property rights, help people plan for the future, and often create work for people who want to keep their jobs. This book takes the deepest two layers of institutions (culture and constitutions) for granted as it suggests reforms to mechanisms that date from a past of abundant freshwater. More important, it assumes that the best solutions for water scarcity are local solutions.

That's because local conditions and customs are more important in water management than in any other area of human activity — more than sports, religion, manufacturing, politics, real estate, you-name-it. This perspective is not just "think global, act local" rhetoric. It reflects water's local origins and the difficulty of transporting water over long distances. "Local" can mean anything from the pond in your backyard to the catchment of the Amazon River; scale is not as important as managing waters that mingle. Good water management requires that one understand local customs and solutions while looking for outside ideas that can be modified and implemented with a creativity that drives at the goal while bending to social, economic and political realities. Yes, waters in one location will be affected by distant management decisions, but we are going to identify good policies first and then work on removing the barriers to their implementation.

This book describes water policies across many topics and how some topics — agricultural and environmental water, for example — overlap and conflict. These descriptions may not match your knowledge, but that's not the point. I hope to encourage you to think differently about how we manage water. You may be an engineer, politician, farmer, environmentalist or concerned citizen. No matter who you are, where you live, or what you know, I've tried to explain how institutions for managing water succeed or fail, what damages may result, and how economic ideas can improve institutions. Hopefully, you will be able to combine these ideas with your own experience to create an improved hybrid. At the same time, the simple framework here should allow readers from India, Australia, Holland or the US to speak on common themes while allowing for adaptations to local tastes.

Ice cubes, waterfalls and civilization

Before we move on, we need to cover some basic scientific facts about physical water. A molecule of water consists of two hydrogen atoms bonded with an oxygen atom. As a molecule, H_2O has unusual characteristics. It can exist as a gas, fluid or solid at relatively mild temperatures. As ice, solid water is lighter than liquid water. That's not just handy for ice-skating on frozen ponds; it's also handy for the fish that swim underneath.

Water is dense and heavy, with a high heat capacity and affinity for mixing with many substances. Although freshwater sources exist all over the world, people prefer to move water from those places to where they live. That takes a lot of energy because one liter of water weighs one kilogram. Water's heat capacity is not just important for water beds and mugs of tea; the oceans function as a global heat sink, moderating and driving the weather. Water's "mixiness" is both a blessing and a curse; sometimes we want to dissolve matter in water; sometimes we don't. Chefs like salt in pasta water, but farmers don't want it in their irrigation water.

Earth's fixed water supply takes different forms. Water can fall from the sky as a solid or liquid, evaporate, puddle up or flow away, be as pure as the driven snow or as dangerous as a poisoned cocktail. Most of Earth's water rests in salty oceans. Evaporation from this enormous source (more than 97 percent of all water) stays in the atmosphere until it precipitates over land to create freshwater flows that join glaciers, lakes, and aquifers; evaporate; or flow back to the sea. Animals and plants also play a role, taking water molecules apart when they grow and creating new water when they respire. This hydrological cycle sustains life, nourishes ecosystems, removes contamination, and moves water from low to high places.[3]

Many human activities have evolved to match water's nature. Civilization developed along rivers (where floods fertilized soil) and natural harbors (where people gathered to exchange goods and knowledge). Then engineers learned how to bring freshwater to cities via wells and aqueducts, flush wastewater down drains and sewers, and build dams and ditches for storage and irrigation. Most engineering has sought to move water from where it falls to where it's useful and store water from when it's abundant to when it's scarce. These engineering works are often massive, but their effectiveness is limited by the amount of energy it takes to pump water over hills and the construction materials necessary to store large quantities of water. These limits mean that most water management decisions are local. People in France do not worry about water storage in China; people in California do not worry about irrigation infrastructure in New York. Localized water management keeps managers in touch with user needs, but it increases vulnerability to local disasters. New Zealand's surpluses cannot end California's shortages.

A note on the metric system

American readers may not be familiar with the metric system, but it's used here for several reasons. First, the only countries that have not

---

[3] An aquifer is an underground layer of water-bearing porous stone, earth, or gravel. Aquifers are often recharged by surface water, but "fossil" aquifers are no longer recharged. I'll say "contamination" when it's a measurable addition to water and "pollution" when contamination reaches harmful levels.

switched to the metric standard are the US, Liberia and Myanmar. Second, liters are easy to understand; a liter is close to a quart, and we see liter-sized bottles of liquid everywhere. Third, most people have no idea how much water is in an acre-foot (af) or megaliter (ML), the basic units of bulk water.[4] Since they are abstract accounting numbers, we can use simpler metric units. Fourth, and perhaps most important, the metric system was designed around the natural dimensions of water. One liter of water weighs one kilogram (at 4° Celsius); one cubic meter of water contains 1,000 liters (and weighs 1,000 kg, or one ton); 0° C is the freezing point of water and 100° C is its boiling point. One food calorie (technically a kilocalorie) contains enough energy to raise the temperature of one kilogram of water by one degree Celsius. The metric system is so useful for describing water that it would be a shame to ignore it.

How much do we use?

Who uses water? First, we need to define when "use" occurs. In traditional accounting, water is used when goods are produced, not when they are consumed. That means a farmer would use water to produce an apple, but a consumer would use no water when eating it. Second, there's the question of whether use results from the withdrawal or consumption of water. Withdrawals happen when water is taken from its natural location; consumption happens when some portion of that water is evaporated or polluted and cannot be used again. Consumption is zero when I bathe in a river; it's 100 percent when I drink a glass of water.

Withdrawal and consumption volumes are nearly the same for urban water because withdrawals are consumed as they flow from taps to toilets to sewers. Agricultural water consumption is lower, since runoff from one field can be used by a neighbor. At the other extreme are withdrawals for thermoelectric power generation. In a typical situation, cold water used to cool nuclear plants, generate hydropower or run steam turbines returns as hotter water to the original point of diversion. Some people claim the returning water reduces consumption to zero; others claim the cool water is "consumed" because hot water

---

[4]One af equals 325,851 gallons, or 1.23 ML. One ML equals 1 million liters, or 0.81 af. A cubic meter (m³) of water, or kiloliter (kL), has 1,000 liters. A gigaliter (GL) has 1 billion liters. Most people use between 100 and 1,000 liters per day at home. A ML of water would fill a cube with 10 meter (33 foot) sides. A GL of water would fill a cube that's 100 m on a side, about the same size as an average city block with 25–30 story buildings.

Table 1: Water use by sector.

Use	US	US (no power)	Med.	EU
Thermoelectric power	41	—	—	44
Irrigation	37	62	64	24
Urban	14	23	14	21
Industry	5	9	23	11
Aquaculture/livestock	3	5	—	—

has a different impact on flora and fauna.

This difference in opinion is pretty important.

First, thermoelectric power diversions are big. As of 2005, the US Geological Survey (USGS) estimates that 41 percent of "extracted fresh surface and groundwater" is used for thermoelectric power generation, 37 percent is used for irrigation, 14 percent is used for urban supply, 5 percent is used for industry/mining, and 3 percent is used for aquaculture and livestock. Second, thermoelectric return flows occur in similar volumes and in close proximity to diversions, but they can represent a large share of local water flows and carry ecologically harmful thermal pollution. Return flows from other diversions — if any — may come much later, at a greater distance, and with pollution.

Thermoelectric diversions can have big impacts, but these flows are not central to debates over the management of consumptive withdrawals for irrigation, urban, and industrial uses. Those uses are in direct competition with one another because each reduces the quantity of water available to other uses. In more mundane terms, different consumptive uses are competing for limited water like different foods compete for space on your plate. Thermoelectric diversions do not go on the plate, but they matter in the same way that food temperature affects your eating experience.

Keeping those caveats in mind, consider Table 1, which shows USGS numbers for water diversions (with and without thermoelectric power), along with similar numbers from Mediterranean countries and European Union.

According to the USGS, these numbers have fallen over time: energy and irrigation withdrawals are flat or lower; urban demand is higher; but total freshwater withdrawals are down 5 percent since 1980. Do these facts contradict the end of abundance? Not really. Supply may be falling if our minimum standard for quality is rising or quality is actually deteriorating. It may also be falling due to past or

continued overuse of resources that recharge at a much slower rate
than they're depleted (the Ogallala aquifer under Nebraska and seven
neighboring states, for example). Finally, we have a huge increase
in demand that the USGS ignores — the demand for environmental
water.

The environment strikes back

The demand for greater flows to rivers, lakes, wetlands and seas is
not the result of Mother Nature sending a telegram to Congress. It's
the expressed desire of environmentalists who have moved from the
fringes to the center of political debates and redefined our view of
water in nature. The water flowing down rivers and into oceans is not
"waste;" it's "in-stream flow." Swamps are not for draining; they are
wetlands providing ecosystem services. Environmentalists are certainly right that healthy environments contribute to our prosperity and
happiness, but their views are too radical for some people (especially
the people losing water to rivers). In California, for example, a little more than half the water flowing in the state is diverted to human
uses. The rest flows from the mountains into the ocean. Municipal
and agricultural users watch these flows with a mixture of envy and
horror, wishing that they could divert just a little bit of that water for human use. Although those diversions were easy 50 years ago, they are
nearly impossible today. In fact, the reverse is more likely to be true.
Environmental policies that increase or restore environmental water
demand leave less water for other human uses. In other words, a major contributor to the end of abundance can be described as either a
decrease in supply for humans or an increase in humans' demand for
environmental flows.

Some economics

The end of abundance is the same as the beginning of scarcity, but
scarcity (falling supply and increasing demand) need not lead to shortage. Although some may try to fight shortages by looking for additional supplies or trying to regulate or talk down demand, economic
methods provide a cheap, quick and straightforward way to bring supply and demand into balance.

    This section explains basic economic ideas that appear through-
out the book. Although some people worry about using "economics"
and "understand" in the same sentence, we are going to keep it simple, looking at markets and prices, behavior in the absence of mar-

kets (within a bureaucracy, for example), and situations where fairness trumps efficiency.

Sometimes it's helpful to use specific economic jargon to explain and explore interesting situations. Most jargon is easy to understand. "Making a decision on the margin," for example, refers to a decision on what to do next given what's already happened. Other jargon gives a narrow technical definition to a familiar word. "Elasticity" reminds most people of rubber bands, but economists use the word to refer to the strength of a response to a change in prices or income. Most jargon is defined when it's first used; recurring words and ideas are also listed in the glossary that starts on page 229.[5]

Demand is driven by costs and benefits

People make choices all the time. These choices are not always perfect, but they reflect each person's version of a benefit-cost analysis that identifies potential actions, assigns benefits and costs (in terms of money, time, happiness, and other factors that cannot be quantified) to each action, and concludes with the choice that gives the greatest net benefit (benefits minus costs) or benefit yield (benefits divided by costs). This process can include benefits to others at a cost to oneself, tradeoffs between the present and future, subjective values derived from an individual's experience or superstitions, and so on.

This process of weighing tradeoffs and making choices leads us to the economic concept of demand. Demand represents our desire for a good relative to other goods. Economists break demand into two parts. Our "demand" for a good depends on income, tastes, other goods, and other factors. In this sense, we may say that we demand ice cream because we like ice cream, have money in our pocket, are at the beach, and so on. This demand leads to a "quantity demanded" that falls as the price of that good rises, just as the quantity of ice cream we demand falls as its price goes up. This inverse relationship is known as the "law of demand."

Figure 1 clarifies these differences. Figure 1(a) shows how the quantity of bottled water demanded falls from 10 bottles a week when the price is $1 a bottle to four bottles a week when the price rises to $2 a bottle. Does this example require that the person drink less water? No. The person can drink more potable water from the tap.

---

[5]See "Notes to the Text" starting on page 241 for data sources and occasional comments. Turn to any economic textbook, Google or Wikipedia for additional background on basic concepts and facts.

Figure 1(b) shows an outward shift in demand for tap water from 400 to 406 liters that has nothing to do with its $1-per-1,000-liters price.

This example illustrates the difference between a slide in demand (the inverse relationship between price and quantity demanded) and an inward or outward shift in demand that has nothing to do with price but depends on the prices of other goods (as here), changes in tastes, changes in income, and so on.

This difference (quantity demanded vs. demand, or slide along the demand curve vs. shift of the demand curve) helps us understand the different ways that "demand for water" can change. As an example of a slide in demand, compare two similar cities in California, Fresno and Clovis. Residents in Fresno do not pay per unit of water; they pay a flat price per month. Water customers in Clovis are charged for the volume of water they use. Consumption in Fresno is 1,140 liters per capita per day (lcd); consumption in Clovis is 920 lcd. From this example, we can see how the mere existence of a price per unit can reduce quantity demanded by 20 percent.

How does a shift in demand work? In 2009, the Australians in Brisbane cut their water use by about 50 percent in a short amount of time, without facing higher water prices. Why was that? The combination of news reports, regulations, community pressure, and concern for future shortages influenced and shifted their demand in. Brisbane residents demanded less at the same price.

It's useful to tackle demand from both fronts. Prices can signal water scarcity and encourage a reduction in quantity demanded. Information can help people decide to demand less, no matter the price. It's not always clear which effect will have the biggest impact. People who care more about long showers than doing the right thing may respond to price signals.

These examples also highlight price elasticity, or the change in quantity demanded resulting from a change in price. Elasticity can be calculated in different ways, but all methods measure the strength of response. Compare an elastic rubber band and how it will stretch with an inelastic piece of string. Price elasticity is high if people dramatically reduce their purchases as price rises; it's low (or inelastic) if quantity demanded drops by only a little after a price increase.

These ideas can be summarized with numbers. Price elasticity of -1.0 or greater (meaning -1.2 or -2.4, for example) means demand for the good is elastic. Price elasticity between zero and -1.0 means demand for the good is inelastic. The important implication of these

15

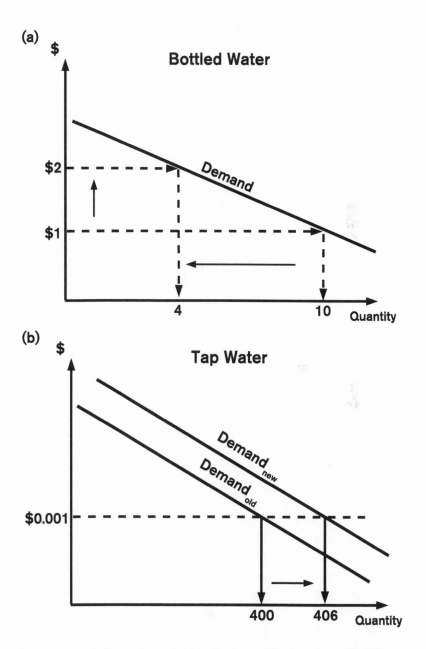

Figure 1: (a) At a price of $1, we demand 10 bottles of water. A price increase to $2 per bottle reduces this quantity to four bottles and increases the demand for tap water. (b) Demand for tap water (at the same price of $0.001 per liter) shifts out from 400 to 406 liters.

numbers is that they indicate whether total revenue (price times quantity sold) will go up or down with a price change. A price increase for an elastic good means revenue will go down (the percentage fall in units sold exceeds the percentage increase in price per unit). Likewise, higher prices for an inelastic good leads to higher revenue. Our bottled water example shows that the demand for bottled water is elastic, because total spending fell from $10 to $8. Businesses pay a lot of attention to elasticity, because they want to raise prices as far as possible, but not so far that their revenue falls.

Although water managers do not usually try to maximize revenues, elasticity is still very important to them. On the one hand, many people claim price elasticity for water is zero: people who *need* water will never use less, no matter how expensive it gets. The people claiming zero elasticity oppose increasing the price of water because such an increase just takes money from people who cannot adjust by using less. They are often joined by like-minded water managers who conclude that higher prices will not address water shortages. On the other hand, some farmers, businessmen and politicians claim their elasticities are so high that they will shut down and relocate if water prices increase.

The truth lies in the middle. The price elasticity for water used for toilets, showers, and other indoor uses is estimated to be -0.2 to -0.4; price elasticity for outdoor water (for landscaping, pools, and other voluntary uses) is estimated to be -0.7 to -1.2. These numbers mean that higher prices lead people to use a little less water indoors (2–4 percent less for a 10 percent increase in price) and a lot less water outdoors (7–12 percent less for a 10 percent increase in price). They also imply that people facing lower prices for water will find more uses for that water while people facing higher prices will cut back on nonessential uses like watering the lawn before cutting back on showers. At retail prices of about $1 for 1,000 liters of tap water, it's pretty hard to imagine that anyone would stop drinking water because it's too expensive. (Average daily consumption of 10–20 liters for drinking and cooking means most additional water goes to life-enhancing, not life-sustaining, activities.)

Finally, let's distinguish between goods that are substitutes or complements for another good. In the earlier example, tap and bottled water were substitutes. As the price of bottled water rose, demand for tap water shifted out. A complement to tap water would be a lawn. A fall in the cost of land and labor for a lawn will increase the demand for water to irrigate it. Likewise, a fall in the price of tap water increases the demand for lawns that are now cheaper to irrigate. These two concepts make it easier to understand how cheap water may contribute to more landscaping around homes or urban sprawl, or how poor quality tap water may lead to an increase in demand for bottled water. Thus, we can see why the average Mexican consumes 169 liters of bottled water per year. Only Italians consume more (184 liters). In both cases, demand for bottled water is shifted out further than in other countries. Italians probably consume more for cultural reasons; Mexicans perhaps for sanitary reasons.

The key points are that people shift their demand in or out according to their tastes and habits; people cut nonessential uses first when prices go up; and people use more water when it's cheap.

Supply depends on cost

The supply side of economics is easier to understand. If I offer $10 to anyone who will mow my lawn, I may get zero responses. If I raise my price to $20, I may get six replies. The law of supply says that people are willing to sell more units of a good or service as the offer price per unit increases.

This model of increasing price, increasing quantity supplied is based on the idea that higher prices attract more participants and make it possible to use more expensive production methods to produce greater quantities of goods. In water, participation is often limited to a single monopolist (more on that soon), but greater production through technology is certainly possible. Engineers are very familiar with the cheap-to-expensive progression of additional water supplies: from groundwater to surface water to imported water to reclaimed water to desalinated water. Chapter 8 has a detailed discussion of these technologies, but the essential point is that supply costs more per unit, the greater the quantity of units produced, as cheaper sources are exhausted and additional supplies come from more expensive sources.

This is true in the long run but not necessarily in the short run, when it may be impossible to pump more groundwater, build a desalination plant, or import more water from distant places. In the short run, the supply of freshwater is fixed, regardless of demand, money on the table, or political pressures for more. In that case, the supply curve slopes up (price per unit rising with quantity) until there's no additional water and the supply curve shoots up to represent how the lack of additional supplies means the last bit of water will sell for a price that depends on demand — like the last concert ticket being auctioned to hundreds of fans.

The next chapter goes into more detail on pricing and shortage, but we can look at a basic case now. Figure 2(a) gives an example of how the price of water rises with each new source. It also shows how the price for that water is set according to the average cost for the amount of water that the water utility expects to provide. Utilities are required to set price equal to average cost so that their revenues cover costs and they make no profit (or slightly above cost, so they make a regulated profit) — in exchange for a monopoly in the service area. This standard method of pricing water has two important implications. First, groundwater is sold for more than cost while desalinated water is sold below cost. Figure 2(a) shows a price set to $0.60 per m^3 — the average of two units of groundwater that cost $0.20 per m^3 and two units of desalinated water that cost $1.00 per m^3. Second, price and quantity based on expected demand are fixed in the short run. A shortage results if they are too low for actual demand. Figure 2(b) shows how a price of $0.60 per m^3 combined with a greater-than-expected demand for water can lead to five units of actual quantity demanded. Given the four unit supply, this excess demand leads to a shortage of one unit.

The economic solutions to these problems are simple. Do not sell water below cost; raise prices in scarcity. Those solutions will create excess revenues or profits, but those profits can be refunded to customers once the shortage is avoided to ensure that profits stay close to zero or a targeted return. Notice how this difference contrasts with a popular, but misguided idea of increasing desalination capacity. Given the norm of setting price equal to average cost, such an idea will merely result in greater financial losses from selling more water below cost and do nothing to prevent shortage. (We'll cover higher prices and rebates and average cost pricing in Chapters 1 and 8, respectively.)

Managing water by its characteristics

Economists claim two characteristics determine the best way to manage a particular good and ensure that the good is allocated to its highest and best use. First, consider water and its use. Does one person's use reduce the amount available to another person? Are they rivals for the same water or not? Second, consider access to the water. Can

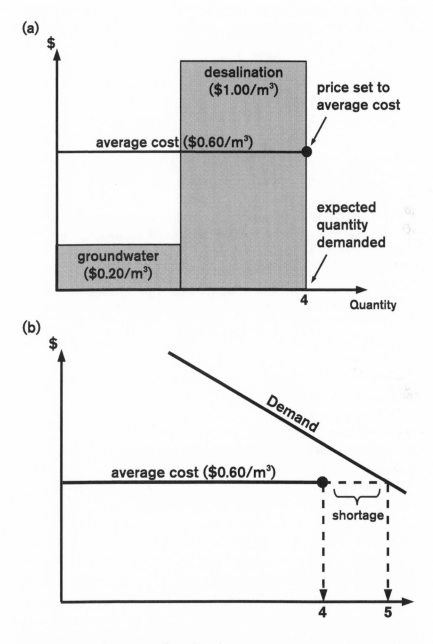

Figure 2: (a) A water utility with cheap groundwater and expensive desalinated water sets a price based on the average cost of the two water supplies. (b) Higher demand may result in a shortage.

Table 2: A good should be managed according to its nature (rival goods are consumed in use) and accessability (people can be prevented from using excludable goods).

	Excludable	Non-Excludable
Rival	Private Goods	Common-pool Goods
Non-Rival	Club Goods	Public Goods

some people be excluded from using the water? Rivalry and excludability can be used to define four types of "economic goods" listed in Table 2. A glass of water is a private good that diminishes with use (rival) and can be kept from others (excludable). Water in a reservoir is a common-pool good that diminishes with use (rival) as each neighbor runs his tap (non-excludable). A pipe network is a club good that can be used by one as well as many (non-rival) but which is available only to residents on the network (excludable). A rainbow over the reservoir is a public good that is beautiful no matter how many look at it (non-rival) and can be seen by all (non-excludable).

This classification of rivalry and excludability (or use and access) can change. Water in a lake may be a public good for two neighbors who are neither rival in consumption nor excluded from using it. The lake can turn into a common-pool good if a hundred new homes all draw water from it. Garrett Hardin's 1968 article on the "Tragedy of the Commons" refers this result, when overexploitation of a resource that can be used by anyone harms everyone. This tragedy can be reversed using two different types of exclusion. Privatization turns lake water into a private good by limiting each owner to a fixed quantity of water per hydrological season, so that enough remains for everyone else. The lake can also be turned into a club that excludes new people from arriving, has rules to ensure that water is not used too quickly, and ejects members who abuse those rules.

It's also possible to think of rivalry in terms of supply and demand, scarcity and abundance. Lake water can be non-rival for swimming but rival for drinking. A bottle of water can be non-rival between two small children but rival between two adults. A good's excludability can also change. A swim club may be able to exclude nonmembers from the pool such that it is non-rival for its members, but that pool can get congested (and rivalrous) if too many members turn up at the same time.

Now consider how water can be either a natural resource or an environmental good. Natural resources are exchanged in markets at prices that tend to reflect scarcity, supply and demand. Thus we may have water resources in bottles, pipes or underground aquifers. Environmental goods are valuable, but they cannot be priced in markets, usually because their ownership and flows of benefits are unclear. Examples include water in the air, soaking a wetlands, or beneath our boat.

A renewable or nonrenewable natural resource is defined according to the relationship between its stock (quantity) and flows (changes in quantity). Oil is a nonrenewable resource because its stocks are being used up faster than they are being created (negative net flows). An aquifer is a renewable resource if pumping extractions are slower than the recharge rate at which it refills (positive net flows). The aquifer is a nonrenewable resource if net flows are negative, because pumping extractions exceed recharging return flows. This overdrafting of an aquifer is akin to mining for coal, a process that ends when the stock is economically exhausted (the value of additional coal is less than the cost of getting it out). Decisions over current versus future use of a stock depend on the simple idea of whether it's worth more now or later, but that value can get distorted if the resource is in a common-pool (Will others use it first?) or subject to uncertainty (Will it be there? Will I be there?).

Although environmental goods are valuable to us as individuals, they are often public goods with a value that represents the sum of our individual valuations. Sunsets and whales, for example, are environmental goods to people who like to look at them. But whales can also be treated as a natural resource and harvested by fishermen who want to sell the whale for meat. In this circumstance, the whale turns from a public good (for environmentalists) to a common-pool good (for the whalers) to a private good (for the fishmonger and his customers).

Change is hard

Definitions help us understand problems and potential solutions, but the real solution to the end of abundance requires that people abandon hard-won traditions that embody decades of distilled experience in exchange for novel ideas and unknown future benefits. A stable institution from one perspective may be rigid from another perspective, but institutions need to evolve with circumstances. In the case of water, good institutions prevent shortage, allowing valuable uses today while saving for tomorrow. Bad institutions make shortage more likely; they can turn abundance into scarcity faster than you can say empty reservoir.

What forces a water manager to change the way his organization manages its water? Not much. In most parts of the world, water service is provided by a monopoly, which means each organization chooses how to serve its local customers without fear of competition. While some managers may pursue novelty and change because they have the internal drive to search for the best ideas, others wait until they are pushed. Politicians may push them if they are not too busy. Sometimes customers push, but customers lack bargaining power. Sometimes drought pushes, but a drought may end before hard choices must be faced. The same can be said for the irrigation districts that serve farmers, the engineers who run dams, and so on. All of these water organizations exist in a world where competition is weak, oversight is intermittent, and customers have few alternatives to taking the service they are given. Although managers may earn gold stars for operating by the book, they may not be doing the best job at managing their customers' resources.

The end of abundance means water managers have more to worry about than recovering costs on the way to delivering water to anyone who demands it. Managers need to either increase supply or reduce demand. Although additional supply can be expensive, the bigger headache comes from allocating the cost of new supply among customers who claim others should pay more. Reducing demand is even harder, since it requires rationing. In a market, rationing occurs through higher prices, but water agencies often ration through bureaucratic rules. These rules may be designed with good intentions, but they can be manipulated, unfair and inefficient. In many cases, they add significant value to rights that were distributed long before scarcity became a concern. We'll see several examples in the chapters ahead.

A local water provider sets prices according to a formula that may lead to imbalances between supply and demand, but price changes require public meetings, political approvals and so on. Most water agencies selling water to urban or agricultural customers factor this pace of change into their operations, starting the process months or years ahead of the day when they need them in place. They maintain buffer stocks of cash and water to handle short-term, unexpected fluctuations in revenue or water flows. Competitive firms also plan and implement changes in their prices and operations, but they face different pressures. First, water agencies face stronger political, regulatory and stakeholder pressures to take actions that threaten long-term viability. Second, water agencies usually make decisions in the absence of market competition. Although monopoly status gives water managers more time to plan and execute decisions, it is harder to compare their decisions and performance with competitors. Monopolistic failure is also more costly. Customers cannot switch water providers as quickly as they can switch food providers. Third, monopolists do not necessarily suffer from their mistakes. A firm that makes a mistake faces lower profits and defecting customers. A monopolist just raises prices.

Markets move water from those who have to those who want, using prices to balance supply and demand. Markets may not be fair in outcomes (rich people can still buy more than poor people), but they provide equal access. Market prices accurately reflect value and scarcity, but they can be high. Can we allocate water with markets and prices — without producing civil war, dry taps, dead ecosystems or thirsty people? Can we do so in the presence of monopoly property rights and other institutions? Yes and yes. The following chapters will explain how.

Overview of the book

This book is not authoritative; there's no single solution to water problems. It's not an economic textbook; some economic ideas are too theoretical for reality. Local situations require local solutions, but some solutions share useful features. This book uses economic analysis to identify problems related to water scarcity and suggests economic tools that can be modified to create these solutions. Stories along the way will illustrate the connections between institutions and outcomes and highlight how incentives lead to actions that create results. The analysis should reveal patterns that make it easier to understand your local situation and perhaps identify some options for change.

Every water basin, urban area and household has a unique water fingerprint that reflects the influence of local hydrology, cultural norms, history, environmental constraints, political and economic structures, and other institutional characteristics. This fingerprint can baffle outsiders, but locals who live with it can find a way to modify outside solutions to fit their conditions. The causes of a water shortage in Atlanta may differ from those of a shortage in Cairo, but their solutions may share similarities.

Any discussion of water starts in one place and inevitably meanders off in interesting directions. This characteristic is fun and interesting, but it complicates the linear narrative of a book. The book has two parts, each containing six topical chapters (tap water, water and human rights, and so on). Each chapter could be expanded into a book of historical developments, case studies, and analysis of relevant factors, but I've kept them short because you probably don't have time to read 12 books and I don't have the expertise to write them. In fact, nobody does. That's the difficulty with water — it enters our lives in so many ways that no one person can understand all its complexities.

Part I (Personal Water Choices) looks at the straightforward topics of water for taps, toilets and lawns. These uses need not affect others since it's possible to design pricing systems that reflect the full cost of individual actions and limit spillover effects on others. Similar systems can be used to regulate the quality and quantity of water used and discharged by businesses, farms, and power plants. Solutions in Part I are slightly idealistic — they ignore some institutional constraints and politicians or managers who serve themselves over customers — but it's easier to work for change when one sees a clear destination than when one sees only a maze of barriers.

Part II (Social Water Choices) expands the discussion to consider political and bureaucratic dimensions of change and topics in which individual or group decisions affect others. These social topics (infrastructure, the environment, climate change, human rights and water wars) are not just complicated by the idea that a majority decides for a minority; they are complicated by the possibility that politicians, bureaucrats and water managers may favor themselves over their constituents. The Afterword has a few ideas of how to change that situation (or any water policy, for that matter) but don't skip to the end just yet — the chapters ahead will make it easier to identify and pursue policies to restore abundance.

Part I

Personal water choices

Personal water choices

Our visits to the gas station are boring. We drive up, buy as much as we want, pay the bill, and drive away. Nobody cares where we drive, or how far we drive. Nobody worries that our fill-up will leave no gas for others. With the exception of pollution (more later), our gas decisions, like our decisions on what to eat for lunch, are satisfying and efficient. We look at prices and choose what we want, without worrying about denying food to others or driving the restaurant out of business.

The chapters in Part I discuss how to make water choices just as satisfying, efficient, and boring — while simultaneously preventing shortages and promoting fairness. Chapters 1–3 focus on demands that respond to posted prices. Chapters 4–6 emphasize how competing desires for business, agricultural and energy uses can be reconciled in markets that generate prices. The discussion of the political process for making these rules is deferred to Part II. Thus, Part I discusses how to price tap water so that individuals choose how much water to consume without creating shortages for others while Part II looks at the way that prices are set and the people who set those prices. Part II also deals with social water uses related to public or communal goods like the environment or a human right to water, where individual actions impact others.

People value water in different ways, just as they value phones, cars, gardens and other goods in different ways. These private, subjective values create opportunities in markets, because different values help buyers and sellers make mutually agreeable trades. I use "subjective" (in contrast to "objective") to highlight how two people may give different values on the same object that are perfectly correct and accurate *for each person*. A dollar is a dollar to everyone, but a liter of water, sunset or garden has different values to different people. An individual's decision to have a garden results from his subjective weighing of the costs and benefits of greenery. Some people want the biggest garden they can get; others don't. These different outcomes do not usually cause any trouble, just as car-fueling decisions do not usually cause trouble (again, caveats to come).

The goal is to design policies that direct water to different users without one person's demand affecting somebody else. Such an outcome will be efficient from an individual and social perspective because everyone gets what they want, without harming others.

Prices and markets are easy to understand, but they are not the only way to achieve these outcomes. Non-price mechanisms can produce better results at lower social, financial and psychological costs. These price and non-price tools will often be compared with bureaucratic command-and-control regulations. Although some water managers may enjoy controlling others, many of them turn to command and control for lack of authority to change existing policies or familiarity with alternatives. Most water managers have an engineering background that prepared them for pipes and pumps but not for determining how much water a customer actually needs or wants. As we saw with San Diego's water shortage, managers' tools for addressing shortages can violate customer expectations of fairness.

The end of abundance means managers can no longer rely on additional supplies to address scarcity. They need to consider demand, and how demand and supply interact. Economist F.A. Hayek said that central planners face a "knowledge problem" when they try to allocate society's resources (water, labor, money, steel, and other goods) without markets or prices. Hayek argued that a lack of price signals would make it hard to direct goods to their highest and best use in production or consumption. Managers who attempt to ration water among customers according to their own definition of want or need risk making the same mistake. People have different subjective values for water, and managers who understand those differences know that the easiest way to serve them is by setting prices that allow everyone to buy water according to their own values, while preventing shortages that affect others. Such price rationing helps managers avoid the knowledge problem; they need to know only how many people are using how much water out of a total quantity. These ideas can also be used in places where water is abundant and prices are low, because they give customers choices.

Now those caveats. Water consumption, like gasoline consumption, can affect others in unforeseen ways. Farmers, for example, affect one another with tailwater running off fields, irrigation in one place that recharges groundwater elsewhere, or pumping from a shared aquifer. Economists call an unintended and unpriced impact of one person's action on another an "externality." A farmer's decision on groundwater pumping usually weighs his own benefits (water for plants) and costs (energy for pumping). That decision may produce positive externalities (runoff that other farmers can use) or negative externalities (less water in the aquifer for others). In either case, we want people to internalize the externality so that their decisions reflect costs and benefits to everyone. This internalization can occur through regulations, taxes, property rights, or changes in community norms.

Some people prefer that the government address externalities (also called market failures) with interventions aimed at a socially optimal level of activity, but "socially optimal" often depends on subjective value judgments. Political or regulatory intervention can help (as with car pollution or groundwater demand), but they can also backfire — producing a "government failure" that worsens the situation. We will address most externalities as they appear in this part, but Part II will take a deeper look at how changes in institutions can reduce externalities, market failures and government failures.

CHAPTER 1

Water from the tap

Water prices that cover costs but ignore scarcity lead to shortages when demand exceeds supply. It's fair and efficient to set residential water prices per capita, not per meter.

Imagine that you're a water manager. At current consumption levels, stored water supplies will last 52 days. You may be able to drill a well in a few weeks; you may be able to borrow some water from a neighboring city, but you are not sure about those supplies or how fast you can get them. One-half of consumed water goes onto lawns, so customers should be able to cut back. You put out a press release: "Please use less water. We have only 52 days of water left." Some people respond, but most don't. You go to the city council, asking for watering regulations. The five gardeners and two real estate agents who show up double attendance. They protest your anti-growth proposals. After a 3 to 2 vote, the council decides to study drought-tolerant roses and the impact of brown lawns on home values. You ask the council to raise the price of water but face numerous objections: What about poor people? What about large families caring for dependents? Why allow the water department to profit off a public service? You're frustrated. The current system wasn't built to restrain demand, and new supplies are much harder to get. Desperate, you go on the evening news, asking people to use less. Some listen, others don't. You have 24 days of water left.

How can showers be antisocial?

The 5.5 liter per minute Earth Massage showerhead "combines ergonomic luxury with peak performance... to save water and energy and reduce your utility bills." Kohler's seven-head "Water Haven" system uses more than 66 liters per minute. We understand how these

31

two products might coexist, but why is it that so many people care about our showerheads, their flow, and how long we sing under them? They worry that we are using too much water, drying out precious ecosystems, withering crops in the fields. Does a shower mean the difference between life and death?

Why are there laws and regulations that specify appropriate water use but not appropriate collar-buttoning or hamburger dressing? Because water is often seen as a community resource (a common-pool good), while other products belong to individuals as private goods. Since water is often financed and managed as a community resource, this view makes sense, but it's based on inefficient water management that has nothing to do with singing in the shower.

The end of abundance requires that we change our individual attitudes toward water; more important, it requires that we change our institutions for managing this community resource.

A change in attitudes can reduce demand and prevent shortage. In some places, people have cut demand by taking shorter showers, flushing the toilet less often, letting their lawn go brown, and so on. Although these solutions are the cheapest (from the perspective of water managers pleading from billboards), they also require the greatest initiative from customers. A few customers will change their habits, but the majority has other concerns (water is still flowing from taps, after all). Activists propose regulations to limit outdoor watering, car washing and showerhead flow. These command-and-control restrictions annoy people who do not see why society should tell them how to bathe. They remove flow regulators from showerheads and water their lawns at night. Although heavy water users may face social condemnation from neighbors, they pay their bills and carry on. It's not worth paying for high efficiency when water is so cheap.

This chapter discusses the economics of tap water, how water is priced to affect behavior and recover costs, and how those prices can cause shortages. It then reviews a fair way to set prices that prevents shortages, recovers costs and allows us to enjoy our showers. It ends with a look at some of the successes and failures in providing drinking water around the world.

How does water get to our taps?

The pipes that bring drinking water to our homes are part of a complex infrastructure. We will discuss wastewater in Chapter 2 and large-scale storage and conveyance in Chapter 8.

Water comes to the tap in many ways. San Francisco, for example, gets most of its water from a reservoir in the distant mountains that's full of water from melted snow (glaciers and snowpack are natural reservoirs). When people in San Francisco turn on the tap, they get water that requires hardly any filtering or treatment to make it safe to drink. As a bonus, the downhill flow of water also generates hydroelectric energy. Dubai has no such luck. Lacking mountains, 96 percent of this coastal city's water comes from desalinated ocean water. Dubai spends a lot of money on treatment plants and energy. Singapore also lacks good local water, but it takes a more economical route of treating wastewater for reuse and drinking.[1]

Tap water comes usually from sources that deliver the most water, of the highest quality, at the lowest cost for moving and treatment. Although everyone may prefer that their water comes from snowmelt (or desalination, or groundwater), the cost of delivering that water may be too high relative to other sources. Many factors determine cost. Some of them are obvious (energy, cement), but others are not. Subsidies, political connections, property rights and other factors can mean that the exact same water is sold to different customers at radically different prices.

San Diego provides a good example. The cost of desalinating nearby ocean water is four times the cost of pumping Colorado River water across nearly 400 km and removing the salts and contaminants gathered on a downstream journey through multiple irrigation canals and wastewater plants. Although San Diego used Colorado River water for years, it now has a desalination plant under construction. Why? Political uncertainty. The end of abundance has increased the complications of moving scarce water across 400 km of ground controlled by thirsty neighbors.

How much does a water system cost?

Most people who live in cities buy their water from a local water agency that has a monopoly on water service in that area. This agency is charged with finding and bringing water to the area, treating it to drinking quality, and then distributing it through a series of pipes that start big and shrink as they get closer to the tap.

Although water systems may be simple in principle ("bring water

---

[1] Recycled water is often called "toilet to tap," but that expression is either inaccurate (it's toilet to treatment plant to tap) or trivial (water has been circulating for millions of years; there is no fresh shiny new water).

from a to b"), they are complex and expensive to construct, maintain and operate. Many people with many years of experience work hard to get water to us. Systems vary in size, due to cultural, geographical, political and engineering factors. In the US, 52,000 water systems serve 86 percent of the population without private wells. Municipalities run most of these systems. Contrast these numbers with those of England and Wales, where 27 investor-owned utilities (IOUs) deliver water and sewer service.[2]

Chapter 4 compares IOUs with municipal providers (the private versus public ownership debate), but all systems have two types of costs. Fixed costs are paid no matter how much water flows through the system. They are the capital costs of building dams and aqueducts, laying pipe underground, installing water meters, and paying the managers and accountants in the head office. Variable costs from treatment, pumping and maintenance go up when more water is delivered and go down when deliveries fall. Fixed costs are much larger than variable costs in the water sector.

But what about the cost of water? Isn't that a variable cost? Almost never. Most water users (urban, agricultural and so on) own a "usufruct right" to use water that belongs to the people.[3] Governments usually distribute these rights for free. Some usufruct rights are rolled into the definition of land ownership, such as the right to groundwater under one's property or the water in a river next to one's property. Other rights are allocated to users who happen to be in the right place at the right time, as is often the case with irrigation projects that bring water to formerly dry areas. The distribution of free rights began when water was abundant and demand was less than supply. Scarcity has increased the value of water rights, but that scarcity is not always reflected in water prices, either because the rights are not traded (the case with farmers that we discuss in Chapter 5), or because the owners of rights are allowed to sell their water for prices that reflect only the cost of delivery — the case with urban water suppliers. Compare this standard with the norm in the oil business, where companies pay an extraction royalty per barrel or purchase a pumping lease at auction.

---

[2]England and Wales have about two percent of the land area of the lower-48 US states. The US would have roughly 1,250 water systems if the industry had consolidated to English levels.

[3]Usufruct rights are separate from ownership rights. Think of the right to use fruit from a tree that belongs to someone else — or the right to use a home that you rent from its owner.

Why omit the cost of scarcity? Because politicians and regulators want to deliver the people's water at the lowest possible price, covering delivery costs and adjustments for policy goals (discussed later). Municipal water managers target long-term profits of zero. Managers at IOUs are allowed to earn a regulated profit based, for example, on the value of their capital investments. Both types of managers set aside money for emergencies and approved future capital spending.

Cost-based pricing explains why the first unit of water from San Francisco's water agency costs $3.50 and the first unit in Las Vegas costs $1.16. Vegas may be in the middle of the desert and constantly on the verge of water shortages, but the price of Vegas water is two-thirds less because its cost of delivery is lower than that of San Francisco's. A family of four using 100 gallons per person per day (380 liters each) would pay $33 per month for water service in Las Vegas (variable costs plus a fixed monthly fee) but $58 in San Francisco. The higher cost of variable water (plus different weather and lifestyle) means the average person consumes 217 liters per day in San Francisco. In Vegas, it's 417 liters.

Compare these cost-based prices with market prices. Gasoline prices, for example, reflect an interaction of cost (oil extraction, refining, distribution, marketing, royalties, expected future supplies) and value (consumer demand). Gasoline prices balance supply and demand, preventing shortages. Figure 3 shows how to use scarcity pricing to end shortages. Figure 3(a) reproduces Figure 2(b), to show how average cost pricing results in shortage. Figure 3(b) adds a scarcity surcharge that raises the total price, reduces quantity demanded and prevents a shortage.

This picture shows the most common economic technique for ending a shortage (higher prices). Any economics student could draw it. But water systems are more complicated, so the next sections will cover details of how prices affect behavior and (mis)match costs, how shortages are managed, and how scarcity pricing can end shortage while covering costs and protecting equity.

It's hard to recover costs and change behavior

Government policies link water prices to costs to eliminate or regulate profits, but these prices can be set in different ways to promote different usage patterns.

Most water systems were established with flat-rate pricing, meaning that all customers with the same connection size pay the same

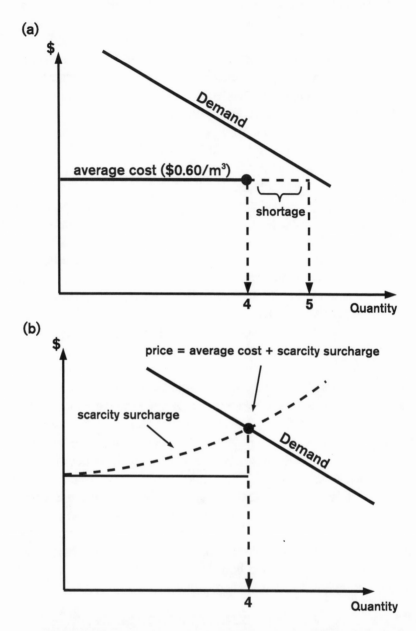

Figure 3: (a) Shortage can result if price doesn't reflect scarcity. (b) A scarcity surcharge reduces quantity demanded to prevent shortage. The surcharge gets bigger as demand approaches the fixed supply to prevent shortage.

amount every month, regardless of how much water they use. This system is easy to manage and works as long as water is abundant. Flat-rate pricing is still very common, but increasing water scarcity has led to volumetric pricing that charges people for the quantity of water they use.

Volumetric pricing is usually combined with a fixed service charge. The theory behind these two-part tariffs (a fixed service charge plus a variable volumetric charge) is that they reflect the fixed and variable costs discussed earlier.

Although it may seem like volumetric prices are better than flat-rate prices in matching costs and revenues, a desire to reduce use can complicate that goal. That's because prices that matched costs would get most revenue from a service charge (because fixed costs are large) and only a little revenue from volumetric charges (because it's cheap to deliver water once pipes exist). Unfortunately, small volumetric charges do not encourage conservation because the cost of consumption is often too low to notice. Higher volumetric prices can discourage use, but they create profits. So water managers lower fixed service charges to return to the break-even point. The result (revenues that are mostly variable when costs are mostly fixed) can lead to wild swings in profits and losses.

Ignoring this break-even, fixed-cost problem for a moment, let's look at the different types of volumetric charges. Under uniform block rates customers pay the same price per unit, for each unit they consume. Thus, a uniform block rate of $3 per m^3 means 5 m^3 of consumption costs $15.[4] Decreasing block rates (DBRs) mean that the price per unit falls as more units are consumed. Thus, the first unit may cost $5, the second unit $3, and additional units $2 each. Five units would therefore cost $14. Increasing block rates (IBRs) rise with consumption. Thus, the first unit might cost $1, the second unit $3, and additional units $4 each. Five units would therefore cost $16. Figure 4 compares these price structures.

Uniform block rates encourage people to use less water than unvarying flat-rate prices. DBRs weaken this incentive by making additional use cheaper; IBRs give the strongest incentive to use less, since additional units cost more. Uniform block rates are simple to administer and easy to understand, but they do not allow politicians

---

[4]Household water use is measured in cubic meters (1,000 liters) in metric systems. In the US, use is measured in units of 100 cubic feet (hcf or ccf), which is 748 gallons or 2,832 liters.

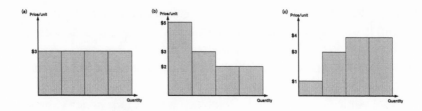

Figure 4: Volumetric water prices can be set in (a) uniform, (b) decreasing or (c) increasing blocks.

and water managers to punish or encourage water consumption.

Under DBRs, customers pay the highest price for the water that is most needed and lower prices for extra water. DBRs generate the greatest revenue because they closely approximate the demand curve's representation of water's value to the user. DBRs also encourage water use through volume discounts, which makes them popular with heavy water users.

Many people think it's unfair to charge people high prices for the basic water everyone needs and low prices for additional water that some people waste. They prefer IBRs that start low and rise with use. IBRs also tend to match the cost curve shown in Figure 2(a), where initial units of water are cheap and later units are expensive. IBRs are popular because they match the triple goals of breaking even (prices track costs), a little cheap water for everyone, and expensive water for water wasters.

But IBRs work only if blocks are tall enough (price jumps by a lot) and narrow enough (the cheapest allocation is small). In the East Bay Municipal Utility District just east of San Francisco, for example, the first block costs $2.15 and the second block costs $2.67. That 24 percent jump may seem large, but it's only an extra penny per 54 liters (about $0.50 per 750 gallons). Las Vegas seems to be doing better. Its first block price jumps from $1.16 to $2.08, an 80 percent increase. Unfortunately, this jump doesn't happen until use tops 625 liters per day, which is so far above essential use (perhaps 300 liters per day for three people) that it's irrelevant. These water agencies are basically using uniform block rates.

IBRs suffer from two operational problems and two philosophical problems. First, IBRs may fail to sufficiently constrain demand, since they are usually based on cost, not scarcity or value. Second, IBRs can cripple revenues, because the price on initial units intentionally or accidentally fails to cover costs. The first philosophical problem with IBRs is that we do not see them in markets. We see prices that are stable with volume and prices that fall with volume, but we do not see companies that sell one unit for $1 but two units for $3. That absence suggests that IBRs should be used with caution.

The second philosophical problem originates with using a meter to charge customers according to their willingness to pay for water (DBR) or right to possess water (IBR). Unfortunately, agencies usually do not know how many people use a meter. Under IBRs, a single guy with a large lawn may pay less for water than a family of six because his use is within the cheap block of water while the family's volume goes into the expensive block. Most water agencies allow for large families, but they use crude rules. The Los Angeles Department of Water and Power, for example, assumes that each household has six people when the average household has three people.

Some water agencies acknowledge this counting problem, but most worry that they will face opposition from privacy groups or do not have the resources to keep track of people. The first worry is overblown when the goal is merely a head count. People who want to protect their privacy can opt out, facing water prices appropriate for a single occupant. The second is more substantial, since it's expensive to count everyone by hand. It's possible to use a box on the water bill to collect head counts, but managers *then* worry about that customers will report higher headcounts to get more cheap water. This fear is perhaps overblown. I did a report for an agency that used head counts and steep IBRs. They had only 10 percent headcount inflation (compared with census statistics), and they didn't even audit customers' self-reported numbers. Some European water utilities use headcount data collected by the government; customers accept their use due to strong privacy laws.

How not to end shortages

> After dealing with a variety of student efforts to amplify the point that Southern California's intermittent water crises are caused by low rainfall, and at times require an elaborate system for water rationing, I stress, "True, it doesn't rain *water* in Southern California, but it also doesn't rain *Mercedes Benzes* in the area either... Have we ever had a *Mercedes Benz* crisis in Southern California?"
> —Richard B. McKenzie (2008)

Water prices based on cost may be too low to reduce demand to a level compatible with supply. When shortage results, water managers and politicians rush to increase supply or decrease demand.

In most parts of the world, it's hard to get more supply. If one community is short of water, it's likely that other communities are also short. That means groundwater and surface water supplies will already be strained. Some communities may commit to build plants to desalinate salty water or recycle wastewater. Although these solutions may be reliable compared with imported water sources subject to political, logistical or climatic variation, they take years to plan and build. More important, they will not prevent shortages that result when demand outpaces supply. The underlying problem is not insufficient supply — it's demand exceeding supply.

How can demand be reduced? Recall the slide versus shift example in Figure 1, where higher prices reduce quantity demanded or a taste or technology for conservation causes demand to shift in. Since institutional norms and political opposition make it hard to raise prices above cost, managers go for customer tastes, asking people to use less. Booklets instruct people to shower with a friend, advertisements encourage people to report their neighbor's green lawn, children learn that running taps hurt baby seals. Water cops give people tickets for sprinkling lawns on the wrong day. Did I make this up? Only the one about baby seals.

These admonitions do not usually work, but sometimes they work too well, and that's how we get the "utility death spiral," where revenues drop faster than costs, prices rise (to maintain breakeven), revenue falls even farther, and so on — until something breaks.

The death spiral originates in the mismatch between costs and revenues. Recall that most costs at a water agency are fixed (pipes, debt, salaries, and so on are paid regardless of delivery volume), while most revenues vary with use to encourage conservation. Prices are then set so that expected revenues match expected costs (at estimated delivery volumes), and expected profits are zero. Unfortunately, this balancing act often goes wrong.

In a typical water system with volumetric pricing, for example, 80 percent of costs are fixed but 80 percent of revenues are variable. These numbers mean that a family with a $100 water bill is paying $20 in fixed (monthly service) charges and $80 in variable (water consumption) charges. At the same time, the water utility's cost of delivering water is $80 fixed and $20 variable.

Now look at what happens when these family members do their fair share and shift in demand, so that their use falls by half. Their new water bill will be $60 ($20 fixed plus $40 variable), but the utility's cost of delivering that water drops to $90 ($80 fixed plus $10 variable), which means the utility loses $30. Water managers faced with this drop in revenue use financial buffers to fill the gap. When these are gone, managers ask for price increases, which drives customers crazy: "You asked us to use less, so we did. Now you are raising our prices. Why are you punishing us?" Price increases reduce quantity demanded even further (the slide effect), leading to additional losses, and so on.

Water managers who understand this problem may not promote effective water conservation programs. Why not? Consider how the chief financial officer of a water utility sees things. She needs to ensure repayment of infrastructure bonds representing debts of millions (even billions) of dollars. Repayment depends on revenues from selling water. Conservation means lower water sales, lower revenues, and less money for debt repayment. Faced with these conflicting goals, she pays lip service to conservation (press releases, drought kits and a picture of an unhappy water drop on the website) without giving people a strong incentive to use less. Customers can then be blamed for failing to use less at the same time as stable revenues make it possible to repay bondholders and maintain a strong credit rating. CFOs don't get paid for conservation; they get paid for balancing the books.

Some water for free, pay for more

Most of us have great water service provided by competent water managers who work under the supervision of elected officials or appointed regulators. This means the problems we've examined that result from deliberate policies can be solved by deliberate change. My suggestion for change, "some water for free, pay for more" (or Some for Free), is designed to cover costs, maintain equity, and prevent shortages for residential customers (businesses are in Chapter 4). Some for Free works like this:

First, every household (every meter) pays a service charge equal to the fixed cost of the water connection.

Second, the number of people in the household determines how many units of cheap (or free) water the house receives.[5]

----

[5]Policies often aim at delivering a lifeline or human right allocation of water to

Third, the price of additional units is set high enough to reduce demand and prevent shortages, not cover costs. Higher prices will also produce revenue in excess of costs (making CFOs happy).

Fourth, excess revenue is rebated per capita to reduce the impact of higher service charges on individuals and restore the agency's accounts to breakeven. These rebates transfer money from people who use more water to people who use less water.

Some for Free fits within current pricing routines. Water managers now set prices each year based on past use, projections of supply and anticipated costs. Put differently, they use supply and cost estimates to set prices and hope that consumers will conform to estimates. Small mistakes can be absorbed (by storing and/or spending saved water or money), but large mistakes lead to emergency meetings, price adjustments, groundwater overdrafting, and so on. A system that sets price high enough to keep demand within supply while generating excess revenue reduces the chance of either financial or hydrological shortage.

Some for Free merges two ideas: everyone should pay the same price for water to promote social equality, and everyone should pay the cost of delivering their water to promote economic equality. Everyone faces the same prices, but people who use more from the system pay a larger share of the system's costs.

Table 3 shows how Some for Free might work for three different households. Let's assume a meter charge of $50 reflects actual fixed costs and that the average cost of delivering water is $2 per unit. The width of each block in this IBR structure depends on the number of people at the meter. Water prices per person are set at $1 for each of the first three units, $3 per unit for the next three units and $6 per unit for additional units.

The results in the table match our goals of covering costs, preventing shortages, and fairly rationing water to people. You will also notice the most attractive feature of Some for Free: everyone gets a rebate because prices high enough to prevent shortage are also higher than the cost of delivery.

Now let's consider a few questions.

How do we know that higher prices will generate higher revenue? Demand for water is widely acknowledged to be inelastic: an increase in price results in a percentage reduction in quantity demanded that's

---

individuals. In South Africa, for example, a small allocation is guaranteed by the constitution. Chapters 3 and 11 elaborate on these policies.

Table 3: An example of Some for Free that uses made-up (but reasonable) numbers for three different households. Block width at each price is equal to three units times the number of residents. Rebates per person depend on the excess of water charges over water cost. Here, it's $(147 - 120) \div 9 = \$3$ per person.

People in household	1	3	5
Service charge ($50 per meter)	50	50	50
Block width (units)	3	9	15
Example use (units)	7	24	29
Units in $1/$3/$6 blocks	3/3/1	9/9/6	15/14/0
Water charge ($)	18	72	57
Provisional bill	$68	$122	$107
Water cost ($2 per unit)	14	48	58
Rebate ($3 per person)	-3	-9	-15
Final bill	$65	$113	$92

smaller than the percentage price increase. This means, for example, that the 10 units of quantity demanded at a price of $1 drops to six units when the price is $2, but that revenue rises from $10 to $12. Price increases do not have to be huge to create a financial surplus. Higher service charges will bring more money and existing prices are already set to cover costs. Higher prices will go straight to the bottom line to produce profits.

What about using excess money for deferred maintenance or improved reliability? That's possible, but those expenses should already be included in charges. Sometimes they are not (in an attempt to keep prices down), so maybe that use makes sense.

What happens when everyone uses less? Won't the utility lose money? Won't the loss in rebates harm people who have to pay the full cost of service charges? The utility will hit breakeven if the service charge covers fixed costs and a cheap water price covers variable costs. There will also be no shortage. The main problem is now the fact that everyone is paying the full cost of service. That's not really a problem for people who think it's better to have people pay for the services they receive, but others think that prices should be subsidized to "social" levels for precious water. Those subsidies bring two costs: political interference in water management and higher taxes elsewhere.

But this system is not aimed at subsidies or breakeven. It breaks the link between price and cost by aiming for excess revenues. This feature contradicts the institutional norms of the water business, but those norms were established in an age of abundance, when any and all demands for water were worthy of supply. That norm was possible because there was always plenty of water. Scarcity requires that demand be rationed, and it is rationed in two ways here. Some for Free ensures that every person gets enough basic water. Pay for More sets prices that are high enough to choke demand (recall Figure 3(b)) down to supply.

Since we are talking about choking and price increases, let me add a comment on how to present this idea — or any price increase — to customers, regulators and political overseers. First, review its features: cost recovery, no shortage, reasonable pricing and per capita allocation. Second, reiterate the reasons for a change in pricing: the end of abundance requires higher prices to ration demand because water is scarce. Third, get residential, business and industrial customers together to agree on how to set prices, cover costs, and allocate limited water. (It's hard to ask for subsidies from people in the room.) Fourth, agree on rebate targets and a formula for changing prices when circumstances dictate. Finally, advertise the agreement well in advance of implementation. Most people will agree to changes that address a real problem in a fair and transparent way.

Compare Some for Free with the industry's cutting-edge water budget pricing model. Each household gets an allocation of cheap water according to a formula that considers head count, lot size and irrigated landscaping. Households with similar characteristics get the same budget of cheap water; they face the same higher prices for exceeding their budget. This model is very popular with water agencies seeking to rein in consumption without forcing people to live with brown lawns. Unfortunately, they are very expensive to calibrate (some agencies use satellite mapping to calculate a landscaping budget that varies with the mix of plants and rocks), hard to explain to neighbors ("so, what's your evapotranspiration?"), and may not prevent shortage (prices are set for breakeven). Water budgets are also unfair, since people with big lawns get more cheap water than people with Water Haven showers. Some for Free is simple and fair.

Don't drink water from that fountain

All of this talk takes taps, money and clean water for granted, but many people in the developing world cannot. Nearly 1 billion people "lack access to an improved water source within one kilometer of their dwelling," and the lucky ones who do have "access" may not be able to drink the water. People with taps in their houses may not have 24/7 service (24 hours a day, 7 days a week), which means that they open their taps when there is pressure to fill storage tanks for later use. Unfortunately, intermittent service pressures can result in leaks that allow local sewage or pollution to contaminate drinking water. (Residents who pump water from the mains can increase seepage and pull in more contaminants.) Dirty water needs to be boiled or treated, but fuel is expensive. Disinfecting chlorine tablets cost less than a dollar a month, but many families do not buy them. Lots of people get sick. Residents with 24/7 supply are better off. They save money on storage and treatment equipment, get water when they want, and are less likely to get sick.

Ironically, policies to help the poor get cleaner water can make them worse off. A low price can encourage wasteful use (not turning off the tap) while denying revenue to the utility. Managers neglect poor areas that cost them money, water and effort. Instead, they concentrate on serving wealthier customers who pay higher prices (and who have political power). In Mexico City's shantytowns, for example, people without pipes get water from trucks. Truckers pay 50 pesos (about $4) to get 10,000 liters from city mains; then they sell 500 liters for 28 pesos (about $2), or 10 times the price. This informal service is fair in the sense that any trucker can gain customers by charging less but not in the sense that the poorest pay the most for an occasional water supply. These slum dwellers do not lack money (their truck water costs about four times the price of clean tap water in the US); they lack decent water management.

In rural areas, people get their water from community pumps or wells. Others have to walk to an "unimproved water source" like a lake or stream. Girls and women usually fetch water. In most areas, that means walking long distances, risking attack and rape. Indirect costs are also significant. Girls fetching water are not in school. Uneducated girls marry younger and have more children. The next generation of girls faces a similar cycle of water shortage/fetching water/missed school.

In 2000, the United Nations announced a series of Millennium Development Goals (MDGs) designed to improve life for the world's poorest. MDG Target 7C seeks to "halve the proportion of the population without sustainable access to safe drinking water and basic

sanitation by 2015." In 1990 (perhaps to get a head start with a flat-
tering base year), 77 percent of the world's population had access to
an "improved water source." By 2008 (most recent data), access had
increased to 87 percent. That leaves only 13 percent of the world's
population (884 million people, mostly in rural areas) without access.

Great! Right?

No. The UN redefined the goal from "halve the proportion of the
population without sustainable access to safe drinking water" to "halve
the proportion of the population without sustainable access to improved drinking water sources." That's a big difference in countries
where tap water can kill you. It's often said that "what gets measured,
gets managed" so we can see how people may get "improved water
sources" instead of drinkable water.

How do communities get improved water sources? Well-meaning
non-governmental organizations donate pumps or wells to communities, but these gifts are not always sustainable. It's not uncommon for
the pump to break (Who will fix it? Who will pay?) or for the water
supply to be drained. Local rules can manage pumps and demand,
but they need to work before saviors arrive with presents.

Although MDGs and free pumps may not work, political power
can. In the early 1990s, the Indian government amended its constitution to require that one-third of the leaders and members of village
councils be women. As this change was phased in, it allowed aca-
demics to compare the number of drinking water facilities in villages
where women had power with the number in villages where women
did not. Villages where women had power had 60 percent more drinking water facilities. Women with power help families.

Success comes in many forms

Most communities want a supply of reliable, quality water. The price
of this water can be high (100 percent desalination, used for lawns)
or low (local groundwater, used for drinking), but that outcome will depend on community consensus. In this chapter, I have concentrated
on making sure that everyone gets some water, preventing shortages
and covering capital and operating costs. Here are a few more examples of success.

It helps to start by charging people for the water they use. The
move from flat-rate, waste-doesn't-matter pricing to volumetric pricing immediately reduces consumption. Some people use a little less,
some use a lot less. The people who reduce use by the most are

those who have leaky plumbing but have never bothered to get it repaired. The same holds for water agencies and their distribution systems. In a well-maintained system, the percentage of non-revenue water (from leaks) is 5–10 percent. Poorly maintained systems can lose 30, 50 or even 70 percent of the water that goes into the pipes, usually because leaks are augmented by theft or special favors to certain customers.

After installing meters, it's important to think about how often customers see their bills. It's hard to change behavior when water bills and usage statistics arrive quarterly or annually. Monthly billing is good, but real-time statistics on consumption and volumetric charges give the strongest signals to conserve. Smart meters that measure and display real-time consumption are more expensive to install and operate because they require wireless communications networks to relay data and replace older, simpler meters that last for 30–50 years. On the other hand, real-time meters reduce labor costs (it costs $1–$4 to manually read a meter) and waste from leaks. Real-time meters also make it possible to implement innovative pricing schedules that can reduce, shift or reallocate consumption among customers. People who see consumption data flashing on the wall use less water and pay more attention to signals that raise prices during peak periods of heavy use. One study reported that customers with real time meters actually used more water. Why? Because they could see exactly how much water they could use before hitting the next block of more expensive (IBR) water. This result helps us understand how the combination of feedback and pricing can help the utility manage demand.

The format and layout of the bill also matters. Water bills using hundred cubic foot or kiloliter volume measurements are hard to understand. Bills that tell customers how many gallons or liters they are using each day are better; those that include calculations of use per person per day are even better. Comparisons of use with neighbors send powerful signals that encourage competitive conservation; bills with a happy face for below-average use or unhappy face for above-average use are especially effective. People don't like the unhappy face. It's important, on the other hand, to give the right signals to people who are saving water. Some of them will be proud of their happy face, but others will discover that they can use more without exceeding the average of their peers. Although it's possible to keep use data from these folks (just give them a request to keep doing what they were doing), it may be easier to reward them with some money from their unhappy-face neighbors, borrowing a page from Some for Free.

Here's an example of how price and non-price signals can work together. In the early 1990s, after several years of drought and no end in sight, water supplies were tight in Santa Barbara, California. Local TV stations had nightly updates on the slowly draining reservoir. Responses came from several directions. First, there was a change in acceptable use: green lawns and car washing were out. Second, the water agency instituted very strong IBRs: The first block was priced at $1.09. Additional blocks were priced 200 percent higher, at $3.27, $9.81 and $29.43 per unit. Although the first block allowed for 375 liters per day (which may still be too high, even for a family of three), that amount was smaller than previous levels and led to a much bigger jump at later blocks. The impact of changes in behavior and aggressive price penalties was fast and significant — gross water consumption dropped by 50 percent and median monthly household consumption dropped from 25 to 17 m^3 per month. And that consumption stayed low. After the drought ended and prices were lowered, consumption was still only 60 percent of pre-drought levels.

The Santa Barbara example combined price and non-price responses, but non-price responses can be powerful. Drought and shortage in Brisbane, Australia, led the local government and community to set a "Target 140" for daily use of 140 liters per person. Even without significant price incentives (Brisbane's prices rise by only 6 percent from the first block to the second block, and the first block allows for 700 liters per day), residents responded to a combination of peer pressure and regulations on "responsible use" to cut consumption from 330 to 130 liters per capita per day, a drop of 60 percent.

Nobody died of dehydration in Santa Barbara or Brisbane because people use a lot of water for lifestyle activities, which we discuss in Chapter 3.

No dry taps

The end of abundance means water is scarce and valuable. Unfortunately, the practice of pricing water according to the cost of delivery often ignores this scarcity value. A shortage may result when demand at the full cost price exceeds the supply of water. The easiest solution is to increase the price of water when it's scarce, so that the full price reflects the cost of delivery and the scarcity value of water. Higher prices need not be unfair. A Some Water for Free system gives everyone some cheap water, prevents shortages and covers system costs.

This suggestion offers one way of making sure that water reaches the tap, but demand can also be influenced through billing design, peer comparisons, community coordination, and other methods that do not require water imports from distant places, water cops issuing tickets, or showerhead regulations. It's also important to structure water service around service to *customers*, not meters, lawns or bureaucratic definitions. The end of abundance means we need to update old ways of pricing and allocating water to stop scarcity from turning into shortage.

CHAPTER 2

Dirty water

The end of abundant clean water means wastewater has to be cleaned instead of dumped in the environment. Freshwater scarcity raises the demand for treated wastewater, which will justify the cost of additional treatment.

You're a wastewater manager for a coastal city. In the 30 years that you've been in the business, you've seen progressively tougher regulations on the disposal of your product. In the beginning, you flushed everything a few hundred meters offshore. Then you were required to separate out the solids, selling or donating "sludge" to farmers for fertilizer. Then you had to treat the liquids, to process and kill bacteria and remove chemicals. Then the farmers started to reject the sludge, and you had to pay truckers to haul it to the desert for burial. Now people want the water to be treated to drinking water quality, not for discharge into the sea but for use on lawns. Never mind that nobody is going to drink it; they're afraid for their kids running on the grass. In the good old days, it was easy to get more clean water and it was easy to dump the dirty water. These days, it's harder to find new water sources, so people want your wastewater. Politicians, customers and regulators all want clean water, but they are shocked at the cost and complexity of treatment.

The end of abundance for freshwater means we have to pay more attention to protecting our drinking water and the environment. Our definition of dirty is changing, our rules for discharge are changing, and our perspectives on local and distant are changing.

Even the definition of goods is changing. Economists say that "goods" have a positive demand at a price of zero. Free food? Good. Free water? Good. Free hugs? Good. Bads have zero (or negative) demand at a price of zero. Garbage? Bad. Wastewater? Bad. Or maybe not. Empty aluminum cans are not bads because someone will buy them for their metal. The same is true about wastewater that can be reused. The end of abundance is simultaneously increasing the demand for treatment of wastewater (so that it does not pollute other water) and treated wastewater that urban, industrial and agricultural sectors can use. These demands reinforce each other, creating a virtuous cycle. Pollution is out, recycling is in. Storm water drains are out, recharge basins are in.

In this chapter, we will start with some physical and social definitions of "dirty water" that we don't want to drink, bathe in, or use on our lawns. Dirty water is water from toilets, sinks and other home sources; storm drains, industrial and agricultural discharges; and mines and oil refineries. We'll look at the way that dirty water was treated in the past, how the end of abundance is forcing us to reconsider those institutions, and how costs and benefits shifting under the influence of legal regulations and market incentives are driving innovations in the water treatment sector.

In the US and other developed countries, environmental concerns are pushing these changes. This importance has grown for aesthetic reasons, but also because our toxins are more harmful and more abundant than they were a century ago. In the past, for example, we would discharge wastewater into rivers and treat the drinking water we took from those rivers. We still have to treat drinking water, but we are now treating wastewater because it can cause greater harm and because we care about what happens as water moves between discharge and intake pipes.

Europeans try to reduce dirty water with regulations. Americans put more emphasis on market solutions (cap and trade of emissions) while also relying heavily on regulations. The end of abundance has a stronger impact on people in developing countries because they have less money and worse institutions (laws are missing or unenforced, politicians and regulators are negligent or corrupt). Most of the 2.8 million deaths per year from dirty drinking water happen in developing countries, and more than three-quarters of the dead are children. Although 2.8 million is only 5 percent of total global deaths, it's a big number (only 2.4 million people die each year in the US); it also misses the main impact of dirty water — chronic and acute illness. Waterborne diseases account for 100 million of the 1.5 billion global DALYs (disability-adjusted life years) lost to diseases of all kinds. Those DALYs are the equivalent of "put me out of my misery" illnesses that leave you miserable even if they don't kill you. For children under 14 years, 16 percent of total DALYs are caused by dirty water. The good news is that the world's poor can use a broader range of technologies to help themselves.

Dirty water

Our water rarely consists of just H_2O. Water is the swinger of the molecular world, willing to jump in bed with just about any other chemical, bacteria or virus. Water's affinity for bonding, dissolving and hosting contaminants means a simple glass of water may contain many impurities. Some people say that clean drinking water is "white water" while water from the shower or kitchen sink is "greywater" and water from the toilet is "blackwater," but these labels can be deceptive. The urine in toilet water may be less dangerous than household chemicals washing down the kitchen sink; lead pipes may contaminate tap water. It's hard to know which water is safe.

Water quality tests can help us pinpoint the source and magnitude of threats to our drinking water, but tests can also feed hysteria. Modern tests can detect contaminants in concentrations of parts per billion, trillion or quadrillion! A liter of my tap water, for example, contains 28 μg of trihalomethanes.[1] What are trihalomethanes? According to the US Environmental Protection Agency (EPA), "Some people who drink water containing total trihalomethanes in excess of the maximum contaminant level (80 μg) over many years could experience liver, kidney, or central nervous system problems and increased risk of cancer." That's bad, but I only drink 28 μg. So, I'm safe, right? Or not? I'm not happy about contaminants in my water, and neither is anyone else. Legitimate scientific uncertainty over impacts can quickly spin out of control, as advocacy groups (against industry, in favor of selling purifiers, against over-regulation) turn doubt into propaganda.

But propaganda works for a reason. We have a robust and evolved instinct to avoid dangerous food and drink. Some economists did an experiment in which they dipped a sterilized cockroach into a glass of water and then asked people how much they would need to be paid to drink the (sterile) water. People wanted a lot of money. A sterilized cockroach is still a cockroach.

The EPA enforces the Clean Water Act (1972) and Safe Water Drinking Act (1986), but new threats emerge faster than amended regulations. "Contaminants of Emerging Concern" such as hormones, drugs and other modern chemicals take years or decades to integrate

---

[1] A microgram (μg) is 1 millionth of a gram.

into the regulatory framework. This pace may be deliberate (science takes time), but it also may be slowed by political interference, limited resources, or lobbying from interest groups.

Additional complications come from measurement, reality and caution. The measurement problem arises from our ability to detect parts per trillion concentrations of substances that are harmful only in concentrations of parts per thousand. People have a hard time ignoring "harmless" contamination. Then there's the complication of reality: what happens when different substances that are individually safe combine in living creatures or ecosystems over time? These worries and others lead people to support the "precautionary principle" that any new substance (or process or product) should be prohibited unless evidence shows it to be useful and harmless. That sounds nice, but the precautionary principle can prevent the introduction of *any* new substance. As scientific philosopher Karl Popper pointed out, it's possible to prove that a substance is harmful but impossible to prove that it's always and everywhere harmless.

This discussion does not bring us to any conclusion. It merely highlights some of the factors in the scientific debate over water quality. The economics and politics are much easier. In California, for example, Sacramento and San Diego have exemptions from discharge regulations that allow them to put partially treated wastewater directly into neighboring bodies of water. They claim they cannot afford to pay for treatment. Why are they allowed to get away with this? They have political connections and can get waivers from regulators who are supposed to prohibit these activities. The benefit-cost calculus is simple: politicians, water managers and residents from Sacramento and San Diego get the benefit of dumping partially treated wastewater; neighboring cities and the environment get the costs.

Flushing away those externalities

Flush toilets and sewers are pretty efficient at moving urban waste, but they were designed in an era of abundant water. That era is over in places where regulations and market demand for toilets that use less water have reduced the amount of water in each flush from 13 liters of water per flush to about one-half liter in compressed-air-assisted toilets.[2] The resulting reduction in water flows can lead to un-

---

[2] It's possible to use no potable water by installing a parallel set of pipes (to carry greywater or recycled water) or using composting toilets, but these solutions involve heavy up-front capital costs.

intended complications (San Francisco manually flushes its clogged sewers with bleach). Flushing toilets with drinking water is sometimes a cheaper and better choice.

The costs and benefits of treating dirty water in sewers are also changing. Sewage can either be treated or dumped straight into rivers or oceans. Let's return to Sacramento and San Diego and their partially treated wastewater. What does "partially" mean? Wastewater that arrives at a treatment plant is pre-treated to remove garbage, plants and other floating debris. Primary treatment physically separates heavy solids and oil, grease and lighter solids from liquids. Secondary treatment biologically removes dissolved and suspended biological matter from those liquids using microorganisms that digest organic matter. Sludge solids from primary and secondary treatment are sent off site for treatment, combustion, burial, or spreading on agricultural lands. Tertiary treatment chemically or physically cleans water with chlorine compounds, UV light, ozone, bacteria, and/or filters (carbon, sand or lagoons with flora and fauna). The intensity (and cost) of tertiary treatment depends on where the water is going: natural water bodies, irrigated landscaping or agriculture, groundwater recharge, or even drinking water supplies.

Sacramento residents would have to pay $2 billion (about $1,400 per person) to add a tertiary treatment stage to the wastewater it now discharges into local wetlands (known as the Delta) that border many communities and eventually drain into the Pacific Ocean. The people of San Diego would have to pay $1.5 billion (about $700 per person) to put the wastewater that it currently dumps into the Pacific Ocean through a secondary treatment stage.

Treatment is expensive, but it keeps rivers and oceans cleaner. Although these benefits may exceed the costs of treatment, the real problem comes from the distribution of costs and benefits. Should cities dump untreated dirty water for free or pay to clean it for the benefit of neighbors? The people of Sacramento and San Diego don't think so, but their opinion is decreasingly relevant. Indeed, Sacramento was ordered to pay for an upgrade to its treatment facilities in December 2010. Downstream users lobbied for the order to improve water quality in *their* local environment.

Don't flush on me!

The negative externality of an upstream user's discharge of dirty water on downstream neighbors arises from this benefit-cost asymmetry.

Although many people claim government intervention is necessary to correct this imbalance, the problem can be solved in other ways. Mismatched benefits and costs are an ancient problem. The relevant question is how to reduce the harm from that mismatch at the lowest cost.

The right to clean water has been protected in Anglo-American common law for many centuries. This right, for example, says that an upstream user cannot harm a downstream user by diverting quantity or degrading quality. The common law has been used to stop farmers from polluting a stream with animal waste and to stop gold miners from filling streams with sediment, arsenic and mercury. The common law requires that the downstream user show harm, which is defined to suit local circumstances and custom, but it gives them a right to not be polluted. The establishment of harm gives the pollutee the right to be free of that harm, which means the polluter has to pay the pollutee if he wants to pollute.

But what about a failure to establish harm? Interestingly, that result merely shifts rights, from the right to not be polluted to the right to pollute. In that case, the pollutee has to pay the polluter to reduce or stop the polluting activity. In either case, the size of the payment depends on the relative costs and benefits of pollution (as defined by the interested parties) and efficiency increases as costs and benefits align more closely.

Many people do not like the idea of a right to pollute or payments to continue pollution, but payments extend the range of possible choices and outcomes. We don't want to ban any action that has costs; we want to make sure that most or all costs are reflected in decisions to undertake that action. We want to internalize the externalities, and sometimes internalization requires a little creative thinking.

Ronald Coase won the Nobel Prize for economics for making these points in his 1960 article, "The Problem of Social Cost."[3] He argued that either the polluter or the pollutee could receive the right to pollute. If the polluter has the property right, then the pollutee will pay him to pollute less, until she decides that additional reductions in pollution are not worth the price. If the pollutee has the right to be free

---

[3]The prize's official name — "The Sveriges Riksbank Prize in Economic Sciences in Memory of Alfred Nobel" — was a clever ploy to associate it with the older Nobel prizes in chemistry, literature, peace and other disciplines. That ploy has succeeded in popular perception, but I also use the shorter name to save space.

of pollution, then the polluter has to pay her if he wants to pollute, until that cost exceeds his benefit from further pollution.

These ideas explicitly ignore the value of the right to pollute or be free of pollution to the individuals. Coase, like many economists, considers the transfer of money between individuals to be irrelevant to social efficiency, since a dollar in the pocket of one person is the same as a dollar in the pocket of another person in the same society. The key is to set up a mechanism that delivers the efficient amount of pollution and avoids inefficiently high or low pollution that raises social costs. Such a goal underlies existing markets for water pollution that allow existing polluters to trade discharge permits, so that those polluters who reduce their pollution below permitted levels are allowed to sell their excess permits to others facing higher costs for reductions. This system provides a profit motive to those who clean up, gives flexibility to those who cannot do so very easily, and keeps total pollution below an overall cap.[4]

Politicians are more interested in the distribution of money, so that may explain why the right to pollute is not just scattered among citizens. It's given out very carefully, according to institutional norms that we will address in Part II.

Coase did not dismiss another important point. He reminded readers that the transaction costs of negotiating an agreement had to be small, relative to the costs and benefits of pollution. A deal between neighbors over a common stream is easier to conclude than one between many neighbors sharing a lake.

This leads us to regulation of pollution and dirty water. Regulation works best when transaction costs are large. For example, when pollution affects a common-pool good whose ownership is vaguely defined, crosses political or judicial boundaries, or affects many people in different, hard-to-quantify ways. Regulated water quality, for example, makes it easier for customers to know what's in their tap water or bottled water, because a few independent experts can perform complicated tests and publish results for all to see, eliminating the need for every household to test its water. The regulation of aerial spraying of chemical pesticides and herbicides that persist in the soil and water for long periods also makes sense, because these chemicals affect many places. That's why Rachel Carson's *Silent Spring* had such an

---

[4]These negotiations will factor in the positive value of pollution in a way that regulations may not. Farmers, for example, may prefer to use wastewater fertilized by human waste.

impact in 1962. Her thorough and passionate exposure of the poisoning of America's soils and waters by widespread (and ineffective) spraying of DDT, Aldrin and Heptachlor led to regulations and bans on the use of those chemicals, without requiring individuals to fight their use many times in many places. In fact, regulation may have been the only choice in the matter, since the Department of Agriculture was responsible for abusing those chemicals. It's harder to sue the government than forbid it from taking certain actions.

But not all regulations are effective; they can be outdated, unenforced, politically manipulated, based on bad science, hysteria, or excessive caution. The biggest problem is that regulations can displace more efficient methods of minimizing the cost of pollution.

Regulators are useful when they are representing us, the masses, but they can get in the way of a bilateral negotiation between upstream and downstream parties who have better incentives to accurately measure harm and costs. On the other hand, regulations can complement common law and property rights institutions by defining and quantifying harm and the relative property rights of polluters and pollutees, which will reduce the transaction costs that inhibit negotiations.

The growing value of dirty water

Abundance can have objective or subjective meanings. On the one hand, there may be less water, of lower quality. On the other, the definition of "less" can change. Both of these factors affect our perception of dirty water and their interaction in our minds, homes, and communities creates demands for action and change.

From an objective perspective, wastewater from residential, industrial, and agricultural users is dirtier than it was a century ago. We use more chemicals, even if modern chemicals are safer than earlier versions. These dirty water streams are not always treated before they are mixed into natural bodies of water. Offshore dead zones (where algae have absorbed all the oxygen, leaving none for other creatures) can be traced to nitrogen in agricultural runoff. Resource extraction industries have polluted vast amounts of water while refining crude oil and shale oil (tar sands), extracting metals and minerals in hard rock mining, breaking rocks with high-pressure water injections to get at natural gas (fracking), processing coal into low-carbon fuels, and so on. Excessive volumes of dirty water from these activities can be traced to a combination of weak regulation and missing prices for clean water as an input or dirty water as an output.

Subjective perceptions explain the "things are better, we're in trouble" paradox in wastewater, where the move from primary to secondary or tertiary treatment improves quality, but not by enough to meet higher expectations of clean. These expectations can lead to over-treatment from an economic or environmental perspective, as when treated water is cleaner than the water it's discharged into.

For many years, "the solution to pollution was dilution" because there was enough clean water for dilution and adequate natural filters to process pollution. It was also the solution because downstream water users already needed to treat water before drinking. But higher volume and lower quality changed that norm. Higher wastewater volumes overwhelmed natural filters, creating cesspools. Natural processes could not filter new sources of artificial pollution. These new sources increased two costs: the cost of treating water for drinking and the cost of damage to the environment. The environmental movement launched by *Silent Spring* gained strength as people started to see nature as more than a place for wastewater. The end of abundance that began then is growing stronger, as our subjective definition of "clean" waxes and tolerance for pollution wanes. An important side effect of the pursuit of cleanliness is the increase in supply of water that's clean enough for industrial processes, thermoelectric cooling or agricultural irrigation. These sectors are willing to pay some or all of the costs of getting treated water. Their purchases of dirty (but useful) water save them money and leaves more clean water for drinking and the environment.

Technologies to reduce dirty water

Most residential water customers do not pay for wastewater by volume. Instead, they pay a flat price that reflects the average cost of treating sewage in the entire system or a volumetric charge that depends on their tap water consumption. Both methods are easy to calculate, but neither method gives an incentive to reduce wastewater volume or pollution. People with low discharges subsidize people who discharge heavy volumes or add oil, pharmaceuticals, chemicals or other substances that are expensive to remove. Rates based on intake mean that people with big lawns pay more than their toilet flushes would justify. Although it's expensive to monitor volumes or detect contaminants now, technology can lower the cost of measurement at the same time as higher treatment costs make such detection attractive. We already know that this works: industrial users facing wastewater charges that rise with volume or pollutants increase their recycling and cleaning to lower their bills.

People who divert greywater from sinks and showers to toilets and gardens conserve potable water and reduce their drinking water bill. Such clever conservation makes sense to some, but water managers don't always like greywater. First, greywater may be polluted or unsafe. Second, greywater reduces water flows in sewers, which increases the unit cost of treating wastewater. Third, more greywater means less wastewater, which can be valuable. Las Vegas, for example, can take more water from nearby Lake Mead when it discharges treated wastewater into the lake. These new withdrawals can be treated and sold to customers, increasing revenues and lowering the chance of a shortage. The example of Prescott Valley, Arizona, is even starker. Prescott sold treated wastewater for more than $20,000/ML to real estate developers who needed to secure water supplies before they could build new homes. Prescott Valley's water managers don't want people to reduce wastewater flows that they can sell.

The high cost of additional treatment (recall those billion dollar costs for Sacramento and San Diego) worries water managers. Many of them want federal subsidies for municipal wastewater treatment. These subsidies are not economically sound. First, they are targeted to public agencies, not private companies that also serve the public. Second, subsidies hide the true cost of pollution from the people who create it, reducing the incentive to reduce waste. Third, subsidies targeted at secondary or tertiary standards may be inefficient if they require too much or too little treatment relative to local conditions. It makes more sense to compromise with neighbors on certain pollutants (assuming that all interested parties can be identified). Finally, subsidies narrow choices. For example, wastewater can be moved through a constructed wetlands full of plants, trees, insects and other processing beasts that function as a "living machine" for removing organic and non-organic pollutants (even heavy metals). These systems may deliver results that meet the goals of local communities (restore damaged wetlands, nurture insects and fish for food, buffer floods, and so on) at lower costs than systems eligible for subsidies. Wastewater subsidies are not a good idea.

The end of abundance (and rise of nasty chemicals) means sludge remaining after primary and secondary treatment is more of a liability than an asset. Farmers have put human waste on their fields for centuries, but today's sludge is contaminated with pharmaceuticals, household chemicals, pesticides, herbicides, and other nasties that we don't want on our salad or in our milk. Unfortunately, half of America's sludge is put on fields as fertilizer. Los Angeles used to truck 450,000 tons of sludge a year over a mountain ridge to neighboring Kern County, a rural area with big farms. Los Angeles spread its sludge on its own farm (charmingly named "Green Acres") until 2006, when 86 percent of Kern voters decided to ban sludge. Los Angeles is now fighting to get that ban overturned, claiming that the extra cost of taking its sludge elsewhere is too high. How much? An extra $8 per ton. Fortunately, there's a market solution to this issue. Los Angeles can auction its sludge; whoever wants it can buy it (or be paid to take it). Market prices reflect the cost of pollution, but they also provide incentives. Technologies for extracting energy and processing wastewater and sludge are gaining market share as traditional dumping, burying and discharging options disappear.

Lower quality municipal sludge has also made personal sludge more attractive. Modern composting toilets that don't use water have updated the outhouse model for collecting human waste for compost. Like solids from septic tank systems, this compost is safe to spread on agricultural land, because it normally lacks the contaminants of municipal and industrial sludge.

Localized recycling of solids has its equivalent for liquids, in closed-loop, Toilet-to-Tap systems that return treated wastewater to customers as potable drinking water (it's called NeWater in Singapore and also sold in bottles). What's interesting is that this recycled water is cleaner than the natural water people have been drinking for years, but many people don't like the idea of drinking it (remember the cockroach). People would rather drink dirtier water from a stream than clean water from a machine because the stream's connection to toilets is abstract, but the machine's connection is all-too-real. In response to this fear, water managers often take recycled water that's gone through three or four stages of treatment and mix it with natural (dirtier) water in a reservoir or aquifer. The mixed water is then withdrawn, treated to drinking quality standards, and distributed to customers. This process (called Indirect Potable Reuse or IPR) has nothing to do with quality or safety and everything to do with perceptions.

IPR reproduces Earth's closed-loop system for cleaning, evaporating and precipitating water. The key difference is speed. The end of abundance means we need to spend money and energy to hurry up that process. We need clean water now, not later.

Dirty hands kill millions

Several years ago, I was hiking in Nepal. Every day, I passed another lovely stream, and every day, I didn't drink the water. I put iodine tablets in the water I got from taps. The water looked cool and fresh, but I had no way of knowing whether it was clean. Rural Nepalis, like 2.5 billion people worldwide, do not have access to good sanitation. Many of them defecate in the open, increasing the chance of contaminating water that will sicken people. Ironically, the global total of 2.8 million annual deaths from dirty water could be reduced by bringing water closer to sanitation facilities. That's because the majority of sanitation-related deaths can be traced to inadequate post-toilet hand washing.

Germs and dirty hands remind me of some interesting statistics about people in developed countries. Researchers have confirmed that men wash their hands less often than women (one study found that 75 percent of American men and 90 percent of women actually wash; fewer than the number who say they wash), but it's also true that women's apartments have more germs than men's. Why? Women spread germs around when they clean. Men don't clean so much, so their germs are localized. Is the dirtiest place the toilet? No, it's the sponge next to the sink, which is warm, moist and full of germs.[5]

Meanwhile, urban people in developing countries face the same problems with wastewater that they do with tap water. Facilities do not exist; money for infrastructure often disappears into corrupt pockets; and pollution is literally dumped on poor people. It's common to see poor people living next to drain pipes, open sewers and other dirty places. That happens for three reasons. First, the poor cannot afford to live in clean places. Second, waste managers can ignore poor people who have little political power. Third, managers can save money by routing sewage through poor neighborhoods where land is cheap. Poor urban Indians, for example, sometimes live next to treatment plants that do not handle their waste, either because they are not connected to the system or because the system is so badly maintained that it cannot move waste to the plant.

What adds insult to this injury is that the poor are often presented

---

[5]Cleaning hint: Wet and microwave your sponge for two minutes. The sponge will be hot, so don't get burnt when removing it.

as the beneficiaries of subsidized wastewater services that they do not even receive. The subsidies go to service clients with greater political or economic clout. The poor are often able and willing to pay for sewerage, but they are not given the chance. That's because the bureaucrats who provide service often have zero incentive (higher salary or profit) to increase their workload by extending sewerage into slums.

Private companies may better serve the poor. Economists who studied Argentina's 1990s water privatizations concluded that "child mortality fell 8 percent in the areas that privatized their water services; and that the effect was largest (26 percent) in the poorest areas." Contracts allowed profits, subsidized the poorest households, allowed for disconnection for nonpayment, and required private operators to extend their service area for both drinking water and sewerage. The poor benefited the most because they finally got service that they could also afford.

Turning black water into blue gold

The end of abundant freshwater has increased the importance of treating dirty water. We have higher expectations in our definition of clean water and want a healthier environment, but we also have greater problems with industrial, agricultural and urban contaminants in wastewater. The increasing value of clean water has increased the benefits from cleaning dirty water, facilitating higher expenditure on advanced treatment techniques that increase clean water discharges. (Sacramento was ordered to clean its wastewater, but it's planning to sell the treated water to partially offset higher charges to customers.) Higher costs from more dangerous contaminants have also made it easier to decentralize wastewater handling. Localized treatment may cost more per processing unit, but it can be cheaper than subsidizing treatment of a neighbor's nasty wastewater. The end of abundance means that contamination is more costly, clean water is more valuable, and polluters should pay the cost of cleaning up their mistakes.

CHAPTER 3

The liquid lifestyle

Water scarcity will reduce water consumption for lifestyle uses. Regulating water uses is inefficient and unfair — it's better to raise prices and let people pay for the uses they prefer.

Water managers have a love/hate relationship with their accountants. On the one hand, they document managers' ability to deliver clean water to customers at very low prices, about $1 for 1,000 liters. On the other hand, these accountants require that managers charge a price linked to that cost, a price that's so low that customers demand more water for pools, power showers, lawns and other lifestyle features with heavy demands that reduce supplies and make shortages more likely. Cheap water policies mean that it may be possible to buy a thousand liters for $1 today but no water at any price tomorrow.

The end of abundance means prices based on cost need to be upgraded to include scarcity charges. Scarcity-based prices may not keep people from wasting water on lifestyle habits, but they will prevent shortages and ensure that people pay the full cost of their choices.

This chapter on lifestyle water is not devoted to the water we need to stay alive, clean and fed. It's not about the water that businesses need to operate. It's about the optional water that we use to improve our surroundings or have fun. Lifestyle water is different in three ways. First, it represents a large component of our water demand and consumption; more than half of the residential water in Southern California (an arid region) goes for landscaping; across the US, the average household uses about one-third of its water outdoors. Second, lifestyle water has the lowest value to us, by definition. It's the first use that we cut when we want to use less water. Third, lifestyle water is at the heart of water shortages, and our consumption patterns are the result of the way we price and manage it.

The end of abundance will have a stronger impact on lifestyle water because most lifestyle uses are optional. Consider a green lawn in the desert. The average "Scottish lawn" in Southern California uses 110–200 cm of water per year (the number varies with heat and humidity) to stay healthy and green. Rainfall in Southern California averages 25–50 cm per year. If we assume demand of 130 cm and rainfall of 50 cm, that means a healthy lawn needs an extra 80 cm of water. That's 800 liters of water per square meter of lawn per year — ignoring the frequent problem of overwatering. Although an average American lawn is 1,350 m^2 (one-third acre), let's assume that this Southern Californian lawn is only 500m^2. That's 400,000 liters of water per year (more than 1,000 liters per day). That huge volume is typical for Southern California, and it's the reason that outdoor irrigation accounts for more than 50 percent of residential water consumption in the area. A thousand liters per day is enough to keep 20 people alive and healthy in a typical developing country. Although it doesn't make economic or environmental sense to reduce Southern California lawn irrigation and export the saved water to people in Sudan, it does make sense to think of why we use so much water.

The economics of lifestyle water are simple. We use that water for fun, so we should have to pay the full cost of that fun, including the cost of scarcity. These higher charges have two virtues. They limit demand (making shortage less likely) and provide revenue to subsidize basic water service. This Some for Free policy (described in Chapter 1) is not necessarily efficient from an economic perspective (most people can afford to pay the full cost of their basic service), but it would ensure that the highest charges are associated with voluntary uses, without passing judgment on the correctness of those uses. High prices on lifestyle water that reduce demand for pools and lush landscaping in wet periods also reduce the need for painful cutbacks during dry times when supplies are short (people fight for lawns they've invested in). Revenue from lifestyle surcharges can be used to maintain infrastructure, improve reliability or reward water conservation. After all, it doesn't help to have a dead lawn and a dry tap, does it?

Prices based on cost lead to shortages

Institutions for managing water can be confusing to people from outside the industry, because they reflect an evolution of policies aimed at particular political, bureaucratic and social objectives (generally in that order), as opposed to arising in response to market forces. Thus, we have water policies that distort familiar ideas into unusual shapes. First, consider the basic definitions of supply and demand for a good such as gasoline. Our demand for gasoline expresses a *value* relationship between price and quantity. When gasoline is expensive, we buy some for our most important uses. When the price drops, we buy more for less important uses. That's how we get the demand curve in Figure 1. The supply of gasoline, likewise, expresses a *cost* relationship between price and quantity. When the price is low, it makes sense to sell gasoline that's the cheapest to find, refine and bring to market. When prices are high, it makes more sense to go look for oil in other places, even when that oil is more expensive to bring to market as gasoline, because the prices are high enough to pay costs and make profits.

These two relationships lead to the familiar interaction of supply and demand, a process that adjusts quantity and price until quantity demanded equals quantity supplied at a price where value equals cost. At that point, additional quantity is too expensive to supply, relative to market price. Likewise, additional quantity is not worth demanding because the value is less than the price. Figure 5(a) clarifies these relationships. Compare them with the scarcity pricing in 5(b) that we first saw in Figure 3(b).

An efficient market needs many consumers and many gas stations to create competition. It also has prices that change as often as necessary to balance supply and demand. An increase in demand, for example, leads to an increase in prices, which quickly attracts gasoline from other places (even other countries).

With the exception of demand (we use more water when it's cheap), none of these dynamics are common with water, and that's why water allocation structures (they are not markets) are prone to shortages and surpluses in water and revenue.

The most important reason for these problems is the practice of pricing water according to the cost of supply, not scarcity or value. Prices are not based on a market equilibrium because urban water markets do not exist. Local monopolies sell water to cover their costs. Cost pricing made sense when water was abundant because the only goal was to recover the costs of building and running the system that had plenty of water but it doesn't when water itself is scarce.

Let's pause a moment to focus on this important point: prices based on the cost of delivering water may not reflect the costs of tak-

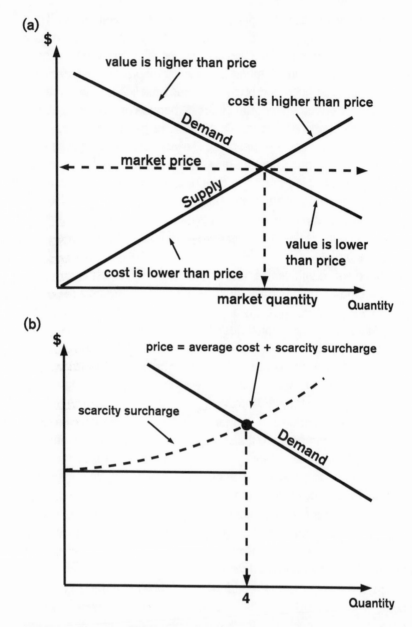

Figure 5: (a) We demand more and more of a good while its value to us exceeds (or equals) its price. Similarly, businesses will supply goods as long as price exceeds production cost. Supply and demand are equal at the market price and quantity. Beyond this point, additional quantity will not be demanded (price exceeds value) or supplied (cost exceeds price). (b) A scarcity surcharge produces this equilibrium by increasing price to reduce quantity demanded.

ing that water from one place and depositing it elsewhere, in terms of the flora and fauna affected by those changed flows or future scarcity. Cost-based pricing may also fail to allocate water to the most valuable human uses, because non-price rationing during shortages does not necessarily reflect our subjective personal priorities. Prices that reflect and reconcile these costs and values more accurately are going to increase our wealth and health and happiness.

Now consider how cost pricing can lead to water shortages in the short run and an expansion in demand that makes shortages more likely in the long run.

Figure 2 shows how average cost pricing combined with an unexpected outward shift in demand can result in a shortage. This problem does not arise from setting price to average cost as much as not being able to change prices when a limited quantity of water becomes scarce. A gasoline seller can respond to higher demand by increasing prices or trucking in more supplies from elsewhere. Under current institutions for water management, neither of these responses is possible. It's hard to raise prices or get more water in less than a few months. What we see instead is a desperate attempt to cover shortages by borrowing from stored supplies, but those stores may not be sufficient.

The case of long run shortage begins with average cost pricing, which simultaneously underprices expensive water and encourages use. Different patterns of average cost pricing (flat-rate, uniform block and decreasing block prices discussed in Chapter 1) do nothing to reduce demand — increasing the likelihood of shortage. Increasing block rates (IBRs) rise in steps that reflect the marginal (additional) cost of each new source of supply within a portfolio of sources. IBRs are thus meant to mimic the supply curve that ensures that we have gasoline for our cars. Does that mean that IBRs will limit demand or prevent shortages?

No. The main problem with IBRs is that they cannot limit demand. Even worse, they actually reflect average (not marginal) costs, which means IBRs — like other average cost pricing models — subsidize overconsumption and encourage the expansion of demand by selling water at prices below real cost.

Figure 6 illustrates these ideas. First, remember that IBRs are calculated to deliver total revenues that cover total costs. This means demand must be estimated and prices set so that the quantity demanded equals supply. These estimates are shown as Average Demand, $1/3/4 per unit prices and Q(average) in Figure 6(a). Now, say that a drought occurs. With less rain, customers want more tap water, and their demand shifts out to Drought Demand. Water managers can respond to the drought by asking customers to use less or rationing customers (voluntarily or involuntarily shifting demand back in). They can also raise prices, but that takes time and may fail to work, since prices still need to reflect real costs — unlike the case in Figure 6(b), where scarcity surcharges can prevent shortages. Finally, they can pray (the "March Miracle" that broke California's 1987–1991 drought dropped six-months' worth of rain in a single month). If customers still decide to use water, they pay $4 per unit for Q(drought) units. Managers are forced to draw down stored water to meet this demand because it's impossible to get new water fast enough. Unlike gas stations, water utilities need months or years to get more supplies. This pattern reveals the problem with IBRs: The top block of water that supposedly reflects the cost of acquiring new water cannot meet all demand at that price. The most expensive block of water is limited in width (quantity) and cannot be increased on short notice. When it's gone, the price should shoot up to choke demand — as the vertical arrow at Q(average) does in Figure 6(a). If prices do not increase, then excess demand is either served with stored supplies or ignored via rationing.

Water managers try to avoid rationing by storing extra water. They also keep extra money on hand. Why? In a normal year, Q(average) is sold and revenues equal costs. In a drought, more water is sold, reducing stored supplies, but more revenue comes in, adding to financial reserves. The opposite happens in a wet year, when sales fall (revenue down but storage up). Over time, these fluctuations in money and water balance out around the average quantity of supply that meets average demand, generating average revenue that covers average costs. In other words, IBR water is really sold at prices that reflect long run average cost, not the marginal cost of new supplies that do not exist.

To recap (and simplify), water managers who cannot quickly raise prices to reflect water scarcity either ration water (creating a shortage) or deliver emergency water (allowing demand to expand, which increases the chance of future shortage).

Why don't shortages happen all the time? First, because managers build large and expensive water storage infrastructure to meet demand. Second, because many people are willing to restrain them-

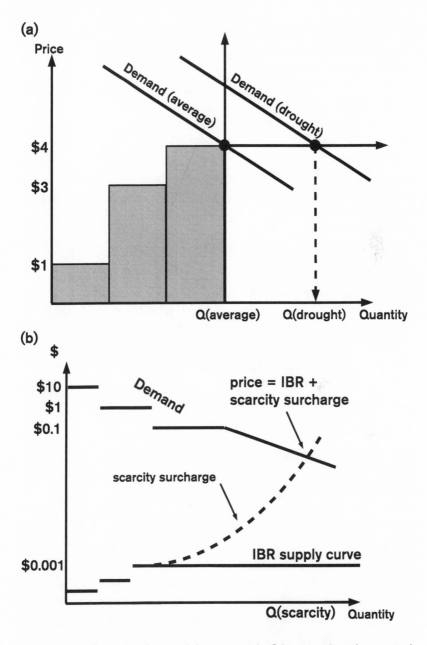

Figure 6: (a) Drought demand that exceeds Q(average) at the posted maximum price of $4 requires that emergency supplies be used, at a cost that shoots up far above $4. (b) Shortages can result when the value of water is much greater than the cost of water (per liter prices and values on the vertical axis are reasonably accurate but are not drawn to scale). A scarcity surcharge on cost-based prices can lower demand to available supplies.

selves — until it rains somewhere, and water is psychologically abundant. Third, because we've been lucky to have cycles of wet years and dry years.

But sometimes we aren't lucky. A drought persists, demand sucks down supplies, and everyone panics.

It would be easier to use Some for Free scarcity pricing (Figure 6(b)) to prevent the shortage, ensure that everyone gets a fair share of cheap water, and double-reward water misers with lower water bills and rebates of excess revenue.

That's how cost-based pricing encourages demand to grow. Let's look at some of the interesting ways that this growth manifests.

Desert palms, desert lawns

Palm trees are strongly associated with the sunshine lifestyle that people enjoy in California, Nevada, Arizona and other hot dry states. What's interesting is that most of these palms are not indigenous. Only one palm species (out of the 2,500 worldwide) is native to the western US, and it's not the one we see in Beverly Hills. Even more interesting is that these palms cannot live without irrigation.

Then how did they get there? Beginning in the 1920s, real estate developers started planting palms in dry areas, providing the water that those thirsty trees needed. People who came to buy houses were struck by the "native vegetation" that has been associated with abundant water supplies for thousands of years. They bought houses and continued to water their trees from Southern California's bountiful imported waters. Palms became a non-sustainable liability as demands from people and vegetation outpaced supplies and abundance ended. A palm tree needs about 250 cm of water per year to stay alive. That's about double the local precipitation in Southern California, and much more than the 10 cm that falls in Las Vegas. (The California white oak, *Quercus lobata*, lives in areas with 40–100 cm of precipitation.) Despite palm trees' thirst for water, their existence is not the main driver in urban water use. Neither is the water used for toilets, showers or swimming pools. The biggest source of demand for lifestyle water comes from lawns. Indeed, America's largest crop is lawn grass, not corn or wheat.

In some parts of the world, indigenous green grass survives on rainfall. That's the way it is in Scotland, where men have spent centuries learning how to exploit the rolling hills, rocks and deep turf. Besides being a great place to make whiskey and raise sheep, Scotland is also a great place to play golf. Fairways and greens are everywhere. Sand traps, water traps, sheer cliffs, stubborn trees and strong winds make it a challenge to walk from here to there, especially while bashing a little rock with a stick.

The trouble came when those Scots (and their English cousins) went overseas to expand the British Empire. No matter where they went (Australia, India, New Zealand, North America, South Africa and so on), they brought their notion that a house wasn't a house unless it had a proper garden and lawn. In some places (Boston or Christchurch, New Zealand), it was easy to grow those familiar plants. In others, it required a lot of work. But the colonials got their lawns.

Most of the landscaping that we associate with "native" or "natural" has nothing to do with what was growing in the area 100 or 200 years ago. Many of us grew up with lawns, sports fields and golf courses, but those grassy places are more habitual than normal. Phoenix, Arizona, gets about 20 cm of rain per year, but homeowners water their lawns by flooding them. That's right. They open a little gate and allow water to flood in, until 4–6 cm of water laps against little dikes on the edges of their yards. How can people do this with Colorado River water that comes from 200 km away? Because the Central Arizona Project (CAP, built between 1973 and 1993) brings so much water that it's possible to sell it at cheap prices. This example makes it easy to see how water economics worked in the era of abundance. Everyone worried about the big fixed costs from infrastructure, not whether there would be enough water to fill the pipes and canals. Revenue covers infrastructure debt and delivery costs. The water itself was free, but limited to Arizona's quantified rights to Colorado River water. For many years, CAP managers did their best to find new customers for their abundant water, to make sure that they could generate enough revenue to cover their costs. But the end of abundance means they are now trying to find ways to limit demand and ensure reliability: they recently announced an auction to allocate new supplies and a plan to leave water in storage on the Colorado, to prevent future cutbacks in the event of extended drought. Lawn owners may soon face the choice between dead lawns and expensive water bills instead of a choice between a 5 cm or 6 cm pool on their lawn.

Many cities and planned communities force homeowners to keep green, lush lawns. Landscaping laws are not meant to protect neighbors from dead lawns. They're designed to protect property values, so that potential home buyers see a nice green neighborhood. But that common sense explanation often turns into micromanaged laws and ordinances on landscaping. Sacramento's 1941 Front Yard Landscape Ordinance 17.68.010 required "primarily low groundcover or turf" in the front yard (not just a clean or healthy yard) until it was amended in 2007 to allow for tall plants and other features. Unfortunately, the amendments still required a front yard that was "irrigated, landscaped and maintained." In June 2008, California Governor Arnold Schwarzenegger declared a statewide drought from his office in Sacramento. Shortly thereafter, a local couple was given a $746 ticket for failing to irrigate their front yard in accordance with 17.68.010. It took about two seconds for local media to pick up on this bureaucratic violation of common sense, and a public outcry forced the city government to cancel the ticket.

Anti-lawn activists point out that lawns use a lot of water, are frequently the source of nasty runoff from over-application of pesticides and fertilizers, and are not even native to most parts of the world. These points are all true, but they are being used to create an entirely new set of command-and-control regulations that are just as bad as the old regulations. Now communities force homeowners to plant native vegetation, give tickets for watering the sidewalk, and prohibit lawns that are too large. Other communities defend mandatory lawns: the city council of Albuquerque, New Mexico, voted against proposal that would *allow* homeowners to have no lawns in August 2010. Stuck between "green" cactus and green lawns, some homeowners split the difference and spray their dead brown lawn with green paint.

This is not really progress. Regulations and laws may make people think that they've accomplished something, but they are costly to write, enforce and obey. Regulations can favor certified landscape professionals over homeowners with shovels, but their real weakness is the way they impose an inflexible one-size-fits-all solution on everyone.

Lawns are not the problem. The problems are overconsumption of water, pesticide and herbicides that can be solved by charging people for using more water, weed spray, or bug killer. It doesn't matter if a higher price is set in the market or through a bureaucratic tax. People should be able to choose whether they want big lawns, small lawns, vegetable gardens or basketball courts, according to simple rules. The problem is water that's so cheap that people use it without thinking. Expensive water that reflects the cost of scarcity may mean that a lawn costs $50 per month, but the decision to have a lawn belongs to the homeowner, not the city council.

Fountains, follies and fish

Palms and lawns may not be the best idea when water is in short supply, but we can hardly blame people for having them when water is cheap. Don't blame the consumer who overuses cheap water. Blame the monopoly water provider that sets a low price. Unfortunately, many water managers (and their political bosses) do not seem to connect use with price. Instead, they seem to think that people need to be told that water is precious and — worse — how to use water.

Public Service Announcements tell us to shower with a friend, pee twice before flushing, and grow native plants. Water cops give people tickets for watering on a Monday or Wednesday when watering is permitted only on Tuesday and Thursday (I'm not kidding). Some people are given tickets for breaking this law:

> Residential car washing is only allowed if a bucket and/or a hand-held hose equipped with a positive shut-off nozzle is used. During a water emergency or during Stage 3 drought restrictions, washing of vehicles will only be permitted at commercial establishments equipped with treatment and recycling systems and approved by the El Paso Water Utilities. Fundraising car washing events can only be held at commercial car wash establishments.

El Paso, Texas, is not the only place with this kind of command-and-control structure. Quite a few full-time employees are paid to tell us how to use water. Why are water cops, watering ordinances and do-it-yourself toilet-tank-reducing kits all over the place? Because the price of water does not reflect scarcity and the people who manage our water work for monopolies that pump water, fix leaks, and charge prices based on the cost of running the system. When it comes to "Oh crap, we're running out of water," they don't know how to respond because their institutions do not connect water prices with water scarcity. Insulated from the threat of bankruptcy from a water shortage and the incentive to maximize efficiency, they ask us to change our behavior instead of sending a price signal that gives customers the freedom to choose their response.

Advocacy and persuasion can work, but it's useful to have price signals that reinforce the conservation or scarcity message. Sure, laws that restrict and regulate prices can make it difficult to charge for scarcity, but these laws can be changed if they impede reliable water service. That will happen as soon as water managers decide that they want to use price tools to prevent shortage.

Remember Las Vegas, where water consumption is double that of San Francisco? Water managers there will pay people to rip out grass lawns, but they won't raise the price of water to cut consumption. Their lawn program doesn't stop cheap pools and power showers from causing shortages.

Culture is hard to change. Try to get a Frenchman to drink wine from a bottle with a screw cap or an American to eat french fries with mayonnaise. Water managers and bureaucrats are trying to end shortages, but they work for monopolies that will stay in business whether or not their policies are effective. Managers are smart and mean well, but they don't have much experience with changing consumer behavior. Their culture is deep with experience in moving water and charging costs.

Lawns and water cops and shortages — all of these topics come together in a perfect example of government failure, where costly interventions do not fix problems. Water managers see scarcity coming. They cannot get more supply, so they try to reduce demand. They may tell everyone to use less, pay people to tear out lawns, or give tickets for watering on the wrong day of the week. Failure comes in two parts: failure to prevent shortage and failure to minimize the costs of rationing (inconvenience, staff time, and so on) by using the wrong tools. Failure is relative — in some cases, no action may cause less harm, but in most cases another action would have been more effective. That action was not taken because politicians, bureaucrats and regulators do not face punishment from consumers and competitors in markets, so they are neither accustomed to looking for the best solutions nor rewarded for finding them. It may take political hearings and require more staff hours to prevent shortages, but these costs are not relevant. The costs of shortage to citizens and customers are all that matter. (Part II has more on these themes of accountability and incentives.)

It's not an accident that the people who have the most to teach water managers are folks who have worked in the oil business. They know how to move a precious product from one place to another, adding value on the way, so that end users can enjoy it. They also know how to raise and lower prices as demand and supply conditions change, to keep enough of that precious liquid around. Finally (and most important), they work hard to find the most efficient way to move those liquids, for fear of competitors who will take their customers. Consumers would know how to respond to water prices that moved up and down. We'd consume less water when prices go up in the same way that we consume less gasoline when prices go up. We'd take shorter showers, install high efficiency appliances, kill our lawns, turn the pool into a roller skating rink, whatever. The key is that nobody would need to tell us to use less water. We would naturally do that because water would be expensive.

Why do people get angry when they see a neighbor's sprinklers watering in the rain but shrug their shoulders when the same neighbor drives off in an SUV, burning enough fuel to keep a dozen Eskimos sweating in a hot tub? Probably because fuel wasters pay at the pump. The same cannot be said for water: its price doesn't reflect scarcity or market value. Neighbors who waste water leave less for us. A price that reflected scarcity would reduce waste, balance supply and demand in the community, and charge heavy users their fair share.

Some water managers may be reading this right now, and they may wonder, "Sounds good, but how do I get my boss or the public to accept higher prices?" That's a good question, and the easy answer is to aim higher prices at heavy water users — to lower demand, cover costs, and maintain reliability for everyone. Of course, prices should fall when water is abundant. Fluctuating prices will increase reliability, make shortages less likely, and reduce the need to spend vast sums on storage projects or desalination plants. They will also make water managers' jobs easier.

Appropriate prices for water will not only prevent shortages and ensure reliability for all of us. They will also push water toward the highest and best uses that maximize our wealth. Notice that full pricing does not mean giving a preferential rate to a certain type of use in exchange for the promise of more jobs, tax revenues, or campaign contributions. Every business, like every farmer, should face the same price for the same water. The price of water in Chicago may be different from the price of water in Buenos Aires, but the price should be the same for all businesses in the same place — unlike the variable prices in Some for Free that are designed to balance equity and efficiency in personal water consumption. Every business can make a claim to providing more jobs, positive publicity or community services, but those claims are half propaganda and half impossible to measure.

A level playing field means every business faces the same prices and regulations. After that, success is up to hard work, luck and plain dealing. No business deserves special treatment. Just like we don't deserve special treatment (except from our moms).

Recreational water

Speaking of businesses, let's talk about the business of golf.

Lots of people love hitting little balls around those Scottish lawns, and they are willing to pay a lot of money to keep doing so. As everyone knows, golf courses use a lot of water; even worse, they tend to be in hot places. There are 900 golf courses in California, about 60 in Las Vegas, and even a few in the desert kingdom of Dubai.

Should this be allowed? Maybe golf should be banned so that we can use that precious water to grow food? Or maybe not. In California, golf uses 1 percent of the state's water to generate $7 billion in economic activity; farmers use 75 percent of the state's water to generate $32 billion in activity. That means every liter of water used in golf generates about 16 times the economic output of a liter used in farming. But this doesn't mean that we should turn our farms into golf courses. The best way to reduce water waste is by making it profitable to use less water or expensive to use more water. Water markets would probably reduce water consumption in golf courses, but they would reduce agricultural consumption by even more. Why? The value of the output per unit of water at a golf course is greater than the value of output per unit of water at a farm, which makes it easier to pay more for water that's going to be used on the putting green.

The most important aspect of business water service is the bottom line. Businesses that cannot make a profit while paying full market prices for water deserve to fail because they are not managing water (and much else) correctly. That's good. That's capitalism. There's certainly no excuse for giving a failing business access to cheap or subsidized water. The same can be said for water skiing, swimming pools, and other water-hungry facilities. All that matters is that these places face the true cost of their water, a cost that reflects scarcity.

Vanity projects take water from the poor

Poor people in the developing world don't worry about getting enough water for their swimming pools and putting greens. They worry about getting enough water that's safe to drink. That's not true for their rulers. The French kings built enormous fountains at Versailles; Russia's Peter the Great liked them so much that he built his own fountains near St. Petersburg. In both cases, the peasants were more involved with moving earth than splashing in fountains.

Many projects in the developing world are devoted to generating power, ending floods or irrigating fields, but they are also presented as nationalist symbols of the ruler's might and intellect. They often end up costing more and producing fewer benefits than promised. The winners are often wealthy and powerful friends of the regime; the losers are often the poor who face flooded land, lower water supplies and higher taxes. Chinese governments have forced peasants to build vanity water projects for millennia. Some people claim Three Gorges Dam (the biggest in the world) was built as party propaganda. China's plan for the South–North Water Transfer Project is as much about ending drought in the North as it is about competing with grand works built more than 2,000 years ago. National pride may increase, but wasted water means less food — and you can't eat pride.

Other leaders promise to give free water to the poor and soak the rich to pay for their largesse. In South Africa, the poor residents of Soweto did not have decent water supplies until the end of apartheid. After that, the ANC government gave them nearly unlimited supplies at low or zero costs. Their neighbors in Johannesburg had to pay for that water delivery. Not surprisingly, free water led to heavy use. At one point, Soweto used one-third of the water but paid 1 percent of the costs. Between 2003 and 2008, Johannesburg Water installed 95,000 water meters (out of a total target of 170,000 meters); these meters have reduced waste (unmetered losses) from 42 to 30 percent and use per customer by 81 percent. These meters ran into resistance from people opposed to making people pay for water, but courts have ruled them legal. The only change is that the free allocation of water (a basic right in the South Africa Constitution) has been increased from 25 to 42 liters per capita per day (lcd). With a reduction in heavy use and increase in revenue, it's more likely that the residents of Soweto will be able to drink and bathe, instead of standing, thirsty and dirty, next to a dry tap with a sign saying "free water for all."

The joy of wetness

Lifestyle water makes people happy. It makes homes into oases, helps us relax, and makes us laugh. All of us want to drink and wash and keep ourselves healthy. After that, we can use water in many different ways. If we pay the full cost, no way is right or wrong; it's a question of personal choice. Some of us want lawns; others want fish tanks. Some of us will pay to wash our cars; others will pay to ski. In all of these circumstances, we can ensure that scarce supplies go to highest and best use by allowing prices to reflect scarcity or abundance, not just the cost of pipes, pumps and personnel. No use should be privileged, since it's impossible for a politician or bureaucrat (or anyone) to decide what's best for the public. The key is to make sure that we pay the full cost of our fun, just like we pay for movie tickets, chocolate bars and vacations in exotic places.

CHAPTER 4

Water for profit

*Bottled water is a consumer product unworthy of moral-
ity discussions. Public or private water service providers
fail because they are monopolies, not because of their
profit structure. Businesses need simple prices and reliable service.*

Tap'dNY sells purified New York City tap water in bottles with the
promise that "no glaciers were harmed making this water." Some people are charmed ("Ah, the honesty tactic"); others are not so pleased
("It's still in a plastic bottle"). But no single company captures so well
the public/private, tap/bottled, and bureaucracy/business contrasts in
this chapter.

The end of abundance is attracting many businesses to the water
sector. Reductions in water quantity and quality (or the perception
of these reductions) have created scarcity, which creates profit opportunities for innovative businesses. The demand for bottled water
has grown as people have looked for convenience, healthy alternatives and guaranteed purity. Bottled water companies have responded
to this demand, while using advertisements to encourage its growth.
The demand for private management of municipal water systems has
grown with the need to increase efficiency and pay for infrastructure.
The demand for reliable supplies has grown among businesses that
cannot operate with shortages. These forces are stronger in developing countries where weak governance leads to poor service and
business opportunities. This chapter is about money and profit in an
era of scarce water.

Profit in a bottle

McCloud is a little town of a thousand people in the far north of California. Springs next to the town gush with water from nearby Mt. Shasta.

These springs attracted Nestle Waters, a division of the Switzerland-based food giant that is the largest seller of bottled water in the world. In 2003, Nestle signed a contract with the local government to bottle and export nearly 1,900 ML of McCloud's water per year (about 1,500 acre-feet).

The people of McCloud were upset that their leaders did not ask them before signing a deal that effectively privatized a portion of the community's water. Their reactions varied with their concerns. Most worried about Nestle's impact on their environment, hundreds of daily truck trips on their narrow roads, or Nestle using some legal trick to take more water. Others hoped that jobs in the bottling plant would be as good as the jobs that left when the lumber mills closed. The biggest benefit for the community should have been revenue from selling water that is clean enough to go straight into bottles. Alas, Nestle was going to pay the same price that residents paid for their tap water. Nestle would pay 15.5 cents per m^3 for water that would retail for about $1,000 per m^3 ($1 per liter), a markup of more than 6,000 percent.

Residents' worries quickly turned into worries for Nestle. The company already had problems with relations in other communities where it pumped water. McCloud became a rallying point for people who disliked corporations, bottled water and capitalism — a protester's trifecta.

From an economic perspective, some deal should have been possible. McCloud had good water and few jobs; Nestle was willing to market its water and employ locals. The troubles came from Nestle's miserly price, uncertainty and mistrust over the contract, and potential environmental damage. Nestle's mistake was to sign a big contract without sufficient debate among residents. Nestle could have started small. Nestle could have paid more; even one penny per liter would have generated 65 times more revenue for the town. But moderation arrived too late to the battle; Nestle and McCloud canceled their contract.

The bottled water scapegoat

The Nestle-McCloud story is symbolic of a greater battle over water, who owns it and how it should be used. Bottled water is similar to Coke or Pepsi, a convenience product that consumers want, a soft drink without added colors, flavors, caffeine or sweeteners. The companies that sell bottled water may be selling filtered, treated and repackaged tap water at prices that are 100 times more expensive, but they also listen to what customers want.

It's interesting that these companies find themselves in a debate over bottled water with activists instead of customers. These activists see bottled water as a nexus of evils: an attack on tap water, the environment and their health. They are unhappy that people may turn from tap to bottled water, reducing support for funding the maintenance of municipal infrastructure. They dislike plastic water bottles. They claim lax regulations allow bottled water (and bottles) to contain more contaminants. They want to ban bottled water, as the people of Concord, Massachusetts, did in the summer of 2010. Unfortunately, a ban does not fix these problems and may make them worse. The only obvious result would be a municipal monopoly on drinking water and a reduction in consumer choice. Although activists play an important role as leaders in organizing collective actions that benefit us all, it's also possible that they are protecting us from baseless fears. Let's look at them one by one.

Activists claim money spent on bottled water should instead be spent on repairing infrastructure. In 2009, Americans spent $10.6 billion on bottled water. Government and industry sources estimate that we need to spend $17–$50 billion per year to maintain and repair municipal drinking water infrastructure. These numbers help us explain four flaws in the activists' logic. First, there's not enough money to repair infrastructure, assuming that those numbers are not inflated (the organizations that provided the estimates would also do the repairs). Second, the bottled water industry doesn't even make $10.6 billion; it has costs. Third, it's not like bottled water buyers would just send in $10 billion to repair someone else's pipes. Bottled water consumers tend to be wealthy and urban; repairs tend to be in poorer, rural places. Buyers voluntarily exchange their money for value; they are not donating it to charity. The activists' logic implies that people should stop watching movies, so that the movie industry's $10 billion revenues can be directed to pipe repairs. Finally, money can't fix everything. The Los Angeles Department of Water and Power (LADWP) suffered a series of major blowouts in its main pipes. The cause? An LADWP order that people irrigate their lawns only on Mondays and Thursdays. LADWP's solution to their mismanagement was an increase in prices to pay for repairs.[1]

Environmentalists dislike that plastic bottles are made from oil and

---

[1] LADWP also changed the regulation so that watering occurs on six days.

can end up as litter. In the US, it takes about 17 million barrels of oil per year (one day of US oil consumption) to produce the plastic water bottles Americans throw away every year. The cost of oil, like other production costs, is included in the price of our bottled water, but what about the costs of disposal and litter? Although environmentalists concentrate on plastic water bottles, half the plastic bottles are filled with soft drinks, fruit juices, sports drinks, and so on. We will therefore consider all plastic bottles.

In the US, about 25 percent of plastic bottles are recycled into other products (not usually new bottles); about 25 percent are exported; and most of the rest go into landfills. But some bottles end up in the environment. This pollution problem is much greater in countries that lack recycling facilities, garbage collection, or a cultural sensitivity to trash that does not decompose. Japanese researchers testing water in the ocean found Bisphenol-A (BPA), a chemical used in some plastic bottles, at every one of the 200 ocean sites they visited. BPA is not good for you or me or fish in the sea — but it's out there, recycling program, landfill program, or not. Plastic consumption can create a negative externality that pollutes the ocean, a common-pool good that has no owner or defender.

How do we address this situation? A ban on plastic bottles would force us to return to glass bottles, but the benefits of less plastic and litter would come with the cost of more expensive transportation (in cash and carbon) from carrying heavy glass. A tax on raw plastic may not work, since industry has been "lightweighting" bottles to reduce their spending on plastic for years. But price incentives could change plastic bottles from trash into treasure. For example, a 5 cent deposit on each bottle would spur people to pick them up and turn them in, as many people worldwide now do with deposits on glass bottles. Even better, the deposit can be used to pay for recycling the bottles. A 10 cent deposit on purchase and 5 cent refund on return would leave 5 cents to pay the cost of processing the plastic into something harmless and useful.

Competition: bottled versus tap

Anti-bottled water folks argue that bottled water threatens tap water by allowing people to avoid drinking it. That reduction in demand, they claim, will reduce support for higher tap water prices necessary to maintain a quality product.

This idea is ridiculous — people use a thousand times more tap water than bottled water — but it contains a useful thought about competition. The bottled water industry listens to customer concerns, but municipal water agencies are not usually so responsive. They react to mission failure (water shortages, for example) by telling customers to use less instead of addressing their own mistakes. Bottled water companies do not have that luxury. If they don't serve customer needs, they lose business; if they tell their customers what to do, they lose customers. Bottled water companies exist only because someone wants them.

Bottled water opponents also claim bottled water companies have an unfair advantage over drinking water providers because they are often subject to different regulations. In the US, for example, the Food and Drug Administration (FDA) regulates bottled water quality and the Environmental Protection Agency (EPA) regulates municipal water quality.

Although this seems to support the idea that one set of standards is weaker, the FDA and EPA coordinate their standards. Standards sometimes vary (the FDA's limit for lead is lower because bottled water is not delivered in pipes, for example), but we can't claim standards make one agency better than the other. Nevertheless, the existence of two standards (and third parties who try to compare them) creates confusion for customers and opportunity for activists (pro–tap and pro-bottles) to denigrate competing water that may be just as good as their preferred source.

A single set of standards (and reporting of results) would help consumers by giving them better information on quality. It would also spur bottled and municipal water sellers to compete on quality instead of claiming that their water passes standards that others don't. Why don't regulators push for a unification of standards? They may claim statutory complications, but they also know that a merger would result in job losses and shifts in power that most bureaucrats instinctively protect. Would a unification of regulation result in a lazy monopoly? Not if various water sellers are competing to show that they are better. They will challenge tests that are inaccurate, infrequent or incompetent.

Researchers have found a strong correlation between poor tap water quality and higher consumer demand for bottled water, and competition between bottled and tap would improve quality for consumers. Municipal suppliers who failed to match bottled water standards could be pressured to improve; low quality bottled water would be replaced by municipal supply. Competition would give consumers better choices in bottled water and better quality from their tap.

Consider what happened in 2006: Fiji Water ran nationwide advertisements proclaiming "The label says Fiji because it's not bottled in Cleveland." Annoyed at being singled out (again), Cleveland's Water Department responded by releasing test results showing that Fiji Water was higher in arsenic. Fiji pulled the ad (claiming it was just a joke), but the damage was done. Tap and bottled water can be compared on quality, and people want to see head-to-head comparisons.

Sometimes bottled water vendors harm consumers, not by competition, but through monopoly. Many people spend time in airports, schools, malls and other spaces where food and drink sales are limited to merchants approved by property managers. Many of these properties use merchant rents to cover other costs. US schools that sign exclusive vending agreements allowing Coke (or Pepsi) to sell drinks to kids use the rent to pay for other programs. Many airports charge rent to those selling coffee, pizza, DVDs and other products.

In the past, these controlled public spaces would have water fountains. Those fountains cost money, but they were considered a basic service, like toilets. The rise of bottled water changed the economics of fountains, by introducing a way to make — instead of lose — money on thirst. It was thus very simple to replace fountains that cost money to install and run with vending machines that paid rent. Who wins? Property managers and bottled water companies. Who loses? Consumers who have to pay for what they used to get for free. This abuse of monopoly power can get out of control. California recently passed a law requiring schools to provide drinking water to students — for free.

This law brings up an interesting policy question. Does bottled water compete with tap water or with bottled soft drinks? Although we can see why it competes with tap water (water is water), there's also a reason to see bottled water in competition with bottled soft drinks. That's perhaps why Coke and Pepsi market Dasani and Aquafina brands of bottled water. They want to defend their share of the "thirst quencher" market so they sell bottled water next to their sweetened drinks.

Private companies selling public water

Should for-profit companies be allowed to run the local monopoly on water supply and wastewater disposal? Some people have immediate negative reactions to this question, worrying that companies will abuse their market power to profit from selling a product that people can't live without. Others wonder whether for-profit companies can improve water management in the same way that they've improved efficiency in mail, rail, ports, telecoms, airlines, banking, mining, and other industries often run by governments. Either way, the end of abundance increases the importance of these questions, and their answers. Less water requires better management to avoid shortages.

Let's start by clarifying some confusing terms. Investor-owned utilities (IOUs) are for-profit companies that are owned by stock market investors, private owners, or larger for-profit companies. American Water (NYSE: AWK), for example, has 16 million customers in 35 states and Canada. Paris-based Suez Environnement (Euronext: SEV) delivers water to 90 million people in 70 countries. IOUs are sometimes called public utilities because they deliver water that's public, either in terms of ownership (the people's water) or customer access (water is sold to all members of the public). This naming is why IOUs in the United States are regulated by Public Utility Commissions (PUCs) staffed by political appointees and bureaucrats. Municipal utilities (Munis) are governmental bodies overseen by elected or appointed directors; sometimes they are regulated by PUCs. I will call IOUs and Munis private and public, respectively.

The public/private debate is complicated, so we're going to divide the discussion. In this chapter, we will compare IOUs, which maximize profits based on performance targets (cheap, drinkable) set by PUCs, with Munis, which target zero profits while pursuing performance targets set by their political overseers. We will assume that politicians and regulators do their job (regulating in the name of the public), and that IOUs and Munis obey them. In Chapter 7, we will look at various exceptions to those assumptions.

Now, let's start with the big point. There is not much evidence that either IOUs or Munis deliver better performance, prices or quality. One study of private and public companies operating in the same city in California concluded that the private company was more efficient and the public company charged less, but they were similar in infrastructure investment and condition, water quality, water conservation, and customer satisfaction. Another study of many water companies across the US concluded that private and public companies had similar efficiency and water quality. The study found that the social cost of taxes and political cost of privatizing determined whether water service came from a public or private company. Price, quality, efficiency and jobs didn't matter.

The reason we see both public and private ownership around the world is because neither is always better. On the other hand, both public and private water utilities can fail.

The mayor of Stockton, California, wanted money for downtown redevelopment, and he persuaded the city council to sell the city's well-run water system to OMI Thames in 2003. OMI Thames brought in its own management team, kept some employees, and ran the system on a "run-to-fail" basis (pushing machinery too hard, without maintenance, to save money). Their actions did not violate performance contracts, but OMI Thames was thrown out in 2007. This was an example of a mayor who wanted money selling a good system to a company that preferred short-term profits to long term-service. Both parties to the deal were happy, but they ignored the needs of the residents they supposedly served. Who deserves blame for this fiasco? Both parties, but the weight of the blame falls on the mayor. He sold the system, and he chose the buyer. OMI Thames may have been run by thieves, but the mayor invited them in through the front door.

Do Munis fail the public? Sure. In April 2010, LADWP decided that it did not want to transfer $70 million in excess revenue to the city because the Los Angeles City Council failed to approve a rate increase LADWP wanted. Since LADWP reports to the City Council, this action was not supposed to happen, but it did. In the ensuing political and bureaucratic war, $3.2 billion of city debt was downgraded; Los Angeles' borrowing costs rose; LADWP's general manager resigned; employees were fired; and customers got worse service. LADWP ended up paying the money but the damage was done.

Monopolies do what they want

Several years ago, I believed that public water utilities were staffed by bureaucrats who cared more about their offices and short working hours than their customers or services. I reckoned that for-profit companies would deliver better water and lower costs. But then I learned more about professional civil servants and local public managers who were skilled at balancing different needs (service, employment, environment, sustainability) in their communities. I read a few too many case studies of for-profit companies that cut corners on quality while raising prices in arbitrary ways. I've concluded that success and failure can happen at private or public firms, in developed or developing countries.

In fact, it's not public or private that matters. It's monopoly. A monopoly delivers water to whom it wants, when it wants, at a price and quality it wants. Water utilities' monopoly power comes from two sources. Water distribution is a "natural monopoly" because it's hard for a new company to enter the business in competition with an incumbent company that's already installed the network of pipes for delivering water. The cost of building that network is known as a "sunk cost" because it cannot be recovered. The only value of that network is in delivering water to customers. The incumbent then can choose any price for its water, as long as the price is above the cost of delivery (pumping and treatment, for example). A potential competitor has to charge a much higher price to cover both the cost of delivery and the cost of a new distribution network. Challengers know that customers facing a high and low price for the same water will choose the low price so they stay out of the market, leaving the incumbent with a natural monopoly. The market power of a natural monopoly rises with the cost of the network. In the water sector, roughly 80 percent of total costs are fixed and capital investments often last longer than 50 years. Other natural monopolies (roads, natural gas pipelines, cable TV networks) are not so strong, since their upfront costs are smaller relative to operating costs.

The second source of monopoly power is the legal monopoly that governments award in exchange for a promise to deliver water to all members of the public (hence "public utility") in the service area. This legal monopoly gives politicians and regulators the right to monitor prices, quality, and service on behalf of customers. Sometimes this oversight is motivated by a desire to protect customers from excessive water charges, but low prices can hamper the size and operation of a water system. Politicians may authorize subsidies from general funds to make up for low water revenues, but these subsidies can turn managers' attention from serving customers to serving politicians. In the worst case, they can put the water system at risk of fiscal insolvency (in the event that subsidies end) or operational inefficiency (in the event that politicians decide that subsidies allow them to tell managers what to do). These complications may lead you to wonder why a water utility may be given a legal monopoly when a natural monopoly offers decent protection from competition without prohibiting decent regulation. The easy answer is that legal monopoly gives security to the water provider and power to politicians and regulators. Consumers only get the certainty of one choice.[2]

Virtuous humans

Monopolies can use their market power to raise prices and maximize profits, lower costs and minimize effort, or serve their customers by delivering good service at low prices. The actual outcome depends on what motivates the monopolist. Economists and other social scientists say that motivation results from intrinsic (internal) and extrinsic (external) incentives — otherwise known as love (intrinsic) or money (extrinsic) — that can reinforce or interfere with each other.

These incentives are crucial to understanding success and failure in a water industry dominated by monopolies. Public water agencies may have employees who enjoy working for the public, but those employees can also hide behind vague "performance," secure jobs, or weak oversight. Nonprofit status does not help. Revenues match costs, but prices can be increased to cover wasteful spending. A manager can hire excess staff to reduce his workload or help friends and relatives. Staff may exert less effort: it may look like they are playing poker on Friday, but records say they are in a training session. The purchasing manager may be buying materials from his friend's company, but records say the contract was awarded to the company that promised the best combination of price, quality and service. These shenanigans happen in some places but not in others. We can't see them because many factors influence success or failure in operating a water system that is decades old, underground, and affected by many activities. It's really hard for outsiders to know when failure occurs despite hard work or if success results from luck instead of effort.

Incentives at IOUs are clearer. Companies make profits when they lower the cost of delivering water at prices and qualities that are approved by outside regulators (who face their own combination of incentives). Employees understand this incentive and get paid for responding to it. Intrinsic incentives do not matter so much. Employees who do not work lower profits and get fired. But clear extrinsic incentives can also promote unwelcome behavior. A guaranteed return on capital spending can encourage over-investment, but fixed standards for performance can favor lethargy over dynamism. The OMI Thames run-to-fail strategy may have been directed at higher short-run profits (reduced maintenance) and higher capital spending (replacing worn-

---

[2]On page 155, I discuss a business model for competing with local monopolists in developing countries that will not work if the legal monopoly is enforced.

out equipment). PUC regulators do not have an easy job.

The organizations that manage our tap water may be private, public or a mixture, but they are alike in their monopoly control over the pipes that bring us water (with an English exception below). Sometimes they succeed at serving the community and their employees; sometimes they provide bad service at inflated prices. Customer feedback can be useful, but politicians and regulators play a crucial role in monitoring and improving performance. We will look at the behavior of regulators and politicians in Chapter 7. For the moment, we'll assume that regulators and politicians represent consumers while overseeing organizations that take rules as given (not negotiable) and honestly report their activities. How can we avoid scarcity and maximize efficiency under those assumptions?

Competition is the answer

The real problem with a monopoly is not that we don't know what it's doing or don't know how to make it change what it's doing. Nobody knows what's going on inside of Exxon, Ford or Apple, and nobody cares, because these firms are competing with others, offering quality goods and services in exchange for profits. The real problem is that competition doesn't force monopolies to concentrate on customer service and value for money.

How can we change this situation, to encourage efficiency in a water agency with a natural and legal monopoly?

One idea separates the core monopoly from businesses that can be competitive. That's what happened in 2000 for large water users in England and Wales. The system was legally separated into a monopolistic distribution network and a competitive market to provide water to that network (a structure used widely for electricity generation and distribution). The network is run as a regulated utility, but consumers choose their water vendor. Vendors pay a "common carriage" charge to put water of a standard quality into the network. This system allows carriers to compete on charging the lowest price for sourcing, treating and delivering water. They also have an incentive to monitor the network for leaks and other inefficiencies, since they don't make money on lost water. Unfortunately, this system has not produced widespread competition for customers. Only a few have taken advantage of common carriage; the rest rely on regulation to improve the price and quality of services.

Or perhaps competition should be introduced, so that temporary monopolies work harder for the chance to earn future rewards? Cities in France, a dozen other European countries, the US, and around the world allow companies to compete for 10–30 year service contracts. These competitions bring new management to water services in a variety of private-public partnership formats. Bidding focuses on delivering a specified quality of service at the lowest price. If quality or maintenance fails, the contract may be voided or the opportunity to bid again removed.

Another idea uses "benchmark competition" to compare utilities in different areas on price, volume, leaks and other measures of interest. IOUs compare their own operations in different locations to identify winners and losers, good ideas and strong employees. They use this competition to promote best practices that improve efficiency and profits in the short run and service to customers whenever performance contracts are reallocated. These companies can also watch their competitors and integrate those lessons into their operations. Public managers also learn by doing, but they do not necessarily share those ideas with other operators, and they do not need to translate them into better customer service to keep a service contract. Even worse, they do not negotiate their prices with PUC regulators who can compare prices and performance across many companies; public managers usually get their prices approved by a city council that is often willing to raise prices to pay for mistakes.

Businesses will pay fair prices

We've looked into companies that sell water in bottles, and the difference between public and private operation of water facilities. That brings us to businesses like restaurants, car washes, laundries, hair salons, and food processors that use water to make profits. Many of these businesses worry when water supplies are short, since rationing can shut them down.

Businesses used to get reliable service *and* decreasing block rates (DBRs) that lowered the unit price of water, the more water they used. DBRs make it easy to waste water and create an expectation that water will always be there at low prices. But the end of abundance makes it hard to have both cheap and reliable water. Given a choice between the two, most businesses will choose reliable.

How much should businesses pay if the goal is to provide reliable service at a price that's fair and promotes conservation?

The short answer is that the business should pay the full price for the connection (which will be larger and more expensive if the business uses more water) and the full price for water consumption (uniform block rates that reflect the cost of delivery plus any scarcity surcharges), just like it pays for electrify, fuel, and other services.

But that's not the answer that most businesses, politicians and bureaucrats want to hear, nor the common practice in many places. Certain businesses argue that they need special rates, because they serve food, employ lots of people, and so on. Politicians like to negotiate deals that reflect those features. Bureaucrats require that businesses have big connections to meet health and safety standards; conservation officers want businesses to face IBRs, so they do their share for efficiency.

The mess that results from reconciling special rates to some businesses, higher prices for waste and big meters, and discounts for low use is a mind-boggling version of IBRs. Discounted minimums can depend on office size, employees or customer count, the Standard Industry Code, toilet counts, or a combination of everything. Thus, a restaurant with five tables may pay more for water than an office with 25 staffers but less than a bar with 12 seats. What's right or wrong here?

Since it may be politically difficult to get a simple uniform block rate pricing model, we'll look at a simple IBR model that allows businesses to chose their level of water service while recovering costs, encouraging conservation, and meeting health and safety codes.

Here's how it works.

The business pays a fixed monthly charge based on the size of its service connection. These costs are for water service, not the size of the connection. Although the service connection usually refers to the size of the meter or diameter of the pipe for incoming water (2, 4, 8, 20 cm, and so on), businesses can buy service for a smaller meter than the actual physical meter, either because they are using less water than a past tenant or because they need a high-volume connection to meet fire codes. Thus we may have a 2 cm service connection that costs $100 per month or 4 cm service that costs $125 per month, even if both come to a 4 cm physical meter.

Businesses get a bigger block of cheap water if they buy more service. A 2 cm meter gets 10 m^3 at $1 per m^3 and more water at $4 per m^3, but a 4 cm meter gets 25 m^3 at $1 per m^3 and more water at $4 per m^3, for example. A business that doesn't use very much water will get the 2 cm plan, paying $100 plus $18 for the 12 m^3 of water it

Table 4: How to meter a business.

	Light user (12 m³ demand)		Heavy user (22 m³ demand)	
Service plan	2 cm meter	4 cm meter	2 cm meter	4 cm meter
Monthly charge	$100	$125	$100	$125
Base water @ $1 per m³	10 m³	25 m³	10 m³	25 m³
Extra water	$4 per m³	$4 per m³	$4 per m³	$4 per m³
Water charges	10x$1 + 2x$4	12x$1	10x$1 + 12x$4	22x$1
Total charge	$118	$137	$158	$147
Choice?	This one!			This one!

uses. A heavier water user will get the 4 cm meter, paying $125 plus $22 for its 22m³ consumption, or $147. The smaller meter that costs $158 to use doesn't make sense. Table 4 summarizes the plans and charges from this example.

These numbers can be moved around without weakening the incentive for businesses to minimize their meter class and consumption within that class of service. This simple and flexible plan can replace the existing mess, free managers from the need to know anything about their customer's business, and allow customers who use "too much" to pay more instead of facing a service cut.

Profit from the poor but don't subsidize the rich

Developing countries have weaker institutions. The rule of law may not hold; politicians may be corrupt; statistics may be absent or unreliable; relationships may be more important than contracts. All of these problems make it harder to direct water to its highest and best use. But that doesn't mean that businesses don't do their best to cope.

Some international companies are accused of taking too much water to produce drinks or products and leaving local people with smaller supplies, higher costs and lower quality. These problems may be blamed on the greedy multinationals, but a larger share of the blame goes to the politicians and bureaucrats who allow abuses to happen, either because of laziness, corruption or incompetence.

Some people suggest that these problems can be fixed by forcing multinationals to sign a code of ethics or closing their factories. Those actions are not solutions. Codes are mere words; closure doesn't solve local governance problems or prevent local companies from breaking the same rules.

Multinational companies are not interested in unsustainable practices that threaten their businesses, investments and brands. They want to run sustainable businesses and pay their fair share, but they cannot tell local governments how to work (they risk losing their operating permit), and they cannot do much if local firms are willing to pay bribes and take their water. That's true for bottled water and water used in businesses, but the same can be said for the operation of municipal water by international private companies, and that brings us to Bolivia.

In the late 1990s, the 1 million residents of Cochabamba, Bolivia, had bad water service. The local public agency, SEMAPA, was delivering poor quality water to a fraction of the local population. The World Bank was willing to provide loans to improve the system, but only if SEMAPA was replaced. A 40-year contract was signed with Aguas del Tunari (AdT), a private consortium of four foreign and two Bolivian companies. Activists opposed AdT from the start, but AdT's clumsy price increases and attempts to control local water supplies (claiming to own the rain, for example) led to mass protests in 2000. AdT was kicked out in 2006, and SEMAPA was put back in charge.

Victory for the masses, right?

No. Three years later, a left-wing observer wrote:

> SEMAPA has failed to address its two biggest problems. In a valley still deeply thirsty for water, SEMAPA loses about 55 percent of the water it has to leaks in the pipes and to clandestine hookups. And despite a steady flow of financial support from international donors and lenders, including the Japanese government and the IDB [Inter-American Development Bank], the company still doesn't have a sustainable financing plan in place. One water expert familiar with SEMAPA's internal workings blames the problems on mismanagement. "It is an organization that is completely dysfunctional. They don't generate enough income to cover their costs and they are letting the system deteriorate."

Re-municipalization did not improve service or lower prices. Several SEMAPA directors elected in polls with 4 percent participation were dismissed for giving jobs and contracts to family and friends. Can we blame these failures on Bolivians? No, it's a question of community and accountability. An autonomous cooperative named AP-PAS serves the area next to SEMAPA's service area. APPAS loses 6 percent of its water and serves 6,000 customers. These customers pay their bills and make sure that service is sustainable. When APPAS "holds an Assembly, 95 percent of them show up. If someone isn't happy with their service, they speak up." APPAS delivers good water service because its customers care about staff performance and punish managers for failure. The same cannot be said about SEMAPA, which is operated and managed by people who are beholden to politicians (and sometimes related to them). Good governance delivers good drinking water.

Water service failure can persist in the developing world because the rich and middle classes benefit from the status quo. Water service tends to go to expensive properties in city centers, not outlying slums. The people with service can pay more than subsidized prices, but they do not because politicians (often their friends) claim water is too important to be expensive. The poor people end up paying 10 to 50 times more for water from trucks that drive around neighborhoods without pipes. The rich people who benefit from subsidized public service oppose privatization because new companies try to collect payment for service, expand service to poor areas, and deliver pro-poor policies to people who are actually poor. Ironically, the rich are often joined by anti-privatization activists ("never seen a public utility we didn't like") who persuade politicians not to privatize.

Professor Bruce Yandle of Clemson University calls this alliance of righteous activists and the greedy rich a "Baptists and Bootleggers" coalition. The names refer to the participants in the southern US practice of restricting retail sales of alcohol on Sundays. Baptists think consuming alcohol on Sundays is a sin; Bootleggers who sell unlicensed booze do not like competition from stores. When Baptists agitate to close liquor stores on Sundays, Bootleggers quietly cheer. When stores close, Baptists claim victory for the Lord, and Bootleggers claim victory for their bank accounts. Drinkers are just worse off. These tacit coalitions are often present in sectors influenced by government regulation; the water sector is no exception.

Incentives matter

This chapter discussed bottled water, compared private companies and public agencies that manage tap water, suggested how to sell water to businesses, and described the additional troubles that people in developing countries face. Solutions focused on greater competition and community oversight. Bottled water companies will do a better job if they have to compete with tap water. Water managers will do a better job if they face this competition. Both public and private monopolies provide better service when subject to community and customer oversight. Businesses should be free to choose their payment plan for water, but they should pay the full cost of reliable service. People in developing countries can get good quality water at lower prices if they are allowed to reward and punish the private or public companies that serve them. For-profit companies are experienced in maximizing the value of limited resources, so we should borrow their ideas and methods to ensure that scarce waters are put to their highest and best use for individuals and society.

CHAPTER 5

Food and water

*Farmers make profits with water. Ground and surface wa-
ters should be co-managed. Water markets help farmers
and communities and maximize the social value of water.
Weak property rights harm fishermen and fish eaters.*

Some people claim the end of abundant water means the beginning of food shortage. That's not necessarily going to happen. Food
shortages and water shortages are both caused by prices that are too
low or policies that block trade from surplus to deficit areas.

In the past of abundance, farmers took water for granted, paid
the price of delivery and made their cropping and marketing decisions
based on more important costs (labor, machinery, fertilizers, and so
on). They did not worry about efficiency or its value in use. But increasing scarcity means they now need to consider the cost and value
of water. Some farmers are changing their crop mix; others are selling
their water or rights to other farmers or cities. Some people object to
treating water like land, labor and other commodities, but agricultural
water management requires that we treat it like a valuable input that
should go to the highest bidder and most valuable use. Regulations
that block voluntary water trades or freeze farming in some past version of rural life will make it hard to maximize the social value of water.
The end of abundance is turning farmers' water rights into a valuable
resource, but we do not need to worry that they will sell all the water
to sprawling suburbs or industrial facilities. Many farmers love to grow
crops; all of them like to make a profit from our demand for food. Simple regulations on use and trade are necessary, but they should be
directed at preventing real harm, not interfering with the choices that
farmers make in their local communities.

This chapter starts with an overview of the physical and institutional dimensions affecting agricultural water flows, moves to farmers'

irrigation and crop decisions and the distortions caused by government policies, and speculates on how scarcity can change these decisions. We then turn to water markets, how they succeed or fail and
look at an auction design that can minimize the damage from scarcity.
We then leave port to discuss food in water (fish) and look into agricultural water use in developing countries where corruption, populism
and misguided policies magnify unfairness and inefficiency.

The flow of water for irrigation

In most countries, agriculture uses 60–80 percent of the "developed"
water that is diverted, managed or controlled for human use. Irrigation uses developed water. In the US, 18 percent of irrigated farmland produces 40 percent of total farm revenue. Nature waters the
remaining 82 percent, with timing and volumes that farmers do not
control, to produce the remaining 60 percent of revenue. Worldwide,
about 20 percent of farmland is irrigated, producing about 40 percent
of the world's food. The historically high share of water use by farmers reflects three facts: it takes a lot of water to grow food, farmers
try to grow as much food as possible, and farmers get all the water
left after basic needs (drinking, bathing and so on) are met. Their
historic share is under pressure and falling because the definition of
basic needs is expanding to include everything from suburban lawns,
to water-intensive manufacturing, to environmental flows. This drop in
supply for farmers comes at a time when the demand for food (from
growing populations and a shift to protein-rich diets) is increasing.
Can farmers do more with less? Can they grow "more crop per drop"?
    Yes, but not quite to the degree that some claim.
    Plants combine water, carbon dioxide and nutrients to grow (via
photosynthesis) and transpire oxygen and water vapor as waste products. Transpiration depends on the plant's genetic makeup, but variation in the timing and volume of irrigation can increase yield (more
crop per drop). Farmers have been experimenting with these variations for millennia, and they have been quick to adopt technologies
such as drip irrigation, transpiration-monitoring, and remote sensing
of soil moisture or biomass when technologies are cost effective. Thus
we arrive at the intersection of agronomy and economics. Farmers
will pay for those technologies if the benefits (higher yields and lower
water use) are high enough but not otherwise. That's the first important point.
    The second important point concerns irrigation water that *misses*

plants. That water can be reduced by technology that directs water to plants instead of letting it flow away or evaporate, but this version of "more crop per drop" may not be profitable. Let's explore this idea by stepping back to look at how water flows on a farm.

Water on a field absorbs into plants, evaporates into the air, soaks into the ground, flows to other farmers (via canals or rivers), or leaves to the sea. Evapotranspiration (ET) equals the amount of water that transpires (some of the water absorbed in the plant stays, the rest transpires) and evaporates from a field. ET is a standard abbreviation, but let's add three more letters: G for water that goes into the ground, F for flows that others can use, and L for losses to the sea. Total water applied equals ET+G+F+L. This simple description makes it easier to compare the way farmers and society look at water use. Farmers want to maximize yield (plant growth) via a larger share of T; F and G are not such a problem because they can be used in the present and future, respectively. Farmers want to minimize E and L for a given flow onto their fields, and society puts more weight on F and L that benefit the environment. In some cases, the only "bad" flow can be attributed to E(vaporation).

Taken together, these flows help us see that farmers will invest in technology where E or L are big, G doesn't happen, and F goes to others. Most important, this investment must give improved yield and/or reduce water costs. There's no point in investing if yield does not rise or water is cheap because the cost outweighs the benefits.

It makes sense, for example, to use drip irrigation instead of flood irrigation in a hot place where runoff flows into the sea but not in cooler places where water can sink into the soil or be used by other farmers. In such places, the farmer will only use drip irrigation if cost of the technology delivers enough benefits in yield or reduced water diversions. We'll soon spend more time on the costs and benefits of water diversions, but the point now is that the benefits from technology vary with circumstances.

Water should be managed at the watershed level

It's easiest to think of water flows within a watershed (also known as a drainage basin or catchment area). John Wesley Powell (1834–1902) was a geologist, explorer of the Grand Canyon and the second director of the US Geological Survey. He was the first scientist to think about how to manage water in the western US, a place that has similarities to Spain, Australia and other dry regions with strong seasonal water flows. Powell defined a watershed as "that area of land, a bounded hydrologic system, within which all living things are inextricably linked by their common water course and where, as humans settled, simple logic demanded that they become part of a community." This definition captures the important idea that living things and communities within a watershed share water and affect each other, independent of adjacent watersheds.

Precipitation within a watershed will evaporate, soak into soil, or flow into lakes or the sea, but humans like to move water between watersheds, so they can have enough water to live in pleasant places that happen to be dry. Diversions were common long before Roman aqueducts, but their impacts grew with the advent of powered pumps. Interbasin diversions create big benefits for humans but big costs to the flora and fauna that cannot adapt quickly to radical environmental changes.

Valuable groundwater can be overexploited

Farmers get their water from natural and artificial surface flows and/or storage (rivers and aqueducts and/or lakes and reservoirs, respectively). Storage can be very useful in reducing the risk from variable flows within and across seasons, but it needs to be carefully managed, so that water is not taken by others or spilled through administrative errors. Aquifers are often large and shared by multiple farmers, but their extent, flows and drainage are not usually well understood. Overdrafting an aquifer (by pumping faster than recharge) can adversely affect neighbors; it can be prevented through informal communal arrangements that limit group withdrawals or formal adjudication that awards each neighbor the right to withdraw a fixed amount of water. In the absence of an agreement to limit extractions, neighbors race to pump water. The resulting Tragedy of the Commons drains the aquifer; accompanying land subsidence or seawater intrusion can permanently destroy its freshwater capacity.

In Texas, this race to pump is encouraged by a "right of capture" that gives landowners the right to use as much water as they want, as long as they drill on their own land. This rule worked when farmers were irrigating their own land, but it fails when farmers make deals to export pumped water to thirsty urban areas.

Many California farmers are in a similar race. Their water tables are dropping, their water quality is falling, and their drilling and pumping bills are rising. These farmers resist outside intervention but then fail to coordinate limits on pumping; they appear determined to destroy their aquifers. Texas and California are both dry places, but they do not have good rules for groundwater management, often because water was abundant in the past. Indeed, the pattern is repeating in wet places recently known for abundance, like India's Punjab ("the land of five waters") or the southeastern region including the states of Georgia, Tennessee and Florida. Some farmers hope that their groundwater mining will be alleviated with water imported from other places, but that hope may be in vain. Everyone wants more water.

Tailwater pollution is hard to monitor

Water is never destroyed, but it can be too dirty to be used. Tailwater runoff leaving irrigated land might carry significant quantities of fertilizers, pesticides and other contaminants that people, fish, and plants do not want to drink. In some parts of the world, excess fertilizer in runoff has created "dead zones" where most sea life has perished. The dead zone at the mouth of the Mississippi River averages 22,000 km^2 in size. In other words, it's a New Jersey-sized wasteland incapable of supporting life. [Insert Jersey joke here.]

Tailwater is hard to regulate because it's classified as a non-point-source pollution. Point-source pollution (sewage discharge from a treatment plant, for example) is easier to regulate because it's easy to measure and trace to its origin. Non-point-source pollution cannot be traced to a specific source because it may run across land or underground before seeping into a river. Can we pinpoint which farmer applied too much nitrogen when he shares a tailwater drain with three other farmers? How about identifying the guy in the suburbs who puts too much weed killer on his lawn? Yes, it's possible to find these guys in theory, but it's harder with limited enforcement resources.

Sometimes, non-point sources get so big that they become a point source. That's the case with CAFOs (concentrated animal feeding operations, also known as factory farms). CAFOs are popular with farmers because they quickly fatten a lot of animals in a small area. CAFOs also generate a huge volume of waste that contains natural byproducts that smell bad, antibiotics and other hormones that keep the animals from getting sick in crowded conditions, and viruses and bacteria that thrive in dirty, hot, wet conditions. CAFO waste can pollute water by seeping into groundwater, draining into surface water or accidentally spilling from lagoons of liquified waste that are often several times larger than an Olympic swimming pool.

Regulations can reduce CAFO pollution, but they also reduce profits. Some farmers will comply with the spirit and letter of the law; others will meet minimum standards; and still others will violate the law to save money. Incorrect specifications and loopholes can also weaken the effectiveness of regulations. Monitoring over 20,000 CAFOs in the US requires significant resources that may not be available. Although one chicken producer was fined $1 million for violations, one of the largest pork producers in the US paid only $200,000 in fines. That polluter agreed to change waste handling at 33 of its CAFOs, but it operates in 204 other locations. The EPA and local regulators need to do a big job with limited time and staff. It makes sense to concentrate on bigger operations, but smaller operations can have big impacts in the local area.

Farmers use water to make money

Farmers combine their assets (managerial skills, land, water, machines) with other inputs (seed, labor fertilizer, pesticides) to grow crops that they can sell for a profit. They plant crops suitable to their soils, weather, labor supply, water availability and so on. They choose crops as an investor would choose a portfolio, to balance different risk-reward profiles. Weather conditions may help some crops but not others; market conditions can affect prices in different ways; and so on.

Some farmers make long-term bets, buying an expensive machine that needs to be used on one crop for 15–20 years. They may plant fruit trees or grapevines, hoping that they can wait 3 to 4 years before getting any fruit or revenue. They may switch from flood to drip irrigation, but not if a $1,000 drip irrigation system saves only $10 in water per year. They'd prefer to invest elsewhere instead of waiting 100 years to get their money back. Farmers take all of these factors (capital, inputs, information, financing costs) into consideration and place their bets on the future. Then they wait for the harvest, learn from success and mistakes, and repeat the process.

Government programs distort decisions

Unfortunately, government programs purported to help farmers have disrupted this learning-by-doing cycle. Crop subsidy programs to reduce risk, for example, create predictable financial returns that raise the price of land. Higher land prices make it expensive to get started in farming; they attract absentee landlords who see land as a source of financial yield, not food yield or a career. For American farmers, the most reliable yield comes from "program crops" (cotton, corn, wheat, soybeans, and rice are the biggest) that the government will buy at guaranteed minimum prices. Price supports lead farmers to invest in anything that promises yield: machines, fertilizers, pesticides, fancy seeds, and so forth. They make larger bets on yield with the hope that additional revenues will cover additional costs and increase profits. If they do well, they make money; if they fail, they lose their land to other farmers pursuing large-scale operations. The EU's Common Agricultural Policy also encourages farmers to pursue yield and volume, even as it differs in detail.

In either case, their suppliers sell lots of inputs and buyers get more, cheaper product. Companies in agricultural processing, crop production, machinery and food distribution all benefit from higher production volumes, and their lobbyists make sure that politicians know it. Politicians claim they are responsible for lots of cheap good food, but they are really responsible for programs that benefit a tiny minority (10 percent of farmers, 0.2 percent of the US population, receive more than 70 percent of agricultural subsidies), harm the environment (by subsidizing resource-intensive agriculture), and distort the mix of food available in markets.

These programs also encourage water use. Farmers who pay nothing for water (see next section) do not consider water consumption when they choose crops; they consider profits. Some subsidized crops (corn, rice, milk) use a lot of water, but meat stands out for its water intensity.

The amount of water it takes to produce a product is called its water footprint. A Big Mac has two patties that contain about 100 g of beef. Around the world, it takes an average of 15,500 liters (15 m^3) of water to produce a kilogram of beef from a cow. The cow consumes only 1 percent of that water (155 liters per kg); the cow eats the other 99 percent by consuming hay, alfalfa and corn. Given these numbers, it takes about 1,500 liters of water to produce the meat in a Big Mac. That block of water is 1 meter by 1 meter by 1.5 meters tall, or about enough to fill about 80 percent of a typical phone booth.

Water rights

Recall that farmers and other water users do not own water like they own cars or land. They own the usufruct rights to use water belonging to all citizens. These rights take different forms. We already discussed

(handwritten in left margin: Riparian Rights)

groundwater, the rights to which depend on local management institutions. The same holds for surface waters. (Unfortunately, these rights are not always integrated, even though surface and ground waters are often hydrologically unified.)

Societies with abundant water treated it as a public good. There was no reason to exclude or restrain anyone from taking as much water as they wanted. As demand rose, water in a river turned into a common-pool good vulnerable to overuse. "Riparian rights" made river water into a club good, because people could take water only if they owned land next to a river (exclusion) and if their diversions did not harm their riparian neighbors (non-rival).[1]

Riparian rights do not work so well in places where water flows are irregular or water is used far away from the river. California miners created "appropriative rights" during the gold rush of the 1850s. These rights gave priority access to people who had been using water for longer and allowed water diversions onto non-riparian land. Many arid places use these "first in time, first in right" appropriative rights because they protect senior rights holders against drought (junior holders may receive nothing). These rights can be classified as a private good, since they create an ownership interest in excludable and rival water. But they can be tricky. An appropriative right defined as a quantity that can be diverted ("volume x of water, from this location") is different from the amount of water that will be used. A right that specifies a 20 unit diversion can have a small impact on other rights holders when 50 percent of that diversion returns to the river; it has a much larger impact when only 10 percent of the water returns.

These property rights tended to be identified with individuals, but community rights in water also evolved in water-scarce areas where communities jointly managed water and infrastructure (major and minor canals). In the southwestern US, *acequia* irrigation projects are managed by a community-appointed watermaster who allocates water to farmers based on their crops and location. Farmers have neither quantified nor priority water rights. Historic use is considered, but the watermaster, in consultation with the community, makes final allocations. Families that fail to maintain communal areas (the main canals) get less water. A farmer in need or young family gets more water. These flexible systems are not easy for outsiders to understand, but communities have used them sustainably for generations.

---

[1]The specific rules for determining how much is too much and allocating shortfalls can be complicated.

Farmers with appropriative rights often formed irrigation districts to accomplish the same goals as *acequia*. These districts would manage the farmers' water (in proportion to their acreage or rights) as well as common infrastructure such as dams and canals. The districts were often run as a business, with farmers paying fees for water service and the district hiring staff to maintain and operate the system. The rules and regulations at irrigation districts were clearer than those at *acequias*, but they were also more rigid. It was hard to make exceptions, and easy for someone who did not want a change in operations to block them.

I'll conclude this section with a reminder that expensive water infrastructure reduces the cost of moving water, as long as the water's destination doesn't change for the next 30, 50 or 100 years. You can have cheap water or flexible delivery, but not both. Chapter 8 has more on these issues, but it's important to remember that infrastructure costs need to be repaid — whether or not water flows in the canals.

Markets for water

Some people think that high-efficiency irrigation will reduce waste and free agricultural water for cities and streams. That's wishful thinking. First, we saw earlier that a lot of waste really isn't. Second, farmers often use saved water to grow more crops; they don't leave it in the ground or river. There's one glaring exception to this result: when farmers can sell their water.

Say that Farmer A has the choice of making $100 per unit of water growing alfalfa or selling that water for $200 to Farmer B who wants to irrigate his avocado trees. Farmer A will probably sell his water. Most people accept those transactions, but they get nervous when farmers sell water to cities or environmental organizations that want it to flow downstream and into the sea. Won't those sales reduce our food supply? Ironically, farmers often say that our food supply will fall if they do not get more water. How is it possible that we will starve if we let farmers sell water *and* we will starve if we don't give farmers more water? One side must be wrong, right? Both sides are wrong (with one caveat). If there's not enough food, prices will go up, and farmers grow more food by switching to food crops or not selling water. Starvation over. Farmers do not need more water to keep us from starving. They want more free water to make more money.

Wait. Free water? Remember that governments usually distribute water rights for free. When farmers (or urbanites) pay for water, they are paying for the cost of infrastructure and delivery. In the US, urban water prices are 50–200 times greater than the price of irrigation water. Some of this difference is due to quality (clean tap water is available 24/7), but much of it is due to explicit subsidies to costs and implicit subsidies to access; both subsidies are described at length in Chapter 8.

Now the caveat. We don't need to worry about some farmers selling water and fallowing land if we can buy food from other domestic and foreign farmers. If trade is blocked, then food security starts to matter. Most economists thought that this concern was overblown, until they saw all the political interference with trade during the 2008 food crisis, when world food prices shot up under the influences of higher fuel and fertilizer prices, bad weather, and political demand for corn ethanol. Several countries limited exports of wheat and rice, which led to higher prices and riots in some food-importing countries. Countries with large agricultural exports (the US, Australia, and others) need not use food security to limit agricultural-urban water transfers. Other countries should concentrate on improving trade relations with food exporters (traded food contains "virtual water") and storing extra food for emergencies instead of giving more free water (and excess profits) to domestic producers.

Barriers to trade

But sometimes farmers don't sell their water. Why not? First, it may be the wrong time of the year to make the decision. Second, the farmer may need to get bureaucratic, environmental, political, and/or social approvals to sell it. Third, he may worry that his water rights will be weakened if he sells water for a season. Fourth, he may just prefer to farm.

Let's look into these barriers. Timing is definitely an issue, and it's made worse by the lack of a day-to-day market in water. If farmers saw water prices the same way they saw commodity food prices, then perhaps they would be ready to sell when they ran into their thirsty neighbor at the coffee shop. Approvals are a huge problem. A leading broker in Australia promises to help clients buy and sell water — by navigating through the 19,000 rules affecting trades. Environmental regulations can be useful (preventing a trade that causes problems) but they can also be onerous, taking too long to measure too much of too little value. Water sales would be easier if environmental clearance was faster.

Legal barriers can prevent trade or markets. Politicians interfere when they dislike who is buying water or how much water costs. Many political districts have "area of origin" laws that prohibit the export of water to other places. These laws are often justified as a means of preventing third-party impacts, or harm, to locals who want the farmer to grow crops. These third parties can include businesses that sell inputs, goods and services to farmers, laborers who would work on crops, and so on. It's strange that these impacts worry people when it comes to fallowing land but not when it comes to shutting down a factory. In both cases, people lose their jobs and local businesses lose sales. What's stranger is when these impacts can be positive. That's because the water is sold, not taken, and the money that comes to farmers is often spent in the local area.

Ironically, farmers sometimes do sell their surface water to an out-of-area buyer without reducing production. How do they do that? They may reduce their wasted water by lining irrigation ditches with cement or plastic to reduce leakage, or by installing drip irrigation. These conservation methods reduce the amount of water a farmer needs to grow the same crops, allowing him to sell the conserved water. Unfortunately, such a change in irrigation patterns means the old wastewater will no longer seep underground or into rivers — reducing accidental but useful flows to neighbors and the environment. But the situation can be much worse, as when a farmer sells his surface water and replaces it by pumping more groundwater. Scarcity has also increased the abuse of water rights, as when a well is drilled next to a river. That well's water is classified as groundwater, but it comes from the river, and out of someone's prior appropriation or riparian right. This win-win transaction is really win-lose, since the seller makes money but his neighbors who share the same common-pool source lose some of their water.

Speaking of neighbors, let's also consider some accidental (on purpose) winners from area of origin restrictions: other farmers. If strangers will pay $200 per unit for water and locals will pay only $50, then locals will lose water — unless area of origin restrictions prevent that sale. On the other hand, these neighbors may worry that a neighbor who sells water will stop paying for joint infrastructure, the canals that they share as club goods, for example. As I mentioned earlier, these canals may be managed by informal institutions (as in *acequias*) or through formal payments (each farmer paying his share of costs when he takes delivery of water from the irrigation district). In the formal system, a farmer who sells rights outside the area is not taking delivery. He may stop paying. That problem can be addressed by payment of a severance fee that covers the remainder of his obligation (a fee that can be guaranteed by a lien on his land or water right). The severance fee problem does not exist for informal systems because communal water rights are not sold to outsiders, but those systems can have other problems with underinvestment of time or money in maintaining infrastructure.

Many farmers worry that they will lose their rights if they sell them instead of using the water, based on "use it or lose it" prior appropriation rights. This worry is often unfounded when laws protect rights as long as water is being put to beneficial use. Common sense implies that the water is being put to beneficial use if someone is willing to pay for it. That said, I'm not a lawyer, and lawyers can interpret laws in lots of interesting ways. Farmers won't lease water to cities in a drought if such a deal endangers their rights and future. So they just grow alfalfa.

And some farmers just prefer to not sell. Although some people think that a property right includes the right to not sell, others think that farmers who are using water that belongs to everyone should lose that right if the water could be put to a higher social use in a city or wetland. These claims are made in the name of "public trust," or the idea that the government has a responsibility to make sure that water is put to good use (but not always highest and best use). The trouble with this idea is obvious. For many years, the public interest meant cheap water for farmers. Farmers were given water rights; they paid some fraction of infrastructure costs; sometimes they didn't even pay for the power it took to deliver the water. For obvious reasons, a lot of farmers invested substantial cash, sweat and hope in putting this water to work. It's not right to cancel water rights that have been used for 20 or 100 years.

The obvious problem with seizing rights is that they are worth something, and that value shows up in the land to which rights are attached. Water rights change the value of land according to the difference between the cost of water delivered due to rights and its value. Water rights gave windfall profits to formerly dry landowners, but the next farmer bought the land at a higher price that reflected the value of its water rights. Although it's hard to complain if Mother Nature refuses to deliver water, it's much clearer that a legal or regulatory taking of water will reduce land value and attract energetic opposition.

Farmers should be paid if their water rights are seized. The current distribution of rights may be very costly from a social perspective, but uncompensated seizure would create a toxic combination of bad feelings, lawsuits, violence, business uncertainty, and political disturbance that would probably take at least 20 years to dissipate. It's better to let farmers sell or rent their water.

Markets work and so do community institutions

Farmers in California's Palo Verde Irrigation District (PVID) have senior rights to take water from the adjacent Colorado River, and they use their abundant water to grow alfalfa. These farmers are maximizing their profit from alfalfa (lots of water, little labor), but they have also embraced temporary sales to cities. In 2004, PVID farmers made an agreement with the Metropolitan Water District of Southern California (MWD) in which MWD pays PVID farmers to fallow up to 25 percent of their land and ship the unused water to MWD. (MWD also paid farmers a large sign-up fee.) PVID farmers sell water for $100/ML that they buy for $5/ML, which is better than growing alfalfa for profits that vary widely around $55/ML. The good news is that the 25 percent fallowing limit leaves most farmers busy, while allowing their fallowed land to rest (increasing future productivity). MWD gets water at a lower price than it pays elsewhere. Local non-farmers benefit because PVID farmers spend MWD's money on goods and services.

ML – see p. 10

This trade also illustrates the implicit subsidy that farmers receive when they are given priority to water rights and the social cost of not allowing them to trade those water rights in markets. PVID farmers pay about $5/ML for water that makes them a profit of $55/ML. MWD is willing to pay $100/ML for that water, so PVID's water rights are worth $45/ML ($100 - $55). When PVID farmers use their water, they pay $5/ML and society incurs that $45/ML in "opportunity costs" (an implicit subsidy) because the water does not go to the members of society willing to pay the most. These opportunity costs go to zero when PVID sells water, because water is going to a higher valued use.[2] From a social view, it's important to get water to higher-value uses, through either a government auction of water or secondary markets where farmers sell their water. Unfortunately, water auctions and markets are only active in a few parts of the world. Who is harmed?

---

[2]PVID farmers make a $45 profit from their water rights but that money transfer between MWD and PVID has no net impact on society.

Farmers who cannot sell their water and make an extra $45/ML and society that incurs the $45/ML opportunity cost from misallocation.

The water markets in Australia's Murray Darling basin have been a spectacular success for farmers. These markets allow farmers to sell their (permanent) water licenses or (temporary) water allocations to other farmers. The markets are limited by environmental and infrastructure constraints, but they have thrived with the clarification and open trading of water rights. Water rights have been separated from the land and turned into a given number of ML licenses. In each year, the government announces the allocation for each license. Thus, a farmer with 20 ML of licenses may get eight ML of temporary water from a 40 percent allocation. The farmer can then buy or sell as much temporary water as he wants, with the clear knowledge of water's value to himself and others. Farmers are the biggest buyers in markets, but the government has also bought a lot of water for environmental flows. In 2007/8, the total value of trades was $1.4 billion. The 2008/9 water year saw $2.5 billion in trades.

In Chile, a similar water market has driven farmers to be more efficient and grow more valuable crops. Chile's farmers now produce good wines and export summer fruits during the Northern Hemisphere's winter. Farmers get more money per drop, which is better than more crop per drop.

Water markets are easy for farmers to understand and use, since they already shift their mix of inputs in response to changes in the relative costs of inputs. When water is cheap, they use flood irrigation and reduce their use of more expensive inputs. When labor is expensive, they grow alfalfa or grains. When water is expensive and labor is cheap, they grow strawberries. What we want then, is a price on water that reflects its sustainable supply. Price can be set directly through an auction allocating a fixed water supply, or indirectly, by allowing secondary markets in water and rights. Prices help us understand values and tradeoffs. Without prices, we will misallocate resources, in the same way that the Soviets did when they failed to solve Hayek's knowledge problem.

Culture and indigenous values can sometimes substitute for prices, markets and efficiency. The water temples of Indonesia's Bali coordinate water flows, crop patterns, infrastructure and water rights (like *acequias*), allowing the Balinese to grow two rice crops per year, as they have for more than a thousand years. They do this through a robust, evolved system of coordination. First, farmers apply for permission to divert water; temples make sure that everyone gets enough at the right time. Second, temples coordinate planting and harvesting, so that pests and diseases are starved out of a large, fallowed area. Third, the temples provide technical advice, raise funds for building big projects, and ensure that infrastructure is maintained. Finally, they arbitrate old and new claims to water, maintaining sustainability while maximizing the use of water. The temples do all this with elaborate and constant rituals that coordinate farmers (and burn quite a bit of incense).

In the 1960s, local and international bureaucrats promised that green revolution techniques (new seeds, fertilizers, pesticides and more water) would deliver three rice crops per year. Although yields rose in the first few years, water shortages quickly appeared, and pests and diseases destroyed up to 100 percent of the modern-seed crops. In an unusual step, the bureaucrats realized their failure and put Bali's priests back in charge. Traditional methods fed people.

All-in-auctions for scarce water

These examples of water trades (MWD-PVID), markets (Australia and Chile) and community schemes for managing scarce water (Bali's water temples) are useful in showing that a variety of institutions can efficiently allocate water. In this section, I will describe an alternative way to reach efficiency by auctioning water rights among their current owners. This all-in-auction (AiA) structure doesn't require that water leave an area or that permanent water rights be traded. It's meant to reallocate water in the short term at a fair and transparent price among a group that already shares water. The AiA can be modified to consider environmental water demands, trade with outsiders (other farmers, or cities) and so on.

The key is to recognize the efficiency of markets. When demand exceeds supply, scarcity is increasing. Shortage can be prevented with rationing via bureaucratic rules or prices. Bureaucratic allocations are less efficient than prices because bureaucrats cannot solve the knowledge problem. Markets are efficient because they allow buyers and sellers to meet at one place and negotiate deals at mutually agreeable prices. The most efficient market for quickly settling many trades is an auction.

Here's how all-in-auctions work.

Assume that 50 farmers have different land, crops and quantities of water rights. They jointly control a cooperative irrigation system.

These farmers received 250 units of water in the past, but now they have only 60 percent of that amount (150 units of water). They all have equal priority to that water. How should it be allocated?

The first solution is to prorate water allocations, so that each farmer gets 60 percent of his traditional allocation. But those allocations are too small, and farmers who want more water will buy it from others under a form of cap and trade. Total available water is capped, but buyers who want more trade with sellers who prefer money. Unfortunately, the cap and trade market may not be very efficient. Some farmers will not sell their water; they may choose to grow a less valuable crop. Other farmers may ask high prices because *their* water is valuable. Some sales will happen, but some won't, even if all farmers are invited to the market.

The lack of liquidity (pun!) in this example is costly to individuals and society. It's also typical.

I designed the AiA to address this problem by combining several existing ideas into a mechanism that maximizes the opportunity to move water to buyers who value it, without taking water from owners. It's easiest to explain the AiA with an example.

The AiA requires that farmers have clear title to a known quantity of water rights. From above, we know that each of the 50 farmers has three units of water. These 150 units are put up for sale ("all-in"), so farmers now have zero water. Farmers who want water need to bid in the AiA.

Let's say that the 50 competing farmers make 233 bids.[3] The highest 150 bids win the water. These successful bids are not settled at bid values but a single price equal to the 151st bid. The AiA is a "second-price auction" (or 151st-price auction here) because the highest bids win but pay a price equal to the highest rejected bid. This is how eBay auctions work.

Let's say that the 151st bid is $43. That means the market-clearing price for water is $43.

Who sold water? Everyone (forced sales are discussed in a moment). Who bought water? Everyone who bid more than $43.

The example in Table 5 clarifies how bidding and buying works.

Farmer Alex bids 12, 44, 55 and 67. Farmers Bob and Chris also make bids. Nine of their 13 bids are successful because they are

---

[3]Bidding processes vary, but it seems best to let people bid until they don't want to bid higher prices for more units. This soft ending avoids the last-minute "sniping" problem that frustrates people on eBay, for example.

Table 5: The all-in-auction reallocates water rights to the highest bidders but allows owners to buy back their water at no net cost.

	Alex	Bob	Chris
Units owned	3	3	3
Units owned ($43 each)	129	129	129
Bids	12, 44, 55, 67	40, 41, 80, 100	15, 44, 45, 54, 66
Winning bids (over $43)	44, 55, 67	80, 100	44, 45, 54, 66
Units bought ($43 each)	3 for 129	2 for 86	4 for 172
Change in units (in – out)	+3-3 = 0	+2 - 3 = -1	+4-3 = +1
Change in cash (in – out)	+129-129 = 0	+129-86 = +43	+129-172 = -43

greater than $43. (Other farmers won the other 141 units with bids that were greater than $43.) Alex has three winning bids, paying $129 for three units of water. Bob pays $86 for two units, and Chris pays $172 for four units.

Who gets paid from those water sales? Each farmer gets $129 for his three units.

If we subtract cash paid from cash received, we see that Alex comes out even; Bob gets $43 and Chris pays $43. All of them have the water they bought.

An all-in-auction has several attractive features. First, it ensures that the maximum amount of water is traded. Second, it allows any farmer to "buy back" his water at zero cost, neutralizing any objections of being forced to sell; Alex paid nothing to keep his three units. Third, it makes each farmer think about how much water he really wants. Bob had three units and made four bids, of which two succeeded. Apparently, that third unit wasn't worth it. Would he have sold it outside the AiA if someone offered him $44 at the coffee shop? Probably not. He might think he could get more elsewhere or that it was more valuable to him, but the auction clarified these doubts. Finally, this auction allows farmers to buy water as cheaply as possible. Chris got his four units.

The AiA can work with any group of farmers who need to redistribute their water after a reduction in total supplies. It's probably better to run this auction in every season, so that rights are rented, rather than sold to high bidders. That structure gives more flexibility to farmers making planting decisions now, even as it allows those with rights to defer decisions on future water uses to the future. The AiA takes some time to set up and coordinate among farmers, which means it may have greater transaction costs than trades that now happen at the coffee shop, but these costs will be small, relative to gains, in areas with many farmers, large amounts of water, diverse crops and soils, or too many coffee shops. Note that AiA can also be used inside of other big organizations (regional water distributors or government irrigation projects, for example) where historical rights are not very well matched to current demands.

But let's say that this market is not possible. What should happen when rights are not known (or quantified) but demand exceeds supply? Say that 20 farmers sharing the same groundwater are overdrafting and draining the aquifer. Water quality is falling as the pumps suck deeper water that contains more salts; the cost of pumping is rising as the water comes from greater depths. How can we get a market or price solution and avoid a command-and-control regulation that favors a certain water use or technology?

The solution depends on property rights and effective pumping controls. Groundwater rights that depend on seniority imply that holders of junior rights lose access first. Juniors who want water will have to make a side deal to buy water from a senior holder. If everyone has the same rights to the water, then they can either adjudicate the water, dividing quantities among themselves based on the sustainable yield (turning a common-pool good into a private good), or they can set a pump tax. The tax per mega liter of pumping will depend on the depth of the water table at a reference well. (Groundwater hydrology is complicated, but it's safe to say that each well has water at a different depth and that pumping in one place affects pumping in other places.) The basic idea is that the tax starts at a positive number because the water table is too deep. The tax per ML will then increase if the water table continues to drop or fall if the water table rises toward a targeted sustainable level. Where would pump tax revenues go? Perhaps to improving common infrastructure or subsidizing high efficiency irrigation — or maybe a big party.

What about fish-as-food?

Fishermen are similar to farmers, but fish are like groundwater — a common-pool resource that can be destroyed in a Tragedy of the Commons. That's why 70 percent of worldwide fisheries are destroyed or overexploited. Governments encourage this problem by subsidizing fishermen's equipment and fuel. Sometimes they give them unemployment aid after a fishery crashes. When the fishery recovers, aid ends, fishermen return to overfish, and we're back to square one (or minus one).

Some governments try to control fishing in their exclusive eco-nomic zone by keeping the season short, limiting the equipment on boats or setting quotas for the total catch. None of these regulations prevent fishermen from racing one another and wiping out the fishery.

In the open seas, these regulations are even weaker. In recent negotiations over endangered bluefin tuna, Japan (which consumes 80 percent of the world catch) successfully lobbied the International Commission for the Conservation of Atlantic Tunas (ICCAT, which is sometimes called the International Conspiracy to Catch All Tuna) against any restriction on trading the fish. Japan did this by paying IC-CAT representatives from developing counties, sometimes countries that do not eat ocean fish, to support Japanese demand. ICCAT is supposed to limit catches to a sustainable level but decided to limit fishermen to 30,000 tons. That's a problem when scientists say that no more than 15,000 tons can be caught and 60,000 tons are actu-ally landed. Fishermen catch double the maximum limit because it's hard to enforce quotas. First, it's expensive to monitor fishermen on the high seas. Second, countries have an incentive to ignore world agreements, to help *their* fishermen. A fish caught by a Spanish boat generates money for Spain; if the fish is left in the water for a British boat to catch, then the money goes to the UK instead. In the ensuing open-access race in which any fisherman can catch as many fish as he wants, too many fish are taken. Japan's behavior is likely driven by a domestic preference for keeping fishermen and fish brokers in business. Consumers may be happy about cheap sushi now, but they will be unhappy when there's no sushi at any price.

The solution to domestic and international overfishing is property rights backed by enforcement or traditional rights within a strong com-munity. In Iceland, New Zealand and many US fisheries, for example, fishermen have Individually Tradable Quotas (ITQs) that give them the right to catch a certain tonnage of fish in a specified geographi-cal area. They can sell, rent or use their ITQs. Only quota fish can be landed on shore or sold. ITQs allow fishermen to fish when they want, where they want, using the equipment they want. They end the arms race for bigger boats that takes place in open-access fisheries where boats try to maximize their share of the season's harvest be-fore it runs out. They limit injuries to competing fishermen. They raise catch prices by reducing damage to fish, giving fishermen an incen-tive to get higher quality fish in their tonnage, and allowing fishermen to land fish at different times of the year. They raise the quality of fish for consumers, who no longer face one week of fresh fish and 51 weeks of frozen fish. Best of all, ITQs are sustainable. They are set to make sure that the fishery is healthy, and fishermen prefer that they be set conservatively, since a healthy fishery means ITQs are worth more. (Fishermen with ITQs will help regulators and monitors catch pirate fishermen who reduce the value of their ITQs.) ITQs for Alaskan halibut led to impressive gains for fishermen, consumers and the environment. The season increased from three days to eight months, fish were sold fresh instead of frozen, harvest costs and injuries fell, fresh fish prices fell, and fishermen made more money.

Why aren't ITQs used everywhere in the world? It's not for lack of technology, but political will. We know this because ITQs are implemented in some countries but not others. They are not implemented in poor countries because fishermen from rich countries pay bribes to exploit and harvest local fish. They are not used to protect and improve international fisheries for the same reasons. The Japanese may be the leaders of fishery destruction, but many other countries (Spain, China, Indonesia) are right behind them. Fishermen are also to blame: good fishermen think they can catch more fish in the current free-for-all; bad fishermen need just one more good catch to get out of debt. All of these examples illustrate a self-destructive preference for get-rich-quick exploitation over long-term sustainability. The lack of political action is easier to understand. Politicians prefer that fishermen make money today (and return some in donations and support), because they will be retired when those fishermen are broke and jobless.

Some entrepreneurs have set up businesses to circumvent the property rights problem, growing fish, crustaceans and shellfish on aquaculture farms that are off limits to other fishermen. Unfortunately, fish farms can create new problems. Shrimp farms often replace coastal mangrove swamps (increasing flood risk and local water pollution). Overcrowded fish in pens produce a lot of waste; their conditions encourage diseases and parasites that can harm nearby wild fish. The antibiotics that farmers use to reduce disease encourage bacteria to evolve and become more dangerous. Farmed fish are often fed with other fish caught in the open seas, displacing overfishing to other places and species. Or they are fed with corn, which is not natural. Farmed salmon have pink flesh because of pink dye in their food; they do not accumulate Omega-3s as they would on a natural diet. Freshwater aquaculture can work better — fish eat algae or cheaper food, are isolated from wild fish, and are separated from natural environments — but there's no free lunch when it comes to addressing the end of abundant and healthy fisheries.

More farmers means bigger reforms

Farmers in less-developed countries (LDCs) are poorer, represent a greater percentage of the population, face greater corruption, are subject to inconsistent regulation, and have less access to markets, insurance or technology. Their governments are less helpful and their institutions are weaker. It's amazing that they still manage to survive, but they do.

In most LDCs, farmers use most of the water, often because they are given preferential prices or access. Indian farmers are given subsidized electricity for their pumps. Many have overdrafted their aquifers to the point of collapse; only a few have managed to organize themselves to slow down overdrafting. In Saudi Arabia, groundwater was mined for growing wheat until the government ended subsidies that paid triple the world price (the farmers are now mining the groundwater for other crops). In Libya, meanwhile, the government continues to mine its aquifers for fossil water that's been under the Sahara Desert for several thousand years. Libyan wheat may not taste better, but it sure costs more.

Israel and Palestine are famous for peace problems but also for water problems. Amazingly, water shortages are the result of self-inflicted wounds, not nature, terrorism or religious dogma. The Palestinian government in Gaza charges farmers $0.02–$0.04 per m^3 of water, and farmers consume two-thirds of the supply. Some people think that Gaza needs to increase its domestic water supply through desalination (at a cost of at least $0.50 per m^3), but it is cheaper and faster to reduce the water farmers use, by either raising the price they pay or buying their water in a market.

Farmers in Israel are quite famous for using high-efficiency irrigation and recycled water to grow their crops. Although more than half their irrigation water comes from treated wastewater, they still use 56 percent of the country's water and pay less for it than urban users on the same supply network. Some claim it's important to give farmers preferred access to water on national security grounds, but it's hard to see how Israel's banana crop is a strategic asset when its cost includes reductions in water for Palestinians and new desalination plants.

Many LDCs use dams to reduce floods, generate electricity and deliver reliable water for irrigation. Unfortunately, these dams allow the agricultural sector to expand onto more land, lowering crop prices for existing farmers. The loss of fertility from the end of flooding means farmers need to use more artificial fertilizers. That's what happened in Egypt when it blocked the Nile with Aswan High Dam. Aswan also reduced flooding and outflow to the Nile Delta, which damaged the local fishery and reversed the growth of the delta. Upstream dams can harm downstream neighbors. Dams on the Mekong in China and Laos will stop the wet season floods that increase Cambodia's Tonle Sap Lake to seven times its dry season size. That's a problem because Cambodians get 60 percent of their protein from fish that breed in the flooded lake. No floods, no fish, no food. Sometimes projects to produce more food and help farmers do neither.

The same practice takes place with unsustainable surface water diversions. Uzbekistan continues a Soviet-era policy of diverting water into the desert to grow cotton. The corrupt government forces farmers to grow cotton and then pays them a fraction of the world market price. Government leaders spend the profits from cotton sales on themselves, and the Aral Sea continues to shrink. The world's fourth-largest freshwater lake is now 10 percent of its original size.

In the past few years, some people have claimed that Indian farmers are committing suicide because their genetically modified BT cotton crops have failed. While it's true that Indian farmers do commit suicide, the reasons are home grown. Government subsidies for groundwater pumping mean that a monsoon failure leads to crop failure for poor farmers who cannot afford the deep wells and big pumps necessary to access the lower water table. Some of these farmers cannot repay debts to moneylenders, and they commit suicide. Don't blame BT-cotton for crop and income losses; blame government policies that destroy farmers' traditional insurance policy against drought.

One of the worst programs harming farmers in developing countries originates in the United States. Ironically, it involves the export of surplus food grown with unsustainable water withdrawals. The US Food Aid program (Public Law 480, the Food for Peace Act of 1961) harms recipient countries in several ways. It increases supply and lowers prices (so that local production is disrupted and unprofitable) and damages the recipient country's ability to cope with natural disasters, by rescuing them with outside help that may not arrive in the next crisis. EU countries also engage in food dumping, but they have gradually shifted to cash payments that are used to buy local food. That program encourages local production and local institutions for dealing with trouble. The US does not embrace that model because it wants to sell domestic overproduction that often results from subsidies.

Some people think that the world faces a hunger problem that can be fixed with more crop per drop or a lower population or a switch to a vegetarian diet. While those ideas do make some sense, they are not the best way to stop hunger. It's better to remove subsidies for water consumption, barriers to agricultural trade, and regulations that tell farmers what to plant, where to sell, and what to charge.

Farmers can surf the wave or be crushed by it

Farmers worldwide currently control most of our freshwater supplies. The end of abundance means these supplies are increasingly valuable to farmers, urban dwellers, industry and the environment. The best way to improve water allocation among all these sectors is to make it profitable to use less water, waste less water and save today's water for tomorrow. Markets can make it easier to reach these goals, as can better regulations on quality and common-pool goods and fewer useless regulations on how water is used. Markets also make it easy to reallocate water that's too cheap or misallocated to valuable agricultural, environmental, urban or industrial uses. Government subsidies to certain crops favor short-term exploitation over sustainability, appropriate technology and cropping decisions that would result in the highest and best use of water. Compared with food, the problems of open sea fisheries are much harder to solve, but the current situation is also a spectacular failure of misguided, destructive policies that favor special interests. The end of abundance in water means we need to change policies so that farmers can thrive and prosper in delivering enough food for everyone. Farmers have the most to gain from improved regulations, markets and institutions. Those who resist change will lose many profitable opportunities. They may also be punished by thirsty populists using legal and political weapons to take back the people's water. We need food and water, so we must ensure that policies affecting food production and water use can respond to the end of abundance.

CHAPTER 6

Water for power for water

Energy production requires water; water transport and treatment requires energy. The "energy-water nexus" is a myth: accurate water prices are sufficient for good energy and water management. Water scarcity makes biofuels less attractive.

The end of abundance also applies to energy. Demand is growing, but cheap oil is running out. Carbon consciousness has made it harder to use abundant coal, just as risk and uncertainty has made it harder to use nuclear power. Alternative energy sources are more expensive. The higher resulting energy prices push our consumption down.

The end of abundant water, in contrast, has not often led to higher water prices or lower consumption because water prices reflect the cost of delivery — not scarcity. Markets for water are barely developed compared with energy markets. It's hard to lower consumption without price signals.

"Peak oil" refers to the peak in global oil supplies, when oil consumption outpaces oil discoveries so that total supplies are falling. Most people in the oil industry think that we're near that peak. Some people say that we are close to "peak water," but that analogy is wrong. First, water is a renewable resource that flows from place to place in seasonal cycles; these flows may shift but they do not reduce the fixed stock of water that rests mostly in oceans. Second, most water does not have a scarcity price attached to it, so there's little understanding of relative supply or demand. Third, water is a local good that's managed in different ways in different places. In combination, these three characteristics make it clear that we can price and manage water for sustainable use without ever reaching a peak, based on local supply and demand.

But water and energy also affect each other. Recall from Table 1 that about 40 percent of water diversions are used for thermoelectric energy generation — for cooling, steam power, or falling-water turbines in dams. The end of abundant water can make it very expensive or impossible to generate electricity, especially when water prices or markets do not exist. In 2006, several European nuclear plants shut down when their cooling water supplies ran low; the same happened with a Tennessee Valley Authority nuclear plant in 2007.

A price of water that accurately reflects scarcity will go a long way toward improving the use of water by energy industries. That's the good news. The bad news is that this price will increase the price of power. Those price increases should not be avoided or ignored. They reflect the real cost of using water. The same can be said for efforts to include the price of greenhouse gases (or other pollution) in energy production. The resulting increase in the price of energy is not unfair or inefficient. It reflects the real cost of using energy. The end of abundance means we need to pay attention to how much we use, and the easiest way to signal scarcity is with prices that rise when demand outpaces supply, for energy and for water.

The next two sections look at how freshwater is used to create energy and energy is used to create freshwater. We then turn to the "energy-water nexus" and how most attempts to manage the nexus are ineffective relative to prices and markets. That section segues into a short description of how developing countries suffer from similar mismanagement of water and energy.

The water in energy

In 2009, 83 percent of the energy consumed in the US came from fossil fuels; 9 percent came from nuclear, 4 percent from biofuels and 4 percent from other renewables, including hydropower.[1] Water is used to produce every one of these energy sources, but missing prices for water quantity and quality can encourage water consumption and pollution. Let's look at the uses that have big water impacts.

---

[1]Energy is the capacity for doing work (a liter of gas has energy); power is the rate of using energy (liters of gas used per second). Water's potential energy from its dense mass converts into kinetic energy when it moves. Moving water converts energy into power that pushes on something (hydraulic power) or pushes turbines that transform kinetic energy into electrical energy (hydropower). "Power" and "energy" are technically different — measuring different forces using different units — but we will use them interchangeably. Apologies to the engineers and physicists.

Energy production often pollutes water

Water is used at all stages of energy production. Water is injected underground to force oil into collection pipes. Fracking uses high-pressure water to break subsurface mineral formations and free natural gas for collection. Water is used to move coal slurry in pipelines or separate oil from tar sands. In all of these cases, the discarded water will be contaminated and often polluted.

Hydrocarbon fuels can contaminate freshwater and seawater. The worst freshwater pollution is when an aquifer is spoiled, because it's hard to assess the degree of damage and even harder to clean up. Many freshwater aquifers are economically lost to pollution, because the cost of cleaning is so high. That may not be a problem to humans who can get water elsewhere, but it is a problem to flora and fauna without alternatives.

Mine wastes (or tailings) that contain heavy metals and/or extraction and processing byproducts can pollute water that flows into rivers, lakes and aquifers. Pollution often occurs because it's cheaper to dump tailings into a valley that drains to other places, as with mountaintop removal coal mining, than sealing them off from rain and local drainage systems.

Thermoelectric plants use water for once-through cooling, where cold water absorbs waste heat before being discharged as hot water or steam. This water may not be chemically contaminated, but it is thermally polluted. It's also dead in the sense that few creatures survive the process of being sucked in, heated up and pumped out. Cooling and recirculation can reduce these impacts, but the cost of additional equipment is usually higher than the cost of just taking more water from rivers and other sources. A rise in the price of extractions or discharges can quickly make once-through cooling expensive and recirculation more attractive.

Renewable energy — more water per megawatt

Hydroelectric dams use water's weight to drive turbines that generate electricity. Although hydropower seems better for flora and fauna (because it discharges cool water instead of hot steam), dams prevent fish and other animals from migrating. Dams also interfere with the natural downstream movements of silt and gravel, changes in the location, width and depth of river channels, and changes in the size and shape of deltas. They also tend to discharge water at a uniform temperature. Turbines cannot operate efficiently with unstable water pressure, so winter floods are held back for discharge in summer, ending the natural variance between cold spring floods and hot summer trickles. It's possible to generate power with off-stream and in-stream turbines that do not need dams or with wave-powered hydraulic pumps, but these technologies are new, expensive and represent a tiny share of overall supply.

Geothermal energy uses steam generated when water comes in contact with rocks heated by the Earth's core. This renewable resource is naturally available where the Earth's crust is fractured by volcanic and tectonic action, such as Iceland and Northern California's Geysers field. Oil drilling techniques are now making it possible to create engineered geothermal systems by simply drilling 4–5 km down, injecting cold water from the surface and harnessing the heated water for power generation. The trouble with these schemes is that they need a reliable source of water, and probably freshwater. Free water would encourage too much use.

Biofuels are often mandated or subsidized by governments and produced by large corporations that employ more lobbyists and financial engineers than farmers. Subsidies lead to overproduction that increases the demand for water. Farmers who pay no scarcity price for water and have no need to protect their neighbors from overpumping tend to use too much. In terms of water per unit of energy produced, biofuels use 1,000 to 1,000,000 times more water than other energy sources. That's because water is used to produce sugarcane, corn, soybean or palm crops that are then processed into ethanol or biodiesel. Actual processing requires only a tiny fraction of the water needed to grow the crops. Biofuels also need land for production. This can mean that rainforests are cut down (for palm oil or sugarcane plantations) or that other crops are displaced (as with corn fields). Biofuels need machinery, diesel fuel, fertilizers, pesticides and herbicides to produce. They increase the volume of agricultural tailwater that can pollute the environment: the dead zone at the mouth of the Mississippi River has been linked to corn ethanol production. Biofuels are a lot more like nasty fossil fuels than proponents admit.

The US corn ethanol program offers a useful example of a Baptist and Bootlegger confluence of greed, corruption and moral superiority. Greed can be traced to big agro-processing companies (ADM, Cargill and others) that make money by trading corn and ethanol. Corruption is connected to congressmen who want campaign donations (legal bribes) from these companies and farmers who benefit from congressionally induced demand, via per gallon subsidies, mandated corn ethanol fuel blends, and tariff barriers that block imports of cheaper, sustainable sugarcane ethanol from Brazil. The moral superiority component comes from the environmentalists who demand that Americans use more renewable fuels and patriots who want energy independence from dodgy foreigners. Their clamor for renewables gave farmers, processors and politicians the cover they needed to start another program designed to transfer money from taxpayers and car drivers to the agricultural and political sectors. The worst irony is that this "green fuel" may have done nothing to reduce net CO_2 emissions.

In this Baptists and Bootleggers alliance, environmentalists are happy to have more renewable fuel. Farmers and agro-businesses are happy to sell more fuel in the gasoline market. Taxpayers lose and drivers get lower-quality fuel. Politicians win twice, since they can claim to protect the environment at the same time as they collect bribes from the corn industry. But there's an additional twist: corn ethanol uses a lot of free water, simultaneously increasing scarcity and pollution. Ethanol production would fall if we priced water for scarcity and purity.

The energy in water

We use energy to move water around, pumping it over hills and through pressurized pipes. How much energy goes into moving water? Water transportation and treatment uses 19 percent of California's electricity. Las Vegas uses energy to stretch its small water supply to meet a big demand. Vegas recycles its water several times, discharging treated wastewater into Lake Mead and then pumping water back up the hill to sell to customers. Vegas water managers do this because they get recharge credits. Their pursuit of water resources may be successful, but it comes with a heavy cost in energy resources: 6.5 percent of total electricity consumption in Las Vegas goes to processing and pumping water. Vegas is not even extreme, since its energy consumption per unit of water delivered is average for US utilities.

Although our water bills reflect the price of transporting water, they do not reflect the impact of those energy sources on greenhouse gases (GHGs). Internalizing that negative externality with moderate carbon prices ($20 per ton CO2e) would increase the price of water pumped with carbon-intensive energy sources by $10–$30/ML.[2] That's

---

[2] I use carbon, CO_2 equivalents (CO2e) and GHGs interchangeably in this book.

not much for residential customers paying $1,000/ML, but it's very steep for farmers paying $5–$50/ML. What's interesting is that consumers may not notice this price change: only 20 percent of the price of food in the US represents farmers' growing costs; the other 80 percent represents processing, packaging, marketing and transportation costs. Assuming that water costs are 25 percent of the farmer's production costs, these ratios imply that a doubling of water costs due to the inclusion of carbon prices would increase the price of milk in the store from $1.00 to $1.05 per liter. Higher prices would be more unpopular with farmers and middlemen who count every cent, but they would give a useful incentive to use less water and power.

Turning oil into water

We also use energy to improve water quality. Boiling water will kill bacteria and viruses. It's also possible to treat water with UV radiation, ozone or chlorine, but these techniques (like boiling) cannot remove salt or other robust contaminants that can make water unsafe. To purify water completely, it's necessary either to distill it (converting it to steam and then cooling) or separate water from contaminants via reverse osmosis (RO), which uses high pressure to push water against a surface with holes that are big enough to allow water molecules through but small enough to block organic molecules, ions, and particulates. Both processes use a lot of energy, but technological improvements mean that RO often uses less energy than distillation. With larger or smaller holes, RO can be used for different purposes, such as purifying drinking water (at home, a municipal water plant, or bottled water plant), cleaning wastewater, or removing salt and impurities from ocean or brackish water.

RO-purified wastewater uses less energy than desalinated ocean water, but it's unpopular with people (the yuck factor) and current beneficiaries of wastewater flows (see Chapter 2). Ironically, RO-freshwater is often so pure that minerals must be added to prevent the water from leaching minerals from pipes and joints in the distribution system.

Desalination is one of the most expensive ways to get freshwater. The capital costs of the plant, pumps and pipes are significant. Operating costs (energy and filters) depend on salinity, energy source, plant technology, filter technology and other factors. Environmental costs from entrapment/entrainment/impingement of sea life harmed or killed by suction at intake pipes and saline discharge are important, inexact and occasionally ignored. A typical RO desalination plant turns two liters of ocean water into a liter of freshwater for drinking and a liter of extra-salty water that's discharged. But the biggest cost may be the time it takes to win political and regulatory permission for construction. It's not unusual for pre-construction to take three, five or ten years in the United States. This process will be much faster in countries where water supply is regarded as a matter for national security (Kuwait, Israel, Singapore), shortages are pressing (Australia, Spain) or national pride reigns (Saudi Arabia).

Desalination is often presented as the easy solution to complicated interrelationships. The desalination plant under construction in Carlsbad, California, is not necessary for health and safety or as the next cheapest source of water. Carlsbad residents already use more than 900 liters of water per person per day (an average Los Angeles resident uses about 640 lcd), so they are hardly facing death by desiccation. Why are they building a desalination plant there? Because they like their lawns and pools, and it's easier to spend money on a desalination plant than fight a political war for more water. The desalination plant is not really drought proof as much as neighbor-proof.

Some people propose that we end all of our water supply problems with nuclear-powered desalination plants. Although I spend more time on this idea in Chapter 9, it's complicated by the necessity of building nuclear power stations (unpopular) and doesn't even end water shortages (ineffective). Additional supply will end shortage only if it's combined with policies that lower demand.

What about solar- or wind-powered desalination? Those renewable energy sources are a distraction from the truth: a desalination plant cannot have a zero carbon footprint because desalination increases the overall demand for energy. A new desalination plant powered by, for example, an existing solar array may require a new coal-fired power station to serve former solar customers. Sure, it's possible to build another solar array, but don't forget about the carbon impact from manufacturing more solar panels and the need to get power at night. The only way to be carbon neutral is by reducing existing power demand by enough to offset new demand from desalination.

The energy-water nexus

Water is used to produce energy and energy is used to produce water. Industry people call this symbiotic relationship the energy-water nexus. These nexusites have devoted many conferences, committees and re-

ports to measuring and managing that relationship, but they are missing a big point. The nexus doesn't need to be managed, it needs
prices for water and energy.

Bureaucratic regulation of energy may fail to account for carbon
emissions, pollution, water consumption and other factors. Water regulators may ignore infrastructure costs, environmental impacts, energy consumption and so on. Some regulators and politicians realize
that these omissions impede success; others see the opportunity to
expand their command-and-control bureaucracies over larger areas
because they believe they can solve the knowledge problem.

Prices and regulations both aim to ensure that water users include
the energy embedded in their water consumption decisions and energy users consider the water embedded in theirs. The key difference
is the relative effectiveness of the tools.

Good regulations make it easier for people to understand the costs
and benefits of their decisions and make those decisions; bad regulations reduce efficiency or fairness, by favoring a special group or
impeding useful actions. Take, for example, regulations on energy efficiency. They are not really necessary when the person making the
buying decision is also the person who will operate the product. This
is true for automobile fuel economy, where buyers pay for their own
gas, or AA batteries that we put into our electrical devices. It's not
the same when the greater cost of a high-efficiency appliance goes
to one person but its benefits go to another. It makes sense to regulate the efficiency of appliances in a new house (the home builder will
not be able to raise the home price to recover every additional dollar
spent on efficiency). That's not true for water appliances in apartment
buildings where the landlord pays for installation and water consumption. Some people may argue that buyers don't pay much attention to
efficiency when they should, but that argument can be flipped around:
maybe that "precious" resource is so cheap that it's not worth paying
attention to conservation.

The end of abundance means our past management paradigms
no longer apply. Although we've never ignored the energy used to
pump or treat water (because energy, unlike water, usually has a
meaningful price), we now think that energy prices need to include
the cost of pollution and climate change. By this logic, it seems reasonable to add an adjustment for the quality and quantity of water
consumed, but that's easier said that done with our outdated institutions for managing water. First, power-generating companies sell their

output at cash prices, so they want to think of inputs in the same measurement units. Second, regulations are not flexible enough to reflect either changing conditions or interactions between different groups using water; market prices can reflect those changes. Third, regulations can reserve minimum flows for ecosystems (which are not usually priced anyway) while leaving remaining water allocation to markets.

The bottom line is that the missing market for water makes it harder for energy producers to use water efficiently. Price signals that aggregate scarcity information from many people of many opinions in many places would make it possible for them to decide whether to use more water, less water and more machines, or not operate at all. Regulations that try to reproduce the same matrix of water scarcity and operating decisions across many users are unlikely to be accurate because the knowledge problem is too hard to solve. That doesn't mean that regulators should step back and wait for laissez faire market forces to deliver prosperity. They can enforce pollution regulations, environmental flows and property rights, but they should complement these market-framing actions by allowing water prices to signal scarcity. Although markets with clear water rights would do the best job at allocating water, it's also possible to create a simple "bureaucratic" market in which regulators set arbitrary prices, observe how behavior affects scarcity, and change prices to direct behavior toward a target (the way a market does).

Wasting water to waste energy

A missing market for a good that's allocated by bureaucracy or regulation does not only mean that the good lacks a price. It also means the good is misallocated from those who are willing to pay its true cost to those who benefit from the allocation formula. Missing markets for energy mean that inefficient allocations of inputs and outputs do not reflect the true cost of generation (in carbon or water consumption) or use (in pollution, for example). But missing markets in the developed world are double-missing (excuse the non sequitur) in the developing world, because people with political and economic power change rules and incentives to suit their needs, regardless of damage to the powerless, the environment, or the future. The waste of water to produce or process energy will be worse; the waste of energy to produce or process water will be worse. This analysis applies in Yemen, where cheap energy, a lack of pumping controls and a booming demand for qat (a mild narcotic) threaten to dry out drinking water supplies, or Venezuela, where cheap energy has combined with drought to deplete reservoirs behind hydroelectric dams, or any number of countries where policies ignore water scarcity.

A wise dictator is even less likely to fix energy-water allocation problems than busloads of bureaucrats in the developed world. Developing countries need to develop robust institutions for pricing water and energy if they want to efficiently allocate these essential commodities for the benefit of society.

Prices for water and energy increase efficiency

The roadmap for managing the water-energy nexus is simple: Price water and energy according to supply and demand. In areas utilizing hydropower, for example, the price of energy and water should rise in the low flow season to reflect the lack of water for turbines and consumption. Prices can fluctuate in markets or according to a regulatory rule that considers scarcity and surplus. All that matters is that they go up when water is scarce, so that people have a good excuse to use less.

There's no inherent need to study the water-energy nexus, like there's no need to study the coffee-doughnut nexus. These pairs of complementary goods are connected by interlinked supply and demand, such that the demand for one increases the demand for the other. The clearest way to signal the resulting change in scarcity is with changes in prices, not a memorandum from the Office of Energy-Water Relations. We don't have coffee or doughnut shortages because these goods are priced in markets that reflect present conditions and future predictions. The same could be true for water and energy.

Part II

Social water choices

Social water choices

Democracy is the theory that the common people know
what they want and deserve to get it good and hard.
—H.L. Mencken

Part I looked at water uses (at home, for business, on the farm, or
at power plants) and how simple rules can help individuals use water
efficiently, without creating negative side effects or social spillovers.
Part II looks at complicated decisions that affect all of us, the people
who make these decisions, and how citizens influence and experience
the impacts of these decisions.

A brief tour of upcoming chapters will clarify these themes. Chapter 7 goes to the foundations of government, how we cooperate to
produce it, and what drives the people who make, implement and enforce group decisions that serve citizens (or themselves). Chapter 8
looks at the distribution of costs and benefits for major water infrastructure. Chapter 9 explores the economics and politics of water in
the environment. Chapter 10 is about weather, climate and adapting
to climate change. Chapter 11 considers the human right to water and
how to deliver it. Chapter 12 explains why the popular "water wars!"
headline is more smoke than fire.

All of these chapters have political dimensions. Why do politicians
make decisions affecting water? Because water is a collective good
that belongs to all citizens and must be managed by our representatives. That explains why they are in charge, but their management
decisions are much harder to predict, implement or evaluate because
the impacts of collective water uses depend on individual values. The
end of abundance means some values will not be satisfied, leaving
us with unpleasant choices between "priceless" polar bears and "essential" energy independence that cannot please everyone. Citizens,
special interest groups, politicians, and bureaucrats all bring their private subjective values to the debate over scarce water allocation. Different values create opportunities in markets that lead to gains from

trade, but they can create conflict in a political environment where the majority imposes its values on the minority.

This discussion focuses on the governance problems because we need to focus on correcting failure. Although governments and laws can clearly make everyone better off, policies that are badly designed or directed at special interests can harm the average person, creating "government failure." Mistakes in markets are less harmful because willing participants representing their own interests make smaller trades that do not involve others. In other words, markets work because mutual self-interest helps buyers and sellers get mutually agreeable results. Political actions can succeed, but when they fail, they do so on a scale that affects more people.

Part I was mostly about behavior under laws and informal rules. Part II looks into deeper institutions, describing how politicians, bureaucrats and water managers make laws and take actions. Although representatives often mean well, their behavior can be distorted by the delegated power they possess; they decide how to use our money or affect our lives without the ability to know or reconcile our individual desires (the knowledge problem). Beyond the information challenge is the complication of representatives who favor their own interests (money, effort, fame, beliefs, and other factors) in ways that produce self-serving actions instead of actions in the public interest. People call this corruption; economists call it the problem of "public choice."

These self-interested actions may not violate the letter of the law, but managers who work by the book may violate customer expectations of good water management. Managers who match revenues to costs but preside over shortages can claim they are just following orders. But their bosses, the politicians, can pass back responsibility. They ask managers (the experts) how to prevent shortages. Studies, meetings and outreach can delay change and may do nothing to prevent the next failure, because no individual takes responsibility for reliability.

Some politicians take bribes (campaign contributions, favors, consulting jobs and so on) in exchange for helping special interests. Infrequent elections mean it's difficult to punish a politician making hundreds of decisions for constituents over an occasional abuse of power. These problems are worse in the water sector, where elections are less competitive, appointed bureaucrats make most decisions, and it's hard to understand the costs and benefits of changes in low-visibility policies that create winners and losers. A reduction in water rates in one place, for example, means higher prices somewhere else. But it's hard to know whether your rate increase is the result of a careful decision that balanced the costs and benefits to public welfare or a biased favor to special interests. The economic and political beneficiaries of water allocations who pay "full cost" may be getting water that's much more valuable that its official price.

Water policies can be reformed in two ways. One path sets managers' performance targets to reflect current priorities and allow for future adjustments. Such a path assumes that politicians and managers want to serve the general public. The other path assumes that politicians and managers are corrupt. The goal then is to reduce their power, to decentralize water decisions to smaller, local areas. Decentralization can take many forms, from tradable shares to communal trusts, but they are aimed at matching local waters to local needs.

The key is to find the right tool for the right job. Water use decisions are so complicated and layered that it's nearly impossible for political processes to reconcile citizens' values into effective policies that create expected impacts without significant side effects. It makes sense to establish constitutional rights and basic laws at the political level that maximize choices to individuals who then make decisions based on their private values. It is possible, for example, to set water prices to prevent shortages and let individuals decide if they want to pay for a lawn or long shower. Likewise, farmers should be allowed to buy or sell water in markets — just as they should decide which crops to grow. The goal is to set rules that target big policy goals and allow freedom of choice while preventing negative side effects or favors to specific groups, actions or values.

In developed countries, a strong rule of law keeps corruption in check. Most people in government work hard for us, but sometimes they are fighting today's problems with laws and regulations that reflect old priorities or favor those with power and wealth. Nonetheless, people can use social, political, legal, business and community channels to challenge policy makers and their decisions. Change in the developing world is complicated by corruption but simplified by weak government. A community that's able to avoid crooks can solve its own water problems.

I'll end with a little personal note. Ever since I was young, I've loved to walk along streets in the rain, clearing the leaves and branches blocking the flow of water along gutters and into drains. When I look at the water world, I look for the branches and leaves that are clogging the efficient allocation of water and work to clear them. I hope this clarifies why I spend so much time talking about problems that need to be solved, while ignoring areas that are flowing smoothly. Plenty of politicians, bureaucrats and water managers succeed. This book focuses on increasing their numbers.

CHAPTER 7

Managers and politicians

Managers and bureaucrats may make decisions and policies affecting collective goods for their own benefit — not the benefit of constituents. Community oversight and/or benchmarking outcomes can reduce abuses.

Part I looked at how formal and informal rules affect behavior and considered how to deal with the end of abundance, under the assumption that good rules would be designed and implemented that would allow us to enjoy water today, tomorrow and into the distant future. This chapter looks at how water managers make rules that may or may not be targeted at useful goals or effective in reaching them. This discussion will make it easier to address topics in later chapters on infrastructure, environment and so on.

The discussion builds on the simple fact that individuals have private, subjective values for goods (a glass of water, a rainbow). Our goal, then, is to channel and reconcile these values so that private and collective goods create the greatest social benefits. A good's characteristics determine which management framework is appropriate for reconciling values into outcomes. An economic market, for example, is best for allocating goods that are excludable (private or club goods). Likewise, a political community is best for allocating collective goods that are non-excludable (common-pool or public goods). Put another way, we want to channel each individual's interests (in self, family, and other goals) into a mechanism that reconciles different values at the lowest cost. The key is to choose the right mechanism.

Excludable and collective/non-excludable goods will be mismanaged if they are not treated as excludable or collective goods. The Soviet model of a collective cow was disastrous for milk and meat production because nobody wanted to feed it, but everyone wanted its milk and meat. Private cows are better. Likewise, private ownership of a collective good can have terrible consequences. Many national parks in Africa operate as club goods that exclude the people who have lived, hunted and gathered in the area for millennia. When these people are excluded from their old territories, they go hungry, migrate elsewhere, turn to poaching, or harvest resources — overexploiting assets that no longer belong to their community.

Good water management takes physical and social factors into account. Physical factors may be easy to understand but expensive to address. Water's weight and bulk requires strong pumps and big pipes. Social factors reflect the influence of people, hydrology, and past decisions. These baseline factors are then modified by politicians who represent our collective will and managers who work to turn aspirations into reality. But this theory needs to be modified by the fact that some politicians and managers pursue their own values over community interests. They might work too hard or too little, preempt events or be overwhelmed by them, serve themselves or sacrifice for the community. We want to consider these factors and look for ways to maximize the social value of water to the local community.

Markets for allocating excludable goods

Individuals' subjective values for goods drive allocation of scarce resources in markets.[1] Trades occur because a buyer's value for a good exceeds the seller's value. These values are driven by fundamentals (the value in use of a good or cost of producing the good) but subject to idiosyncratic adjustments. The difference in values represents the potential gains from trade and reallocation (the bigger the difference, the more useful a market). Trade occurs at a price between high (buyer's value) and low (seller's value), a point that depends on market power (competition among buyers or sellers), information, transaction costs, related goods, and so on. It's difficult to predict trade prices or determine who gets a larger share of the gains from trade, but the simple truth is that trade benefits both buyers and sellers and more trade creates more benefits.

Markets aren't always perfect. Some market trades produce negative externalities. A water sale from Farmer A to Farmer B may not be good for Farmer C, for example. Negative externalities can be alleviated by carefully defining the good. An excludable water supply can be traded as a private good because its use or diversion has no

---

[1] If the resource is not scarce, the allocation method and outcome do not matter, since everyone can have as much as they want.

effect on others. The same cannot be said of common-pool water because its use affects others. Farmer A's sale of his 5 m^3 per minute diversion to Farmer B has an adverse impact on Farmer C if Farmer A was consuming only 2 m^3 of his diversion and the remaining 3 m^3 were flowing to Farmer C. The negative effect of Farmer A's sale on Farmer C (also called a third-party impact) can be reduced by limiting Farmer A's sale to his consumptive use.

Water sales can create third-party impacts on laborers, seed sellers, machine vendors and other locals, but these impacts are often based on the subjective personal values of offended individuals and a failure to consider other options (a job lost due to land fallowing can be replaced by working elsewhere). Third party impacts are based on a counterfactual reality, which makes them difficult to objectively quantify, compensate or weigh against gains from trade.

Unfortunately, some people think the potential existence of such impacts gives them the right to prevent trade between consenting adults. It's not hard to use their argument in support of a return to autarky (a world of self-reliance, without trade) in which everyone lives as hunter-gatherers. Yes, trade causes changes, and change is uncomfortable, but change needs to happen if we want to reallocate resources, encourage innovation, reward success, and improve our lives.

Markets and trade are not the only way to allocate goods or balance supply and demand. Members of a group can prevent rivalry by excluding disobedient members — ejecting members whose water use overdrafts a shared aquifer, for example. Water supplies that belong to the people are even harder to trade without affecting others, so they are managed by politicians who face the tricky task of allocating private rights to common-pool water among claimants whose needs are based on subjective values. We may agree we all want the nation's water to be put to highest and best use, but which version of highest and best is right? How do we choose among human rights, social necessity, historic facts, past suffering, and community values? Which is more important? Flushing toilets or irrigating fields? Each of these claims comes from a subjective perspective that can neither be compared with others nor denied to the claimants.

Politicians can choose the right winners, but miscalculation (the knowledge problem) or self-interest (bribes and bias) may lead them to choose incorrectly. A politician/farmer who gives water to farmers is just as corrupt as the politician/environmentalist who leaves water in streams — assuming, in both cases, that some other use maximizes benefits to society.

The alternative is to use markets to allocate water owned by the people to users (with payments for use channeled back to the people). Markets efficiently integrate thousands of subjective value judgments into prices that balance supply and demand. These prices allocate goods in a fair and transparent manner among many claimants to those willing to pay the most. There is no need to measure or weigh the relative merits and validity of individual subjective values.

Markets would not prevent politicians from exercising their authority and pursuing polices on behalf of the people. They could still transfer money to farmers, fishermen, poor people or celebrities with big pools. These interest groups use the cash to buy water in the market. But such transparency would force political beneficiaries to compete for water in an objective market, identify the politically privileged, and reveal the value of their subsidies. These "weaknesses" explain the popularity of political allocations of private water rights: they are hard for outsiders to detect or measure, either in terms of value (price in a market) or opportunity cost (value to others).

Politicians are neither necessary nor efficient in the distribution or management of excludable water, but markets are not quite so good at managing property that's held in common. That's when we need politicians and political mechanisms.

Cooperating to provide collective goods

A lone individual must take care of all his needs, from food to shelter to security. A few individuals can work together so that each is better off. One hunts, another provides shelter, a third watches for danger. All of them are better off from cooperation. In this simple example, we can see two private goods (food and shelter) and one collective good (security). Private goods can be provided by trade (one valuable good for another), but collective goods suffer from a free-riding problem. Everyone benefits from security, even if they contribute nothing to it. Some people try to avoid their contribution. Humans use punishment, ostracism, shame, and other methods to minimize free riding.

Collective action redefines self-interest. In almost every corner of the planet, some form of "do unto others as you would have them do unto you" exists. Sometimes it's called "an eye-for-an-eye," sometimes "tit for tat," but the basic idea is that I start by being nice to you; if you are nice to me, then I continue to be nice to you. If you betray me (taking more than your fair share), then I will punish you, and others will probably help me.

Why do we find cooperation in the provision of collective goods in every society? Because cooperation enhances survival, and survival enlarges a community with cooperative attitudes and institutions. Communal religions, cultures and ethics enhance social cooperation by making it easier to identify with others and work together. Communities protect common-pool goods and create public goods because their members are willing to limit self-interest in favor of others who are similar and will be around to return the favor in the future. In his 1871 book, *The Descent of Man*, Charles Darwin wrote:

> A tribe including many members who, from possessing in a high degree the spirit of patriotism, fidelity, obedience, courage, and sympathy, were always ready to aid one another, and to sacrifice themselves for the common good, would be victorious over most other tribes; and this would be natural selection.

Many scholars study the tit-for-tat process of encouraging cooperation and punishing defection. Biologists study individual altruism toward genetic kin; lawyers use punishment to strengthen business or social contracts; theists talk about good behavior today for a reward in heaven; and CEOs espouse a corporate culture that empowers employees and delights customers.

Evolutionary psychologists claim our social behaviors evolved with our bodies. Cooperation evolved within our communities by rewarding reciprocation and punishing free riding. Cooperation enhances survival when different communities fight over resources. Consider two tribes. The clay tribe sticks together, giving and receiving mutual support and brutally punishing members who fail to give or reciprocate favors. Every man is for himself in the sand tribe, where opportunism trumps cooperation and selfish behavior goes unpunished. If the clay and sand tribes fight, the clay tribe will have an advantage because some members will put themselves at risk to defend others. When they defeat or displace the sand tribe, their cooperative values become more common. Matt Ridley gives a powerful example:

> Hitler perfected the double standard of in-group morality and out-group ferocity by calling his movement national socialism. Socialism stood for communitarianism within

the tribe, nationalism for its vicious exterior. He needed
no religious spur. But given that humankind has an instinct towards tribalism that millions of years of groupish-
ness have fostered, religions have thrived to the extent
that they stressed the community of the converted and
the evil of the heathen.

Political scientists describe collective action from a simpler perspective. Consider the Netherlands. As the country's name implies,
this is a place where many people live at or below sea level, in "polders" that are surrounded and protected by dikes that keep water from
inundating land at a lower elevation. People who live in polders must
cooperate with their neighbors because they will all be under water if
the dike fails anywhere. Everyone knows that each person must do his
job if the others are not going to suffer. These facts have resulted in
frequent and close coordination in maintaining dikes and operating the
pumps that remove seeping water. Even neighbors and communities
that normally dislike one another will cooperate on maintaining their
common polders, and they have done so since the Middle Ages. Behavioral norms are embedded in local culture. When someone says
or does something useless, the Dutch say *dat zet geen zoden aan de
dijk* ("that doesn't put turf on the dike"). The "polder model" is now
used to explain cooperation among Dutch political parties, as when
they enact programs that serve the common good instead of fighting
over short-term political gains.[2]

Managers and politicians

It's usually better to allocate private and club goods in markets with
prices. Likewise, it's usually better to provide public and common-
pool goods through formal or informal cooperative structures. Management must change as the good's nature changes. An aquifer that
once had plenty of water for all (a public good) may attract so many
users that it risks being overdrafted and depleted. Sustainability can
be restored by managing it as a private good (users get fixed and
limited pumping shares) or club good (informal rules exclude over-
pumpers). That's the main idea behind matching the good's characteristics to an appropriate management regime.

Management is not automatically efficient. The managers who

---

[2]No, they haven't stopped fighting altogether; they just have a name for the mo-
ments when they cooperate.

make, monitor and enforce rules play a critical role. Good managers protect us from ourselves, but bad managers magnify waste and inequity. How can we tell good from bad? How can we tell if they serve the public or themselves? The main barrier is asymmetric information. Managers and politicians know their abilities and actions. They understand the mixture of skill, effort and luck that resulted in success or failure, but outsiders will never know the exact mix.

The end of abundant water has increased the relevance of good management. In the past, household water users couldn't tell if an urban distribution system leaked 5 or 20 percent of its water. But water scarcity means that 15 percent can now mean the difference between a long shower and a bath-in-a-bucket. The trouble is that it's hard to know whether 20 percent leakage results from poor management, old mistakes, or some other factor.

Principal-agent dynamics

We do not face an information problem when buying a pencil at the store. The seller takes our money in exchange for a clearly defined product. There's also no problem when a friend takes our money to go buy a pencil. The friend may take a long time, go to the wrong store or lose the change, but we know what we are getting, and the receipt tells us how much it cost.

Asymmetric information exists in transactions where we (as principals) hire agents to take care of business that we could do ourselves, except that we do not know the quality of the agent or their work. We hire a baby-sitter to competently and diligently watch our kids, not to empty the liquor cabinet while they run amok. On the other hand, we will never know whether our kids survived because of diligence (taking away the matches) or luck (the kids didn't find the matches).

We face the same problem when we appoint doctors, lawyers, car mechanics, teachers, and politicians to look after our interests. When our interests coincide with theirs, we know that they will push for what's best for us because it's also best for them. It's a lot harder when interests only partially coincide. Should the car get the expensive or cheap oil? Should the law contain special privileges for politicians or breaks for big campaign donors? Should the kids do homework for five more minutes, or is that enough?

As workers (and agents), we are paid to create value for the company. Does that include calling friends or shopping online? Some of us may justify it, but the basic fact is that we all have discretion at work, and that discretion can be used to advance our own interests over those of the principal (the boss, shareholders or clients).

That's why we tend to stick with the same dentist for years, and the earliest question a recent arrival asks his colleagues is "know a good mechanic?" Principal-agent relationships are everywhere.

Their importance depends on the degree of asymmetric information and competition. A monopoly provider of Coca-Cola has market power, but it's clear that we are going to suffer only from higher prices. We have no idea how mobile phones work, but competition among hardware and service providers has delivered higher quality at lower prices.

Principal-agent dynamics are very important with water management. Citizens and customers (principals) have to trust that water managers (agents) with strong job security and negligible competition will deliver the best water service at the lowest cost. Customers suffer the disadvantage of asymmetric information — managers know far more about their skills, effort and their success relative to other water managers or potential outcomes. Political and regulatory oversight complicates matters. On the one hand, these representatives may solve the collective action problem for the benefit of all customers by carefully screening managers for talent and watching their work. On the other, they may spend less time and energy on oversight that benefits others or — worse — help a special interest group instead of their customers. These politician-manager-customer (principal-agent-beneficiary) relations and interactions get more complicated and unpredictable as the number of people between the customer (beneficiary) and manager (agent) increases, which is why the social management of water is complicated. Professionalism and industry standards contribute to success, but selfishness (the public choice problem) and complexity (the knowledge problem) contribute to failure.

Professional ethics and outdated ideas

Insurance companies pioneered the study of principal-agent dynamics, and they monitor two dimensions of asymmetric information. Car insurers, for instance, worry about skills and attitude. Driving skills improve with age and vary by gender. That's why females get lower insurance rates than males and experienced drivers get lower rates than novice drivers. Attitude doesn't necessarily vary with age, but companies take it into consideration by raising insurance premiums for speeding tickets and accidents and lowering them for safe driving in conservative cars.

We want to use a similar framework to understand whether water managers have the right skills and make appropriate efforts.

The typical water manager is a civil engineer who has worked in the industry since leaving university. He (usually a man) has risen through the ranks, learning how to work with colleagues, political supervisors and others in an organization where the division of labor and hierarchy becomes more formal as the number of employees increases. These managers use accountants to balance the books and lawyers to handle legal obligations, but their primary job is supplying water their communities need using infrastructure that stores, treats and distributes fresh- and wastewater.[3]

In the past of abundant water supply, problems were solved with pipes and pumps, but scarcity has changed matters. Now pipes compete for the same water, and water management puts less emphasis on engineering.

Engineers, lawyers and economists approach problems in different ways. Say that a city faces water shortages while nearby farmers flood their fields to grow low value crops. An engineer may tell people to use less or drill a well into the aquifer farmers use. A lawyer may cite a law that gives urban areas priority access to water in shortage or use political power to change the relative seniorities of urban and agricultural water. Economists might suggest raising the price of urban water so that people use less (cut demand) or buying water from farmers (increase supply). These differences originate in the tools of each trade.

Engineers are more cost conscious than value conscious; more oriented to supply than demand; and more familiar with hard infrastructure constraints than soft human choices. When they raise prices, they do not consider different users' opinions on scarcity, future actions or values. Lawyers specialize in negotiating and resolving conflict, threading a path between people with rights, contracts and power to a negotiated solution that parties will accept, even if they grumble.

Economists also favor a particular set of tools, but the problem of shortage is central to economics. When fixed supply is less than demand, prices rise until quantity demanded falls and shortage ends. Prices are easier to use than limits on customer choices, subsidies for low-flow toilets, reservoir expansion, or taking farmers' water. Prices

---

[3]The same can be said of managers in irrigation, wastewater, power and other hydraulic enterprises.

rise with scarcity and fall with abundance, reliably matching supply and demand. Local conditions determine the exact means of slaking thirst, but the underlying mechanism of adjusting prices has worked for millennia.

Economists also use trade, an everyday event for most of us that's amazingly rare in the water world. Farmers have water rights and cities have money. A money-water trade can leave both better off (assuming that we account for externalities).

These economic tools are widely publicized and known, so why don't managers adopt higher prices and water markets? Probably because the costs and benefits of change are unevenly distributed. Managers with engineering or law backgrounds bear the cost of replacing familiar actions with novel solutions (replacing rationing with price increases, for example), but the benefits from reliable water supplies go to customers. Managers without an incentive to be efficient (fixed salaries and protected jobs instead of performance-based pay, for example) can do what they like. Politicians who are supposed to watch managers are busy, ignorant of management techniques, and able to delegate responsibility for failure to managers. Political overseers can also block good management. Water managers can have a hard time pushing through price increases on water wasters, implementing new metering technology, investing in the long term, or pushing for changes in regulations. These actions require approval from political bosses who may not want to incur known cost in the present for uncertain benefits in the future.

This discussion is controversial. How do we know that managers are not working hard to innovate and prevent shortages? That they are not willing to learn new skills to make us better off? It's hard to measure or encourage efficiency at monopolies that deliver water to captive customers. Maybe they're not working hard, but how can we even know how they are doing? How can a few customers in a service area of millions get them to change? The next few sections address these questions.

Are water managers selfless public servants?

Many people claim water managers and politicians are selfless public servants willing to sacrifice their own time and effort for the benefit of constituents. Most economists are skeptical of this view; they think that water managers work only for extrinsic incentives (like money). Others disagree: managers pursuing self-interest can still serve the public due to intrinsic incentives such as professional pride.

I tested these beliefs with water managers at the Metropolitan Water District of Southern California (MWD), a cooperative established under state law that sells imported water to its member agencies. As a buyer cooperative, these member agencies govern MWD — setting water prices to cover the cost of infrastructure they use as customers.

MWD's 26 member agencies sometimes pursue different goals. One group may want to build a reservoir to store water and increase reliability, but another may not want to spend that money. That can create a problem if the agencies fight or if they vote for the action that suits a coalition instead of all Southern Californians. These actions can conflict with MWD's purpose as an organization established to serve the public interest.

Managers who care about extrinsic incentives are going to work for their private good (their individual member agencies); those who favor the intrinsic incentives of public servants will work for the public benefit. Since MWD is self-regulated, member agencies decide what's in the public interest and take actions that create results. Their decisions depend on the interaction of different managers and those managers' attitudes towards self-interest or the public good (intrinsic and extrinsic incentives).

The question is whether each manager works for the benefit of MWD and Southern California or himself and his member agency.

People from MWD's executive staff and member agencies tested this question when they played a game for producing public goods that worked like this: Four people in a group started with $10 each. Each person divided the $10 between a public good account and their private account. Public good money created benefits for everyone, so that a $5 contribution was doubled and $2.50 distributed to each person. If four managers put in all their money, then everyone received $20 (4 x $10 is doubled and then distributed to everyone). If three of four put in $10 but the fourth was a free rider (contributing zero to a public good), then the three got $15 each and the free rider got $15 plus the $10 he didn't contribute.

This game creates a tension between the quantity and distribution of money, between personal and group payoffs, between intrinsic incentives to play for all and extrinsic incentives to be selfish. People playing this game have their own beliefs but also watch one another. They may put a lot or a little into the public account, but they may change that decision when they see what others do. Although some may put in less when others put in more, the majority will put in more when others do (the Golden Rule).

I ran this game with MWD managers and a comparison group of university students, measuring cooperation by comparing actual payouts to maximum possible payouts. Total contribution to the public good turned $10 into $20 for each player (100 percent efficiency). Zero contribution to the public good meant that everyone kept their $10 (50 percent efficiency). This result often happened when one person tried to free ride, others responded by holding back, and cooperation quickly fell to zero.

The students played with 67 percent efficiency; cooperating to turn their initial $10 into $13.50. Groups of MWD players achieved efficiency of 64–67 percent. This result is especially striking when we consider that MWD groups were composed of people who had worked together for years in a *cooperative* organization. They were no more interested in contributing benefits to their colleagues than random undergraduates who had never met.

Does this result (which doesn't necessarily apply to all water managers) leave customers vulnerable to their whims, or is it possible for them to band together, to demand hard work and quality service?

Collective action is hard

Say, for example, that a water utility sends out paper bills every three months. Most customers pay whatever's on the bill, but others want the agency to reform its system, so that monthly bills can be paid online. The agency knows that it will cost $25 per customer to implement a new system for its 100,000 customers and an additional $8 per customer per year for monthly billing. On the other hand, accurate and timely billing may reduce demand by enough to avoid a new $25 million reservoir. From a social benefit-cost perspective, it seems a good idea to spend $2.5 million plus $800,000 per year to save $25 million, but it may not be a great idea from a managerial perspective. Saved money goes to customers, not managers and staff. Managers might prefer a new reservoir (they are often named after retired managers) over a new billing system.

The project should go ahead, but nobody on the committee that oversees the agency wants to push for change. Can customers force change? Let's assume that a campaign would succeed if 1,000 customers each spent 50 hours agitating for changes that would result in better bills, avoid a new reservoir, and save $14.5 million over a period of 10 years. That's a reduction of $145 per year for every customer, whether or not they worked for change. That costless benefit raises a key question: who would work for 50 hours to save $145 when it's possible to benefit from others' work?

This is the key to a collective action problem. A small number of people in Group A can do a lot of work that benefits many people in Group B. People in Group A will spend 50 hours to save $145; people in Group B will spend zero hours to save $145. Since most people prefer something for nothing, most people will join Group B as free riders. It's easy to see how everyone could end up in Group B, and nothing would get done.

Collective action problems are solved in three ways: activists join Group A for intrinsic rewards (feeling good about communal service, outrage at inefficiency, and so on); members of Group A punish members of Group B for free riding (minimizing the size of Group B as well as individual burdens in Group A); or representatives are appointed to Group A to work for everyone in Group B. Representative government is a response to the collective action problem. Members of a legislature, assembly or parliament are supposed to solve the free rider problem by managing policies and programs that benefit everyone.

These systems are less effective at water agencies because representatives charged with oversight have many obligations, do not necessarily understand operations, or support water managers over customers (the board of directors is often filled with retired water managers who face weak electoral competition). For investor-owned utilities (IOUs), oversight rests with regulators who have more experience and a clearer role, but regulators also lack an insider's understanding of wasteful practices or misplaced opportunities (an asymmetric information problem).

But what if water managers are doing a great job? Is there always room for improvement? No and yes. No, because it is easily possible that managers are driven by an internal desire to do the best job, all the time, everywhere. Those managers are the civil servants that make countries great. Yes, because, first, not every employee will be such a dedicated professional. Some of these people can use a little extra oversight. Second, because even the most diligent manager may not have the tools to face today's challenges. He may be running to keep in place, when a manager with a different skill set could be moving ahead. But desire, effort and talent may not be enough to overcome inertia in outdated institutions that need to be reformed. Institutional change requires agreement and coordination among many people with the power to say no. Water management suffers from a Tragedy of the Anticommons when any stakeholder can veto beneficial change.

The Tragedy of the Anticommons can be solved by a mixture of persuasion, persistence, and piecemeal reform familiar to anyone who has negotiated vegetable consumption with a child. That trial and error process can be solved on a local level, but it's too complex to explore here. Instead, we'll look at an easier problem: helping outsiders understand whether insiders are working efficiently.

Insurance as competition

I started thinking about measuring and encouraging good management in December 2008, after the levees around a holding pond collapsed and spilled more than a billion liters of toxic coal-ash-laden water into Tennessee's rivers. I wanted to find a way to encourage managers to spend adequate time and money on safety, reliability and other performance goals without spending too much money on gold-plated projects and activities.

The sweet spot between spending too little and too much can be identified by "benchmarking" outcomes (or other performance indicators) for the service of interest against similar services. Benchmarks are common in competitive industries (cars, electronics, sports, universities) but rare in monopolistic industries such as water management. That's because most monopolies do not care to be measured for performance, and it's hard to compare a monopoly with anything; monopolies that do not have substitutes can claim to be unique.

But that definition is too narrow. A local water monopoly is unique to its service area, but it shares similarities with agencies in other areas. That means it may be possible to compare different agencies on measures of interest and reward the ones with above-average performance. This method borrows several techniques from the insurance industry where, for example, unique car drivers can be compared by age, gender, driving record and so on. Car insurance works (encouraging good behavior, paying for accidents) because it's possible to assemble data for many customers, charge more to high risk customers, pay for accidents, and still make enough money to employ analysts who can find key values in the data — even without knowing drivers' exact talents or actions.

The US has 52,000 water systems. Few people know what's going on inside these systems, but most people want to improve their performance. Insurance can deliver better performance by creating competition among water utilities. But what kind of insurance?

It's probably not insurance against water shortages. That risk is easy to understand and easy to correct, via higher prices. The more interesting problem relates to that delicate balance between spending on infrastructure maintenance, water quality and emergency preparedness, where it's hard to know whether spending is too much, too little, or just right.

It's important to remember that there's no sure connection between management effort and outcomes. Careful drivers still have accidents; people who exercise and eat right sometimes die young. Some water managers do everything that they can or should to prevent contamination or broken pipes, but some of them are unlucky. Others take extra risks and have more accidents.

It's possible and useful to insure against bad water outcomes. It's possible because outcomes (interruptions, contamination and breakage) can be measured. It's useful because insurance would smooth out expenses. Managers now choose between a system with low monthly charges and a high probability of failure (leading to expensive repairs and a higher rates) and a gold-plated system with high monthly charges and low probability of failure. Insurance against leaks and repairs would raise rates by less — premiums averaged across many systems reflect the cost of repairing an "average" break; gold-plated systems cost everyone more — and pay to repair a future break (preventing a rate increase).

Customers really hate it when water rates jump by 40 percent (even if that's $3 per month), so this system would please them. Insurance would have to be mandatory for water managers because they do not currently have a strong incentive to invest in maintenance that may prevent a problem 20 years in the future. This mismatch of cost and benefits is magnified by "moral hazard" — water agencies know they can get rate increases approved after disasters. Mandatory insurance would give them a reason to invest in preventative maintenance because their premium would fall as the risk of accidents and leaks fell.

Insurance has additional advantages. First, insurance companies would monitor operations with skepticism of promises and actions that do not have meaningful (insurable) impacts. This monitoring role addresses collective action and free-riding problems. As I mentioned earlier, one customer may not be willing to spend two hours to save $0.50 for herself (and $9,999.50 for everyone else), but an insurance company would have no problem spending two hours to save $10,000 for itself. Second, competition among insurance companies would allow water managers to insure at low prices, something that they cannot now do with self-insurance funds that are set by crude, inaccurate calculations (and often stolen by politicians for pet projects). Third, insurance would allow everyone to get a single, objective measure of the utility's effectiveness. With suitable adjustments for service area, client mix and other factors, managers in Los Angeles could be compared with managers in Phoenix, Paris or Phnom Penh. That comparison would alert ratepayers, regulators and politicians to the quality of managers' work and create competition among managers to see who could achieve the lowest combination of water tariff and insurance premium. Fourth, insurance could be combined with a prediction market, so that customers, workers and busybodies could bet if the premium is too high or low. These markets would allow people to profit from their knowledge and effort while exposing good/bad management to a larger audience. As insurance companies gained experience in the business (they would be hiring lots of retired water managers as underwriters), they would get better at setting prices, until the prediction market was fairly accurate.

This idea makes more sense as the end of abundance forces us to improve water management and raises the financial and social costs of mismanagement.

Managers with the power to fail

People in developing countries are keenly aware of the costs and benefits of water. They are more likely to die from a lack of water (drought and starvation) or too much water (flooding and tsunamis). They often have an intimate knowledge of the well or spring that gives them drinking water or the pollution that sickens and kills them. These challenges and many others affect the subjective values that poor people ascribe to water, but those values are more likely to be founded on facts and experience than feelings and ideology. It's therefore a pity that underdeveloped economic and political institutions in poor countries do not reflect these values in economic trade or political decisions. Weak legal rights, social services or political accountability mean that water, as an environmental good or natural resource, is more likely to be overexploited for the short-term benefit of the powerful. Stronger institutions (such as the Balinese water temples described in Chapter 5) create wealth in a sustainable way, but they can take many years to evolve. It's more common for the poor to suffer from government policies that divert rivers, flood valleys, or drain aquifers without warning, permission or compensation.

Non-governmental organizations try to improve water service in line with their humanitarian missions and millennium development goals, but they negotiate in an environment where nobody knows very much and discretion makes it difficult to distinguish brilliance from treachery. These international saviors want to help but do not always have time to understand and untangle complex problems. Many take the easy road — measuring progress by counting reports, wells or pipes — instead of ending the poverty that keeps them employed.

Water managers in developing countries face intermittent power supplies, unpaid bills, demands from the rich and powerful, poorly educated staff, confusing bureaucracies, and other factors that would turn an American or French technocrat's hair white. But they also have more freedom. They are rarely constrained by regulations on construction, worker safety, water quality or environmental health. Sometimes they are given chunks of aid money, to "develop folks." The combination of diverse influences and managerial discretion means there will be more variety in developing world outcomes. Some cities have 24/7 potable water; others have water two hours per week that needs to be filtered and boiled. Some slums have potable water at the pump; others buy murky dregs from roving trucks. An irrigation manager probably prefers to receive a bribe for delivering water to wealthy landowners over upholding the law and getting a machete in the back.

The bottom line is that water service in developing countries is worse extrinsic incentives are weaker (lower salaries and less oversight) and intrinsic incentives are crowded out by an environment of complacency and corruption. These problems can be solved by, respectively, private water companies that lose money if they fail to perform or community water organizations staffed by people who have a personal investment in success.

Ironically, both of these solutions can work in areas where service is poor or non-existent — unlike the case in developed countries where a local monopolist only faces competition from bottled water. WaterHealth International, for example, will install a turn-key facility that uses the best technology to deliver purified drinking water to a community. WHI tests its water frequently and allows villagers to compare water sources using a microscope that shows parasites and other pollutants. The only water that was safe to drink during a May 2010 cholera outbreak in the Indian village of Gurjala came from WHI's facility, not local wells or taps. Three people died and 16 people were sickened in the outbreak, but locals with access to WHI's water were safe. People in developing countries have a developed sense of good water service; they need only the opportunity to use it.

We're all in this together

We have politics because we need a good way to manage collective goods and markets because we need a good way to manage private goods. Each mechanism can be efficient, but each mechanism can be abused. During the oil shock in the early 1970s, the price of oil jumped by a factor of four or five. This was unpopular with motorists in the US, but the government's restrictions on price increases and rationing were even more unpopular. Instead of paying a fortune to fill the tank immediately, drivers paid a fortune after waiting for hours.

It's useful to think of economics as the study of enlarging pies and politics as the study of dividing pies. These studies overlap: The cost of bargaining over slices may exceed the value of the pie. The pursuit of a big pie without consideration of its division can result in destructive conflict.

One way or another, water is a social good that's owned by all simultaneously, used by individuals sequentially, and managed by the few for the many. Water management might easily be the world's oldest (reputable) profession. The end of abundance means managers need to add a few tricks to their repertoire to address scarcity. It also means managers, overseers and customers have more to gain from good management. The ideas in this book are aimed at improving efficiency, minimizing bargaining costs and maintaining fairness. They are neither integrated nor perfect. They are merely a starting point for the discussion, a way to avoid wars over subjective values. Appropriate solutions depend on the balance between individual and social perspectives. In strong communities, informal agreements with lots of discretion and cloudy ownership are possible. In weaker communities, agreements will need to be strong and clear, allowing individuals to manage their property independently. Local conditions will determine which system (or mixture of the two) delivers the best balance between the size of the pie and how it's divided.

CHAPTER 8

Dams, pipes and pumps

Water infrastructure users like to shift costs to others. Misplaced and mispriced infrastructure can encourage wasteful water use and distort development for a long time. Fights over infrastructure increase with scarcity.

Perhaps the greatest irony in the water business is that the solution to shortage — more supply — often comes from somewhere else, at someone else's expense. The end of abundance results when somewhere else runs out of water.

Las Vegas is in the middle of the desert, but it has grown on the illusion that the adjacent Colorado River would always provide enough water. By 2005 or so, Vegas growth had outstripped supply, requiring that Vegas go out to get more water. Just after that, the real estate bust led to a drop in demand. The myth of abundant supply had contributed to a boom that increased shortage and made a crash more likely. In the future, the people of Las Vegas will choose between living with their limited supply or fighting to take water from other places.

But the story of Las Vegas is not unique. Water transfers from wet places to dry places have occurred all over the world. They brought abundance, but they also created the expectation of future supplies to meet growing demand. The end of abundance violated those expectations. As wet places dried out, shortages appeared that could be addressed only by increasing local supply (recycling wastewater or desalinating seawater) or limiting demand.

This simple accounting makes sense, but it raises an obvious question: how did supply and demand get out of balance in the first place? Marc Reisner answered this question in *Cadillac Desert*, his 1993 masterpiece on water management in the western US. Reisner traced mismanagement to a wasteful use of other people's money (OPM). In water systems where people manage their own water with their own money, it's unlikely that they will use more water than they have; they carefully weigh the tradeoff between spending money on new supplies or cutting demands that require additional supplies. The same caution does not apply to people who are given abundant, free water.

The economics of large-scale projects means it's both uncommon and inefficient to be self-reliant in dry regions, but the rules and norms for sharing water and expenses with others were established in an era when water was abundant and subsidies encouraged. That era is over, but the persistence of those institutions causes many problems.

This chapter examines the abuse of benefit-cost analysis for large projects; subsidies that distort behavior; the dynamics of subsidies, urban sprawl, and water shortages; and finishes with examples of large-scale, subsidized infrastructure that do not help the world's poor.

The use and abuse of benefit-cost analysis

Recall that benefit-cost analysis compares options in two stages. In the first stage, costs and benefits are estimated for each option. In the second stage, the relative costs and benefits of different options are compared. That's how we decide what to eat at a restaurant: Do we want the steak for $12 or the burger for $6? Well that depends. Is the steak more than twice as good? If not, then take the hamburger. But what if someone else is paying? OPM, or other people's money, changes incentives and behavior. I'm having steak if you're paying!

Questions of scale

Economies of scale refer to a falling cost per unit of benefit (or an increasing benefit per unit of cost). For example, a little dam may deliver 1,000 units of storage at a cost of $1 million while a big dam delivers 2,000 units of storage for $1.5 million. The $1,000 cost per unit in the small dam falls to $750 per unit with the big dam. Why is this? Although a dam that's twice as big may need double the materials, it doesn't need twice as many people to design, build or run. Sometimes it doesn't need more at all: a big dam still has one operations center, one regulatory report, and so on.

Economies of scale do not work forever. At some point the cost of additional size rises. Dams, for example, store water in one area, but it may be useful to store water in a different area. Likewise, it may be harder to manage a large dam that produces benefits for many groups. They may not agree on water or cost allocations.

Compare train tracks with roads. The tracks cost a lot of money up front, but they make it very cheap to move goods from Point A to Point B. A road is cheaper to construct, but it does not lower the A–B delivery cost as far. More important, it's possible to use the money saved by not building train tracks to build a road from Point A to Point C. The tradeoff between cheap and flexible means we cannot have both.

An early example of scale

In his 1879 book, *Report on the Lands of the Arid Region of the United States*, John Wesley Powell explained some important facts to his East Coast readers. Large western rivers traversed dry places, unlike the numerous eastern rivers that crossed greener spaces. Those occasional rivers led Powell to suggest that people work together to build the waterworks that would take water from these rivers for use in irrigation. Diversions away from rivers required appropriative rights (instead of riparian rights) to the water. Deeply concerned that monopolies over supply might develop, he suggested appropriations be diverted to smaller land parcels, as recommended by the 1862 Homestead Act that transferred government land to individual settlers. Powell's idea was that a group of individuals could work together, using communal irrigation districts to build viable communities.

Some farmers could not earn enough on farms that would be big in the wet fertile East but were too small in the arid West.[1] Settlers found ways to assemble larger parcels into larger irrigation districts. The Reclamation Act of 1902 recognized these new facts, by allowing larger land parcels and absentee landlords. It also created a federal Bureau of Reclamation to help irrigation districts build infrastructure at an economically viable scale.

Other people's money for special interests

Politicians and bureaucrats make OPM-projects possible because they are entrusted with taxpayer money and employed to use that money for producing collective goods. Sometimes they spend our money wisely; sometimes they abuse our trust by funding projects that benefit agricultural, urban or environmental special interests.

OPM-projects do not face tough scrutiny from beneficiaries who do not spend their own money. *Dead Pool*, James Lawrence Powell's

---

[1] An individual could claim 160 acres (about 65 hectares) under the Homestead Act. Acreage limits have changed over time.

2009 update to *Cadillac Desert*, shows how business-as-usual inefficiency continues to plague infrastructure in America's southwest.[2]
The existence and worsening of inefficiency is not surprising. Existence can be blamed on OPM, which makes it easy for a group of
beneficiaries to support a project that others pay for. Worsening results from diminishing returns: early dams had big benefits and low
costs, but the benefit-cost ratio fell as less-attractive sites were developed. Later projects were socially wasteful (benefits were lower
than costs) because organizations such as the Bureau of Reclamation and US Army Corps of Engineers wanted dams. Their goal was
supported by interest groups that wanted hydropower, irrigation, storage, and flood protection. Both groups lobbied politicians to use taxpayer funds on their projects. The same shift from good projects to
bad projects, from socially beneficial to OPM-wastes, has occurred in
Japan, Spain, Australia, China, India and other countries.

Reisner and other environmentalists pointed out that benefit/cost
ratios were falling (all the good projects were gone), that environmental stresses were rising, and projects were distributing too much water
to people who had no incentive to conserve. But these complaints
didn't keep environmentalists from pursuing their own OPM-funded
projects. Consider the movement to Restore Hetch Hetchy (RHH) in
Yosemite National Park. The centerpiece of the park in California's
Sierra Nevada is Yosemite Valley. Hetch Hetchy Valley is Yosemite's
northern twin. In the early 20*th* century, an almighty battle raged between San Francisco, which wanted to dam and flood as a reservoir
for drinking water, and environmentalists who opposed the dam. San
Francisco won, and Hetch Hetchy was flooded. San Francisco got
water rights and access to land for free (such a giveaway was normal
for the time) but it paid for the project's costs. From a benefit-cost
perspective, Hetch Hetchy passes with flying colors. The reservoir
looks like a natural lake. Water generates hydropower as it leaves the
reservoir; it flows in an existing riverbed before going into pipes that
serve 2.4 million people in and around San Francisco.

The environmentalists behind RHH want to breach the dam, move
storage off-stream and end hydropower generation so that people can
walk in a drained valley. Even ignoring the possibility that benefits for
the new project may be lower than the current carbon-negative facility,
the main problem with RHH is its $5 billion cost. The 5,000 or so
proponents of RHH do not want to pay $1 million each for this project

---

[2] J.L. Powell is not related to J.W. Powell.

— they prefer OPM funding from the other 36,955,000 Californians. RHH probably doesn't make sense from a public welfare perspective (cost versus benefits), but it certainly doesn't make sense for the rest of California to pay for a project that benefits 5,000 enviro-activists.

How special interests get OPM

The use and abuse of OPM for projects was not a straightforward transfer of cash from one pocket to another. Benefits and costs can be shifted between groups in subtle ways. Reisner pointed out that 50-year repayment schedules using low interest rates and constant prices ($200 in 1940 bought much more than $200 in 1990) shifted costs from farmers to taxpayers. Farmers got current benefits for later, lower payments.

Larger projects that affect people in different ways also mismatch costs and benefits among individuals. These problems are common with collective goods like dams, roads, parks, you-name-it. This mismatch need not lead to problems — friends often split the dinner check evenly — but gaming such fairness is unwelcome. That's why we object when a friend suggests splitting the bill for their steak and your burger.

Say that a dam is built that will benefit three groups: farmers who will use the water for irrigation, recreationalists who will fish, boat and swim in the reservoir, and people living downstream who will benefit from flood control. Each group should pay based on its share of the total benefits, but what's the benefit of avoiding a flood or eating a fish? It turns out that it's pretty hard to estimate benefits that accrue on summer days or materialize with flood or drought; it also turns out people manipulate estimates to transform benefit-cost analysis into a benefit-cost robbery.

Folks who want the dam will inflate benefits so the benefit-cost ratio looks more attractive. Folks who want to pay less will inflate another group's benefits to increase its cost share. That's where OPM comes in. General tax revenues pay for benefits like flood control and recreation that go to society. An increase in social benefits means lower payments for farmers who use dam water for irrigation. The engineers and bureaucrats who want to build and operate dams don't worry about inflated social benefits because society's cost share doesn't come out of their pockets or budgets. Thus we can see how farmers, bureaucrats and engineers may cooperate to build a dam "for society" that uses society's money but doesn't benefit society.

Some OPM-beneficiaries keep coming back for more. The OPM-funded All American Canal (AAC) that carries water from the Colorado River to farmers in the Imperial Valley is the largest irrigation canal in the world, with a capacity of 740 m^3 per second. But the AAC was built as an unlined ditch that leaked about 83 GL of water per year along 37 km of its 132 km length. Those 37 km were lined with concrete in 2009 so that San Diego could claim the "saved" water. San Diego got the water, but the losers from the deal were the California taxpayers who paid most of the $300 million cost and the Mexican farmers who had been using the seeping water since the 1930s.

Subsidies and opportunity costs

Mexican farmers suffered more from the absence of a market that would allow them to compete with San Diego than they did from OPM, which brings us to a third variety of OPM. (The first was a direct cash transfer or subsidy; the second was a manipulation of benefits to shift costs to others.) This OPM is the award of a valuable right to a special interest group for a low price (or nothing at all). The award of rights may not be socially harmful if trades then move the right to those who value it most, but the absence of trade may result in those rights being used in a way that does not create the greatest benefits to society.

It's possible to waste water resources by selling water below cost or selling water to privileged insiders who do not value it as much as others. These wastes create subsidies and opportunity costs, respectively. Although subsidies are easy to understand (the government charges $5 for a widget that costs $10 to make, covering the loss with tax revenue), opportunity costs are a little trickier.

Since they are so important in water, we will take time for an example. Figure 7 starts us off with subsidies. The figure has three lines. The top horizontal cost line shows the cost to produce, say, a cubic meter of water. The line below it, price, shows how much is charged for that water. The difference between the two is the subsidy, or the amount of loss on every cubic meter that's sold at a price below cost. The third line is a demand curve. Recall from Figure 1 that this line starts high and slopes down because people demand more water as its price falls. Likewise, the figure here shows that Q_P is larger than Q_C — the quantity sold at price is greater than the quantity that would sell if price was equal to cost.

Subsidies that reduce price below cost are one way to increase quantity demanded. This means there will be water shortages if only

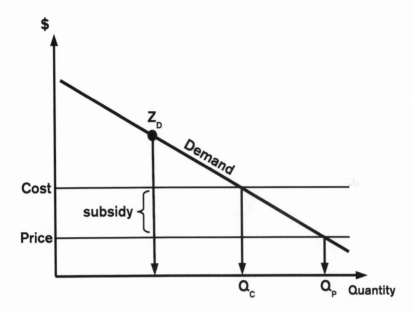

Figure 7: The subsidy to Mr. Z is the difference between the cost of the good and the price Mr. Z pays. Mr. Z's benefit is the distance between his value for the good and the price he pays ($Z_D - price$).

Q_C cubic meters are available. Mr. Z, who is not affected by this shortage problem, is happy to get a unit that he values at Z_D at a price that's less than cost, since his net benefit (the difference between Z_D and price) is greater than it would be without the subsidy. Note that this example does not include any form of special access. Everyone willing to pay the price receives water (assuming Q_P is available). The subsidies are funded by another source such as taxes.

Figure 8 keeps subsidies but limits production to Q_C cubic meters, the efficient quantity to produce when the cost of production is "Cost" per unit. Why is that quantity efficient? Because the values on the demand curve to the left of Q_C are higher than the cost of production. Price does not affect efficiency (because demand is held to Q_C); it reflects the value of the subsidy to the recipients of the good. Although most economists would stop right there, political scientists would continue. They would ask "qui bono?" (who benefits?) from those subsidies. Society as a whole may not be better off (the transfer has a zero dollar net impact), but the people who get part of Q_C are better off than the people who only subsidize its production.

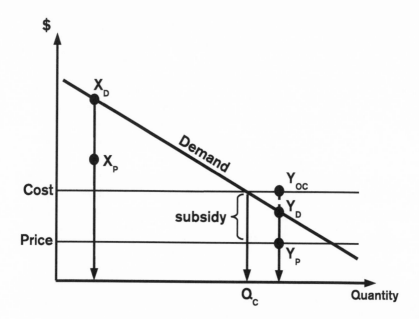

Figure 8: The subsidy to Mr. Y is partially wasted since his value of the good (Y_D) is less than its production cost. That waste, or opportunity cost, of $Y_{OC} - Y_D$ falls to nothing if Mr. Y sells to Mr. X because Mr. X's value for the good is greater than its production cost.

Figure 8 shows that Mr. X values water at more than its price or cost of production; Mr. Y values it at more than its price but less than its cost of production. In a free market, the non-subsidized price would be at cost and the production quantity would be Q_C; Mr. X would buy water but Mr. Y would not. In this political market, the price is lower than the cost of production due to subsidies. More important, the politicians who approve subsidies also gain the power to decide who gets access to the Q_C subsidized units. They take care of privileged individuals like Mr. Y instead of people like Mr. X who have an economic claim on the units but lack political connections.

Mr. Y pays a price for a cubic meter that he values at less than its cost. He gets the benefit of Y_D – price. Society pays a subsidy equal to cost – price. The "opportunity cost" of Y's purchase is $Y_{OC} - Y_D$, or the difference between the cost of production and the value of the cubic meter to Mr. Y.

At this point, Mr. Y either keeps or resells the water. If he keeps it, then society is worse off by the opportunity cost of $Y_{OC} - Y_D$. That waste falls to nothing if Mr. Y sells to Mr. X, who values the water at more than the cost of production. If the sale occurs at a price of X_P, then Mr. X receives a benefit of $X_D - X_P$. Mr. Y receives a benefit of $X_P - Y_D$ (the value he forgoes).

In all cases, society pays the subsidy, but social losses depend on the quantity of water that ends up with people who value it below the cost of production. People like subsidies because they get something for less than its cost, and they can sell their subsidized goods to people without preferential access. Although these sales can reduce the opportunity cost of distributing water to people who do not value it as much as others, it can also encourage games among potential beneficiaries of subsidies and special access. Who benefits from these games? The bureaucrats and politicians who decide the value of subsidies and who gets access to them.

This example demonstrates how preferential access wastefully misallocates valuable assets. Although it would be better to end such practices, a second-best choice (reselling in markets) can eliminate most of the waste. Reselling is also politically feasible, since winners in the current system would continue to win. Society would lose less, because markets would reallocate water to those who value it most.

Access to water and infrastructure is valuable

In most parts of the world, governments gave water rights to settlers and farmers in vacant lands. This popular policy increased rural populations, food production and infrastructure for moving and storing water. Over time, water rights and access to infrastructure have become more valuable for other uses, but new arrivals have a hard time getting access, either because water is not for sale or because the transaction costs of trading are so high. The combination of long holding times and low trading volumes means water and infrastructure are often misallocated.

Las Vegas is the biggest city in Clark County, Nevada. About 1.9 million people live in the region, and their $100 billion of economic activity accounts for about 80 percent of the state's economy. California's Imperial Valley is also in the middle of a desert, just down the river from Las Vegas. Six thousand farmers grow crops worth $1 billion in Imperial Valley, and they use five times as much water as the people in Clark County use.

Clark County and Imperial Valley both get their water from the Colorado River, and their water withdrawals were legally quantified in

1928, when their populations were both about 8,000 people. Imperial got about 10 times as much water as Clark County because its farmers used more.

Clark County now has many more people producing much more value, but their water rights have not changed since 1928. Although it may be logistically possible for Las Vegas to buy water rights from the farmers in Imperial Valley, it's not politically possible, since politicians in Imperial block trade. That means Las Vegas is trying to get water from desalination (at a huge price) or imports from other areas (with much political fighting). The people of Imperial may be happy to benefit from their privileged access, but the opportunity cost of the current allocation is very high for the people of Las Vegas and the country.

Or consider the award of contracts for hydropower at Hoover Dam, which the federal government built near Las Vegas in the 1930s. Although some people might think it makes sense for the government to maximize the return on its investment by selling Hoover power in an open market to the highest bidder, that's not how it works. A press release from Senator Harry Reid (D-NV) describes how Congress manages Hoover power:

> Since its construction, Hoover Dam power has been allocated by Act of Congress. Congress first allocated Hoover power in the Boulder Canyon Project Act of 1928. In 1984, Congress again allocated Hoover power through contracts with state, municipal and utility contractors. These contracts will expire in 2017... The Hoover Power Allocation Act of 2010 allows existing Hoover contractors to continue receiving allocations of Hoover power to 2067.

It's not markets, highest and best use, or willingness to pay that determines who gets access to the 4 billion kilowatt-hours (14,400 terajoules) of hydroelectric power from Hoover; it's Congress. The wholesale value of that power (at the 2009 price of 3.8 cents per kWh) is $152 million per year, but Congress sells power at cost, or 1.8 cents per kWh. The lucky buyers whom Congress allows to buy this power get an annual discount of $80 million; society pays the price in foregone revenue and misallocation of power.

Cheap water increases sprawl and shortages

Does supply lead to demand, or demand lead to supply? Do people wait for water before they move somewhere, or do people who want water get water? Must infrastructure be built ahead of demand, or is there money to be made in buying dry land, adding water and selling it for new homes and subdivisions? It's possible to reconcile these views by differentiating between intensive and extensive demand. Intensive demand is an increase in demand from current customers on the interior of a service area; extensive demand comes from new customers who settle on the exterior of a service area.

In 1840, Americans lived where it rained. By 1990, there was no connection between population and precipitation. Why? Infrastructure projects brought water to arid regions, and people moved from wet cold areas to dry warm areas. Once they got there, they found that water was also abundant and cheap. Their demand for water grew to include lifestyle uses — for lawns, swimming pools, long showers and washing the car and driveway.

In other words, water projects increased population in dry areas (extensive demand), and cheap water increased water consumption in these areas (intensive demand). But Powell told us more than 130 years ago that it's not possible to bring abundant water to every arid region (American Southwest, southeastern Spain, coastal Australia, and so on), so politicians direct managers and bureaucrats to bring water to certain places. How do politicians decide? Maybe they look where water is most valuable, or maybe they ask real estate developers who understand that the biggest profits come from adding water and houses to dry land? A charitable view would have it that developers are interested in building robust communities to serve residents; a political-economic view predicts that an iron triangle might form: developers make donations (bribes) to politicians in exchange for new water services to their land; politicians take these bribes and give managers budgets for the projects; and managers build projects in exchange for bigger service areas. Who loses from this system? People who may deserve new water, people whose existing water supplies are now less reliable, people who care about the environment, and a society that fails to maximize the benefits of its scarce water.

How does this work in practice? A few years ago, the Southern Nevada Water Authority (SNWA) was selling new water service permits for only $6,300 per house. Low fees made it cheaper to build new houses and fed the boom in local housing construction. In 2006, Las Vegas collected nearly $190 million in hookup fees for new homes, much more than its operating revenues of $120 million. Big revenues from hookup fees encouraged SNWA to issue a lot of permits (increasing extensive demand) and reduced the cost of delivering water (increasing intensive demand). The average monthly bill in Vegas is $32. Unfortunately, hookup fees are only one-time contributions, and Vegas started to see them (and the growth behind them) as an ongoing source of revenue.

The global real estate bust hit Vegas harder than any other municipality in the US. Growth reversed. Hook up fees fell to $60 million in 2008, $27 million in 2009 and $3 million in 2010. Vegas had built too much, too fast, and housing prices dropped by 37 percent. Water demand fell by 15 percent between 2008 and 2010. The bust would not have been as bad if the boom had not been encouraged by cheap water and cheap meters, but Vegas politicians and real estate developers wanted to turn desert sandlots into green lawns and cash.

Now the revenue is gone, supplies are not increased, and customers face a nasty combination of lower reliability and higher bills. Water managers gambled on growth and lost. Or did they? New building returned to Vegas in 2010. How could anyone build in the presence of so many empty houses? Those houses are tied up in foreclosure complications, and the drop in labor, material and land costs means new houses are cheaper — especially when water managers are willing to accommodate new growth with cheap hook up fees.

Average cost pricing also subsidizes demand growth. Recall from Figure 2(a) that a price based on average cost underprices the expensive source of water by averaging its cost with cheaper supplies. That same principle applies to the cost of connecting to a network. Customers in the center of the network (near the source of water) are cheap to connect. Newer customers on the edge of the network are more expensive to connect, since they require new pipes and more energy to pump water farther. In extreme cases, new customers may require additional water treatment plants. How much should they pay for their water or water service? The economically efficient price would charge them the real marginal cost for service.

But the industry uses postage-stamp pricing (PSP) based on the average cost of service instead of the real cost of delivery. PSPs are well known for letter postage, where the price of mailing across town or across the country is the same. With water, PSPs mean that someone at the farthest edge of a service area will pay a service charge that's less than the cost of building pipes to get there and a volumetric price that's lower than the cost of moving water there. These people are being subsidized by people at the center who pay more for service and water than the real cost of service. PSPs can encourage consumption on the edges without the offsetting prices discouraging it in the center. That's because people on the edge of town with lawns have a higher elasticity of demand for water; they use more with low prices. People in the center do not usually have big lawns, so they have lower elasticities of demand; higher prices do not discourage them to reduce indoor water use by enough to offset higher demand from their suburban neighbors. These cross-subsidies get bigger as the service area increases: wholesale water is distributed using PSP across an area of nearly 14,000 km^2 in Southern California, but the entire state of South Australia uses retail PSP across 980,000 km^2. That's a lot of subsidy.

Infrastructure projects involve hard choices

The infrastructure projects that convey water from wet Northern California to arid Southern California started more than 100 years ago, and the water that they brought increased the population, economy and agricultural output in Southern California. By many accounts, California's development miracle of the 1920s to 1960s was driven by imported water. The trouble was that this new supply encouraged an unsustainable growth — the demand curve shifted out and kept going. Shortage problems started to surface in the 1970s and worsened in the 1980s and 1990s. In the past 10 years, problems have concentrated on the Sacramento-San Joaquin Delta in Northern California, where huge pumps redirect water flowing toward the Pacific Ocean into aqueducts headed to Southern California.

Stop for a moment and consider an idea that applies in California and everywhere else: the decision to build a dam, aqueduct or water distribution network can be made for good or bad reasons, but once made, it changes the course of future decisions. Infrastructure changes the cost of water storage, conveyance and distribution; it alters the costs and benefits of farming or living in one place versus another. It is in this sense that infrastructure can lead (or drive) demand for water, and the impacts of that process can last for decades (creating what's called "path dependency"). Sometimes those impacts will be benign (people like living in Los Angeles, cheap water or not); in other times, the ongoing impacts will be negative (some parts of Los Angeles have big lawns that use a disproportionate share of scarce water). Remember path dependency when you consider the complications of deciding who can use less water when it comes to scarcity and rationing.

In the Sacramento Delta, for example, three interest groups are fighting over management options. Environmentalists dislike pumps that export water; Delta inhabitants want their communities protected from flooding and earthquakes; agricultural and urban groups want exports to continue. These groups often disagree, but their conflicts are slowly moving toward a resolution in the form of a Peripheral Canal (PC) that will direct freshwater around the periphery of the Delta, to reduce harm to the environment from the pumps and maintain water exports (people who live in the Delta face numerous problems that the PC doesn't really help). The PC was originally suggested in the 1960s, but voters prevented its construction in 1982. It's back on the table for the good reason that it does the best job of meeting different goals.

I looked at the economic and environmental justifications for the PC in 2008 and concluded that the PC would improve the Delta's environment while maintaining exports to urban and agricultural interests. A few months later, I reversed my support, partially due to some careful critiques by other scholars but mainly because I stepped back to look at the bigger picture. I already knew that cheap water had driven growth and sprawl in Southern California and that shortages were the result of unrestrained demand. It was clear that the PC would do nothing to reduce sprawl or prevent shortages. Why spend $10 billion to perpetuate an unsustainable and non-economical status quo?

Although some people think that Southern California would have never developed without cheap imported water, it easily could have. Growth patterns would have been different and population may have been a bit smaller, but we're talking about the difference between cheap water and full-cost water — not sand dunes and Los Angeles. Median water consumption for residents of urban Southern California is 300 liters per person per day (much of it used outdoors). Urban Australians use about half that amount.

Of course, I may be totally wrong on the PC (the Delta recovers, Southern California never has a shortage), but it's important to say something. Big policy choices benefit from an open debate that considers different views, facts and values. That's true for projects in California, Sydney (desalination), Jordan (the Red-Dead canal), or anywhere else in the world.

Corrupt dams hold back progress

Infrastructure projects in developing countries face OPM and externality problems, but corruption makes them worse. Benefits go to smaller groups while costs fall on poorer majorities that are less protected and more vulnerable to harm. Outcomes are more extreme — rivers are drained; pollution poisons water; displacements shift millions — the effects damage economic activities, social stability, and environmental sustainability.

China moved more than 1 million people to build Three Gorges Dam. Those people received little compensation and certainly had no ability to protest their exile. The richest 20 percent of Mexican farmers get 70 percent of the irrigation subsidies. Corruption in China has so impeded enforcement of environmental regulations that the water in 75 percent of urban rivers is unsuitable for drinking or fishing. These results are highlighted in Transparency International's 2008 report, which also gave a handy formula for understanding how these facts arise:

Corruption = discretion + monopoly - accountability

Politicians and bureaucrats in developing countries have more discretion because the rule of law is weak, the press is not free, and official information is propaganda. Rulers are monopolists who face no opposition and do what they please, without any need to consider *their* people. Combine these ingredients for corruption with a sector that is huge, complex and (literally) underground, and we see why nobody knows who spent how much on useless results.

Sometimes corruption is more about incompetence than intention. Hugo Chavez, Venezuela's populist dictator, lowered the price of energy and water, increasing demand for both. In 2009, these policies led to power and water shortages. The country has one meter of annual precipitation per year and the facilities to store water through drought, but mismanagement lowered storage in reservoirs and reduced flows through hydroelectric turbines. Venezuelans unhappy with three-minute showers started to complain about the government's mismanagement, but Chavez was saved by the return of rain in 2010.

International development aid makes all of this worse. Outsiders usually know very little about the politics, culture or economics of developing countries. They are not sure whether one farmer or community is poor or needy (statistics are often missing or biased). They can't tell rulers where to spend money (assuming they know where it should go).

Rather than worry about these problems, many big aid agencies (World Bank, USAID, Asian Development Bank, and others) concentrate on shifting cash. Loan officers with big projects are successful; final performance evaluations or mid-project cancellations are rare; it's hard to ask questions of (or find) stakeholders. Everyone knows about these problems, but change is hard when celebrities like Bob Geldof and Bono insist that countries send 0.7 percent of GDP to these poor miserable people.

What about the demand for water projects? When asked to choose between cleaner water and an electrical connection, people in developing countries choose electricity. That's for two reasons: everyone has access to some water (otherwise they'd be dead), and the men who usually answer these surveys care more about TV than reducing the workload for women. That said, the proposed big projects often offer poor value for money. Local projects that use cheap and appropriate technology could deliver results at a fraction of their cost, but governments and aid agencies prefer big projects that involve lots of money, press releases and jobs for their friends to small-scale projects managed by communities.

In India, for example, politicians used international financing to build large, inappropriate and corruption-laden dams that put rivers at the service of the wealthy and left the poor high and dry. Many of these projects were started in the 50s and 60s. Many of them are acknowledged failures today. It is therefore impressive and hopeful to see how Indians are returning, on their own, to traditional methods of catching and storing rainwater and communal management of groundwater resources.

Local projects and local money for local people

The end of abundance means it's important to maximize the benefit of our limited water supplies. Existing projects and water rights may have been built and allocated under sound economic, environmental and political guidelines in the past, but costs and benefits change over time. The opportunity costs of misallocation can be reduced by reallocating capital improvements and/or water rights to the highest bidder and the resulting revenues to the public purse (or historic owners, depending on property rights). All-in-auctions (see Chapter 5) are one way to reallocate water or infrastructure. Although an iron triangle of politicians, bureaucrats and special interests may try to protect its privileged position, it's possible for a dedicated group of 10–20 people to cause change. Most water management is local, and locals can do a lot to make sure their water is well managed.

CHAPTER 9

Water and the environment

Environmental water flows are increasingly valuable. Special interests support policies that ignore values, waste water, and harm the environment. Technology will not save a misvalued environment.

Americans have a "water income" of 27,000 liters of water per day per person. Haitians have 4,000 liters; even Israelis have 600 liters. Most of this water is in the environment, flowing from somewhere to somewhere else, often without any human contact. Environmental water transports fertile soil to land downstream; it cools and moistens dry and hot areas; it is a moving landscape. Trees need it; animals need it; wetlands and other ecosystems need it; and we need it. We are dead without an environment. For most of history, these flows were taken for granted or treated as a nuisance to dam or divert away, but the more we took from the environment, the more we missed what was no longer there.

The end of abundance hit the environment first. The Colorado River failed to reach its delta in the 1930s, when Hoover Dam blocked the river to fill Lake Mead. The Aral Sea shrank dramatically after the Soviets began diverting its recharging rivers in the 1960s. The 1969 fire on Cleveland's Cuyahoga River got people's attention, but the polluted Cuyahoga had been catching fire since 1868. These events have led to an increase in demand for environmental water, not from nature but from the people who want more water left in the environment.

The debate over how much water nature needs or deserves is complicated from a scientific perspective and controversial from a philosophical perspective. Some people think that all water should be left in the environment, since that's the way we found it. Others think that the environment should get leftovers, even if that means dry rivers and wetlands. Both sides have a point, because we benefit from a healthy environment as well as diverting water to direct human uses.

Environmental water's character as a non-excludable collective good means we need to manage it with political or community institutions that reconcile many private subjective views, just as we do with other uses in Part II. These institutions need to reconcile and reflect changing priorities that change over time — not the consensus of 50 years ago. Missing prices, poor incentives, weak property rights, or inappropriate management structures can lead to adverse impacts that are costly to detect and take years to reverse.

This chapter looks at how economic tools can reflect and reconcile our priorities into sound policies for managing environmental water. Chapter 10 discusses weather and climate change (a global problem that requires a global response) but this chapter sticks with solutions aimed at local sustainability.

Managing environmental goods

People have different subjective values for goods, and the characteristics of the good (excludable or not) determine the best way to reconcile those values. The first step is to assign appropriate property rights; the next step is to establish the right mechanism for reconciling personal subjective values in determining how to allocate those goods in a way that maximizes social wealth and minimizes waste. Property rights and mechanisms can be combined into many different institutions to produce useful results, but useless combinations can increase misallocation and waste. These inefficient institutions can persist if they create winners who fight to preserve them.

Recall the example of the whale in the introductory chapter. As a public good, the whale had a value equal to the sum of values from all the individuals who were happy to know the whale was alive. As a private good, the whale had a value equal to the highest bid of the person who bought it from a fisherman. The goal is not to decide which set of values is more important or valid; the goal is to make sure that institutions reflect and reconcile these values to create the greatest possible social benefit.

Many environmental economists are working on this two-sided problem of valuing "environmental services" and finding ways to reflect those values in policies and actions that affect the environment. This work focuses on the value of in-stream flows in rivers (to fishermen, to local water quality, to ambient conditions); the importance and impact of harmful and beneficial "non-commercial species" to agriculture, forestry, livestock, and other primary commodities; the impact of pollution on human health and industrial activities; and many other areas. You might say that environmental economics is relevant wherever we go and whatever we do, except in 100 percent artificial conditions such as virtual reality. (Ironically, designers spend a lot of time trying to program the environment into virtual reality games, to make them "more natural.") The economics of the environment, like flows of environmental water, are not always obvious, but they can have significant impacts. Ignorance of environmental costs and benefits puts you at risk of unpleasant surprises in the same way that ignorance of rising flood waters puts you at risk of an unintentional swim. As the saying goes: Mother Nature always has the last move.

We have subjective values about the environment

The past had too much environment. Nature was a nuisance to be survived and conquered. But abundant water, air, wildlife, and landscapes have become scarcer, nature is no longer so scary, and the environment's value has risen as its quantity has fallen (there's a demand curve for environment). These local and personal values reflect nature's transition from a wild force that will crush us to a tamed ambiance that we enjoy to a vulnerable innocent that we must protect. Some people believe they have a personal relationship with Mother Nature in the same way that others believe they have a personal relationship with God. In 2009, an English High Court judge recognized that "green beliefs deserve the same protection in the workplace as religious convictions." Others want to protect nature so that nature can protect us.

People often prefer to spend $100 to save a few local trees instead of using the same amount to save hundreds of distant trees. This provincialism may seem natural, but it can result in strange priorities for self-proclaimed nature lovers. It's likely, for example, that the 2010 Deepwater Horizon oil spill in the Gulf of Mexico — the biggest leak off US shores in 40 years — will halt offshore drilling in the US. Where will replacement oil come from? Perhaps Nigeria, the fourth-largest supplier of oil to the US. Americans consume 40 percent of Nigeria's exports, or 800,000 barrels of oil per day. Nigeria has had a major oil spill in every year for the past 40 years. In the rush to protect their own environment, Americans may cause greater pollution elsewhere.

Here's why. Oil is a natural resource that can be controlled as a private good and sold in markets for a price. Clean ocean water is a common-pool good that is rival (it can be used up by pollution) but shared by all (it cannot be priced in a market). From these characteristics we can guess that oil (a private good) will be managed for maximum value while water pollution (the negative externality from oil production that affects common-pool ocean water) may not be. But good institutions can compensate for poor incentives. Ownership of the Gulf of Mexico is just as vague as ownership of the Niger Delta, but the US government is better at managing drilling and pollution than the Nigerian government. The US government collects oil royalties, tries to prevent and clean up pollution, and compensates people harmed by pollution. Nigeria's corrupt politicians take oil royalties for themselves, allow dirty pumping, and do not worry about spills. Their greed means their oil is sold for less than its true cost. American drivers may be pleased to have cheaper fuel, but they are increasing pollution in a distant place.

Appropriate property rights lead to sustainability

Around 1800, Thomas Malthus (a reverend and economist) predicted that population growth would outrun increases in food production, leading to food shortages and starvation. The Malthusian trap is famous for its pessimism and for being wrong. We've avoided mass starvation because the supply of food has kept pace with demand.

Malthus' mistake was not that he misunderstood demand, supply, and scarcity. It was that he applied his analysis to the wrong good. Food, like natural resources (oil, fish and so on) can be priced. Scarcity will lead to higher prices, and higher prices will both reduce quantity demanded and increase quantity supplied, preventing shortage. But Malthus' ideas make sense for environmental goods, which are non-excludable and thus hard to price or manage efficiently. Most water is taken from the environment free of charge. In many places, the cost of discharging pollution into water is also free.

Can we put a price on water in the environment? The amount of freshwater per person is falling (more people, and less clean water), so scarcity is rising. We didn't starve because food had a price, so maybe we need to look at prices to prevent water shortages. But pricing cannot be used unless excludable property rights turn water into a private or club good. That's easy with a river or lake but not a common-pool good like an ocean or aquifer.

Nobel Laureate Elinor Ostrom points out that a common-pool good can be managed as an open-access good that may be overexploited or a collective good that need not be. Common property is often sustainably managed through a combination of formal agreements and informal social norms that arise and evolve from within a community. Anyone who shares the bathroom with others knows that there's a tension between emptying the trash, changing the towels, and lifting the seat. The formal and informal institutions that evolve to cope with these tensions may not work all the time, but they do not require property rights. It's in this way that local institutions can prevent aquifer overdrafting or oceanic pollution.

Ostrom wrote her PhD dissertation on groundwater management in Southern California. She studied how institutions evolved with failures and successes to prevent overpumping and seawater intrusion while fairly and efficiently allocating water among many claimants. Her husband, Vincent, studied urban water management of the Metropolitan Water District of Southern California in the 1950s. The Ostroms brought an institutional political-economic view to their analysis, examining the incentives, rules, social norms and historic precedents that limited changes to the status quo. Their work highlighted an alternative path to sustainable management of the commons that did not require private property rights (a Coasian paradigm described in Chapter 2) and led to Elinor Ostrom's Nobel Prize in 2009.

Changing the incentive to use too much

It's basic human nature to exploit opportunity, until the cost of further action is too high. That's why we walk as close to the edge as possible to get a good view, eat until we are full, and drive as fast as is prudent. When we stand on these margins, we consider how far we've come and stop when the cost of the next step exceeds its benefits.[1]

Institutions affect these decisions. Subsidies lower the cost of consumption, encouraging us to push the margin out further. Taxes reverse that direction. A lack of property rights makes it cheaper to consume property belonging to everybody and nobody, which can lead to a Tragedy of the Commons. Monopolies with property rights, on the other hand, often lower the supply of consumable goods to

---

[1] Many people can be persuaded to spend $20 on a project that has already cost $5 — to "save" the $5 investment — even when the project is going to produce only $10 in benefits. Economists denounce this "sunk cost fallacy," but it may have some evolutionary function.

increase prices and profits. When these monopolies control private goods like cat food or telephone calls, they reduce social welfare, but they can limit over-exploitation of common-pool goods. A monopoly over a fishing commons, for example, would bring fewer fish to market at higher prices than numerous competitors but also extend the life of the fishery (perhaps indefinitely). The bad news is that a monopoly doesn't always try to maximize the value of its resources. Workers in Soviet monopolies often wasted resources, polluted the environment and subtracted value — turning $100 of trees into wood products worth $20. Incentives drove these results: managers and workers were paid to fulfil production quotas for goods sold at prices that reflected the cost of materials, so they wasted materials and produced the wrong products.

A spoonful of sugar makes the wetlands go down

Missing environmental prices result in greater pollution from private consumption decisions (that's why storm sewers are often clogged with old plastic bags and food wrappers). They also encourage the conversion of land providing non-monetized environmental services to uses that generate more cash but less social value. This is the case with wetlands in Florida and Louisiana that have been converted from useless swamps to productive sugarcane fields. According to the US Department of Agriculture, 570 farms in those two states grow 93 percent of the country's sugarcane acreage (sugar beets grown on about 4,000 farms account for about half of total US sugar production), which means the 28 million tons of sugar that those 570 farms produce represents 44 percent of total US sugar production.

Now here's the interesting part. The US protects domestic farmers from cheap foreign sugar produced by farmers in Brazil and other countries by taxing imported sugar. Wholesale sugar prices in the 10 years to 2011 were about 76 percent higher in the US than in the world (51 cents vs. 29 cents per kg). Given annual sugar consumption of 25 kg, protection of domestic farmers costs every American $5.50 each per year.

The gain per farmer is much greater: an extra 22 cents per kilo on 28 million tons of production increases revenue to those 570 farms (probably fewer than 570 individuals) by nearly $11 million each. US sugar farmers don't collect every penny of those millions. They are less efficient than international farmers, so their production wastes resources and costs more. They also need to make political contributions (the US Department of Agriculture helps by tracking agricultural output by congressional district).

Money goes from the pockets of consumers to the pockets of farmers, lobbyists and politicians, but this theft of the many by the few is hard to stop. The many have a collective action problem. Who's going to spend weeks or years fighting to remove trade barriers that cost $5.50 per person against special interests earning millions from their existence? But wait, it gets worse. Higher sugar prices also increase the demand for high-fructose corn syrup (HFCS), which comes from irrigated corn that uses more water than Brazil's rainfed sugarcane. Higher prices also make it profitable to grow sugarcane in wetlands that could protect coastal communities from high winds and surging waves caused by hurricanes like Katrina.

That's our little case study of how cheap water, an unpriced environment and special interest politics combine to produce too much domestic sugar, deplete water supplies, increase agricultural pollution, destroy wetlands, and cost us billions.

Technology versus cooperation and politics

It's difficult to replace a policy that favors the few (sugar farmers) at a cost to many (sugar consumers, environmentalists, citizens), but creative thinking sometimes helps. Consider, for example, an industry whose lobbyists argue against a tax on pollution — claiming that it will destroy jobs, kill babies, open the borders to invasion, and so on. Their lobbying can be overcome by replacing a tax per unit of pollutant with a "zero net tax" (ZNT) that works by measuring average pollution per unit of output, taxing companies that issue above-average pollution, and rebating those tax revenues to below-average polluters (taxes and rebates rise with distance from the average). This scheme breaks the coalition opposed to taxation in half, makes it more likely that taxation will be enacted, and creates a virtuous circle in which firms compete to lower their pollution and receive greater tax rebates. Besides its political attractiveness, ZNT is a form of flexible cap and trade for which the government doesn't need to set a cap (it's set according to average pollution) or specify a rate of improvement (the cap falls as fast as pollution reduction techniques advance).

Technology will not save us

But aren't all these policies a waste of time? Can't technology save us, as it saved us from the Malthusian trap? Maybe, but we have to remember that the No. 1 driver of innovation, the profit motive, will not effectively protect an underpriced environment. That doesn't mean that market incentives cannot be created. Cap and trade pollution controls, for example, create an incentive to innovate because firms that find ways to lower their pollution can sell their excess permits.

That example requires that the government create a property right or tax on pollution, but what about a pure technology play? Can't ocean desalination end water shortages caused by competing demands for limited supplies in Australia, the Middle East, California, Spain and other places?

As a thought experiment, let's consider the cost of sourcing all the water used in California from desalination. That solution would allow all the state's precipitation to run down the rivers and streams, rebuilding and nourishing ecosystems that have suffered from the impact of 38 million people. Take out the back of an envelope and write down these numbers.

Californians now demand 49,000 GL of water (40 million acre feet). The conventional wisdom is that it costs about $1 to desalinate a cubic meter of water, so the annual cost of producing that much water would be $1,300 for every man, woman and child in the state, or $3.50 per day (on top of the current cost of delivery, which does not include water costs). The 640 desalination plants supplying that water would cost about $500 billion, or $13,000 per Californian.

But these numbers hide an obvious fact: farmers use 80 percent of California's water. Under this system, they would face a price of $1,000/ML, which is roughly 50 times what many pay now. That means they would either fallow most of their land or shift the cost back to non-farmers who would pay for their tap water *and* the water farmers use for wine, cheese, almonds, alfalfa and the other crops that contribute to California's $36 billion in agricultural output (2 percent of the state's economy). Most crops are exported, but we will ignore that exporting-water-and-money complication and the logistical challenge of building 640 major installations throughout the Golden State.

What about replacing only municipal and industrial water? That would require one-fifth the desalination capacity, or a mere 128 plants that would cost each person $2,600 for construction and $0.70 per day for operations. Although these prices are more reasonable, they also miss the point, since agricultural diversions would continue to take water from the environment. Some people like that idea; they propose that cities switch to desalination so there's more water for agriculture! (Don't laugh — it happens all over the Middle East!)

But the real problem with this proposal is that replacement of natural with desalinated supply does not guarantee the end of shortages, because it does nothing to reduce demand. But what if the price of water was increased, to cover the $3.50 per person per day charge? Yes, if farmers could be persuaded to pay and if activists would accept high prices for a good "too precious to price." That price would probably reduce quantity demanded by an enormous amount for farmers (say 90 percent) and less for households (say 60 percent — down to the level of urban Israelis). In total, the reduction in demand (from 49,000 GL to about 10,000 GL or 3,500 lcd to 720 lcd) would reduce the number of desalination plants by 80 percent.

But if it's possible to get approval for this kind of project and raise prices so far, then why not just raise prices and skip the project? Higher prices would leave more water for nature, save a lot of money, and still leave humans with adequate supplies. Even if that's not likely, at least the point is clear: the policies affecting supply and demand are more important for ending shortages than technology.

Local water management

Let's turn away from expensive fantasies and consider environmental water management institutions that can reconcile the values of diverse communities on a scale that includes everyone experiencing the costs and benefits (in cash or opportunity costs) of water-use decisions. This scale is likely to match hydrological boundaries of the watershed (or catchment) — not political boundaries — allowing people in the area to manage water flows for highest and best use. Although such an idea may seem unwieldy — the Amazon, Nile and Colorado rivers cross many political, cultural, social and economic boundaries — it's foolish to manage water in one area while pretending that upstream or downstream neighbors are not experiencing the costs and benefits of local decisions.

A useful framework for reconciling different water demands within a watershed would include traditional stakeholders (farmers, bureaucrats, water managers) and recent arrivals (environmentalists, industrialists and civil society). It would establish rights in baseline quantities and qualities (probably in line with historic rights) and then facilitate reallocation of those rights. These sessions would be difficult to organize and run, but so is reality. Yes, all-in-auctions could be used for private rights, but reconciliation of interests in a common-pool good is harder. A mechanism for reconciling warring interests is described in the next section but consider a simple idea recently implemented in Michigan — a law that makes all water users responsible for *not* impacting a watershed. Property owners and riparians have a right to use water under or adjacent to their property, but any new use that may cause environmental harm needs to be offset by changes to existing uses. The key to this system is a web-based tool that allows anyone to estimate ecological impacts from a new well, for example. If no impact is predicted, the system approves a permit and the well is registered. If impacts are predicted, then neighbors discuss how to reduce it. In the 25 percent of cases where neighbors cannot agree, a state employees gets involved; they reject only 4 percent of the cases they see.

Voting with money

The Michigan system shows how stakeholders can take charge of their own watershed, how most changes in use are acceptable to all, and how disputes can be resolved under an existing property-rights and regulatory framework. The results allow new uses, minimize adverse impacts and resolve conflicts at a low cost.

Neighbors in a watershed do not always agree. Should a rainforest be cut down for plantation ranching or left intact to deliver ecosystem services? Should a river be restored for fish or drained for agriculture? These conflicts are usually reconciled with a benefit-cost assessment that chooses the alternative with the greatest value, but this assessment requires assumptions on the value of fish, ecosystems and farms. Further, it assumes that a given constituency for that option exists and that 100 percent of that constituency agrees on that value. These factors create a huge range of feasible benefit-cost values and a huge opportunity for arguments.

Even so, benefit-cost calculations are better than leaving the decisions to politicians and bureaucrats who are influenced by special interests, lobbyists, activists and consultants. Politicians may benefit from this lobbying (they can accept money and attention from everyone), but their subjective decisions often upset losers who then argue, file lawsuits or turn violent.

My idea for reconciling different interests and compensating losers requires that alternative scenarios are identified, costs of implementing these scenarios are estimated, and that the proponents of these scenarios vote for their choice with money.

Let's take a simple example. Farmers want to put river water on their fields, but environmentalists and fishermen want to leave it in place. Let's assume that each proposal costs nothing to implement. Let's also assume that both sides agree that some baseline water flows should be left in the river, to make it easy to move water (farmers) or keep the channel alive (environmentalists). The decision then is to choose whether or not to pump the remaining water out of the channel for crops or leave it in for fish. What's the highest and best use for our water?

Everyone in the watershed votes at a cost of $1 per vote. Say that pro-diverters vote $500,000 and anti-diverters vote $400,000. Pro-diverters then win the right to divert all the water; they pay the net difference in votes ($100,000) to the losers as compensation that's divided in proportion to their votes.

Some people may complain that money drives this "opportunity cost auction," but money *already* influences policy decisions. This decision process is more transparent in clarifying the role of money; it also means nobody gets their way with a few well-placed bribes. The process also assigns a clear value (through monetary votes) to a living ecosystem, an environmental good that is difficult to value using people's subjective statements or opinions. This value is not infinite. It is limited by voters' financial resources and compared with alternative uses of the water supported by others' votes.

Environmentalists may claim the diversion will support low value crops and weaken an ecosystem, true, but they need to show the color of their conviction. Farmers, likewise, need to bid at levels that match their claims of service to the community or food security. (Note that both groups tend to claim public support for activities they personally favor.) Bids will direct water to a use that is objectively more valuable. This mechanism puts people in charge of the people's water, instead of politicians or bureaucrats whose allocation decisions may not represent the people's interests.

Survival first, nature last

Developing countries with weak institutions for making collective decisions, defending minorities, and protecting public assets suffer more from environmental problems. Politicians sell fisheries, forests, oil concessions, dam permits and other goods to the highest bribers, not to those who would contribute the most to national wealth. Bidders are often foreigners with no stake or concern about the country's future, but local rich people also buy assets for exploitation through oil drilling, deforestation, overfishing, unsustainable water diversions, and so on.

The activists who protest this corruption and reporters who expose it are targets of intimidation and violence. Pro-environment activists are routinely murdered in Brazil; anti-mining activists have been killed in the Philippines and Mexico; anti-oil activists were executed by the government of Nigeria; the list goes on. Murder is often condoned or supported by politicians, police and bureaucrats who privately benefit from exploitation; they rarely distribute payments and royalties to the people living in affected areas. These problems also occur in the "developed world" (West Virginia, for example) — development is not always a done deal.

But people in developing countries also face the brutal choice between making a living and protecting the environment. Indian farmers in arid Rajasthan who wanted to irrigate their crops blocked the release of water to Keoladeo National Park, a world heritage site famous for its wetlands and migratory birds. The park dried out, leaving the birds with no place to rest or breed. In September 2010, politicians overruled the farmers and flooded the park for the first time in two years.

The people of Kenya face a similar problem. The floral industry centered around Lake Naivasha exports to Europe. Massive increases in irrigation reduced the quality and quantity of water, creating a Tragedy of the Commons for flower growers that threatens their future and a negative externality for other farmers growing food. It's necessary to reduce withdrawals and pollution before the ecosystem collapses and no benefits are left for anyone, but how does one persuade Kenya's notoriously corrupt politicians to intervene on the side of sustainability when they can be bribed to allow pumping to continue?

It's our environment to manage

The end of abundance forces us to consider flows in the environment as we try to balance competing claims. These flows are clearly valuable, but there's no easy way to establish an agreed value. Further, it's hard to reconcile evolving values for environmental water with existing water uses, rights, and management institutions. Reconciliation and choices must be made, and they are best made within the watershed, among those who experience the costs and benefits of water stocks and flows. Local management institutions can use formal property rights, informal channels for collective action, or some mixture of the two. The goal is that institutions minimize the cost of expressing and reconciling different values. This process will involve political actors and decisions that can advance or retard progress. Hopefully, they will reflect the values (and valuation) of the majority; if they do not, then the majority needs to solve the more basic problem of accountability first. The destination (sustainable environmental water management) is clear, but the journey past broken bridges, barriers and brigands requires travelers to exert themselves with patience and creativity.

CHAPTER 10

Weather and climate change

Human adaptation can reduce harm from bad weather and climate change. Markets and prices make it easier to implement robust, decentralized systems of protection.

Take a moment to look out the window. It may be bright or dark, dry or wet, cold or hot, calm or blustery. The weather is always now. Climate refers to average weather. London may have sunshine right now, but its climate is basically damp, with mild temperatures. The "change" in climate change refers to a departure from past trends toward better or worse weather but also more fluctuations, larger extremes and less predictability. Water plays a central role in weather and climate, as the gears of a global solar-powered hydrological cycle or the buffer and transmitter of changes in climate.

The end of abundance theme for weather and climate is not a straightforward case of dry places get drier and wet places get wetter. The global stock of water is fixed, but the timing, location and intensity of circulating freshwater flows are changing in uncertain ways. Changes in flows and stocks will affect the weather, not just by moving average temperature or precipitation but also by changing the variation around those averages. Atmospheric and hydrological cycles are going to accelerate as greater quantities of heat are redistributed from the equator to the poles, leading to heavier rains, longer droughts, colder nights and hotter days. Winds will be stronger, waves will be bigger, and we will have to deal with that variety.

The tricky part is that we do not have an accurate estimate of the intensity or frequency of these events — or even a consensus guesstimate, mostly because we don't really understand how water touches everything, everywhere. The move to a "new normal" makes it difficult to apply knowledge from the past, to reduce the impact of novel disruptions. Weather will be less familiar. Scarcity may appear in disconnected episodes or long-term droughts.

Abundant water made it possible to live and thrive without needing to understand the weather. Knowledge and technology made it possible to maximize our use of water, even while maintaining a margin of safety. Climate change brings new trends that will eat up or exceed these margins. It's therefore necessary to adapt, changing physical infrastructure and social institutions to increase flexibility. Some flexibility will be rewarded (flood protection that saves a city, for example), but other adaptations will be too little, too late, or too much, too soon. Institutions need time and money to build into robust, functioning systems (compare eight dead in Australia's 2011 floods with 1,500 dead in Pakistan's 2010 floods). Both market and non-market tools of adaptation need to be used: Auctions, insurance, and other tools that create and display prices, costs and values will make it easier to understand and cope with change. People will need to cooperate more, sometimes with distant strangers who are climate neighbors.

Nature is responsible for rains and droughts, but man determines if they turn into harmful floods and shortages. This chapter investigates how to keep our mouths wet and our feet dry.

Water and the weather

Most conversations about the weather are actually conversations about local water conditions: rain, snow, sleet and floods from falling water; fog, cyclones and hurricanes from the interactions of ocean and air; heatwaves from a cloudless sky; and so on. The sun delivers energy and the Earth receives it, but water determines where the energy flows and how its impacts are felt. The greenhouse gas effect refers to the retention of heat in the atmosphere by carbon dioxide, water vapor and other gases that reproduce the effect of a glass roof on a greenhouse that traps heat and moisture to keep plants warm and wet. Perhaps 75 percent of the greenhouse effect is due to water vapor and clouds; the rest is due to CO_2, NO_2, CFCs and other GHGs whose increase underlies climate change.

For most of human history, weather was a fact to enjoy or endure. Knowledge of the weather grew over time, as we began to understand how clouds might lead to rain or tornadoes, how summer brought warmer days and winter cold, how the monsoon would deliver annual precipitation within a few weeks, and so on. These patterns shaped cultures, religions, economies, diet, and settlement — most every dimension of human existence.

In a sense, we had an abundance of information on the weather that helped us minimize costs and discomforts. The end of abundant information means the costs of dealing with weather will rise, as change renders obsolete our institutions for understanding and responding to seasonal variation.

Scientists talk about a move from stationarity to non-stationarity, or a move from a pattern that's repeating or predictable to no pattern at all. Non-stationarity means our understanding of climate is going to be less accurate, with more randomness and fewer patterns. Hundred-year floods will happen more or less often than once per century. Temperatures will vary in a greater range, even as average temperatures increase; droughts will get longer; floods grow stronger; and so on. These changes will be inconvenient and/or dangerous. At best, we will have to spend time and money on robust defenses and better responses to dangerous variation. At worst, we will face more conflict, suffering and death.

Risk and uncertainty

This is a good time to clarify the difference between risk and uncertainty. Although most people use these two words interchangeably, economists separate them to clarify different ideas. Risk refers to something that is quantifiable. A coin flip, for example, has a 50 percent probability of landing heads up. Thus, we say that the "risk" of heads is 50 percent. Uncertainty does not fit into a distribution of probabilities, which means we have a hard time knowing how often to expect an uncertain event. That's because the event is unique (like a sports final) or subject to too many interacting events (like a chess game). Put another way, the risk of heads in 1,000 tosses is roughly 50 percent but the outcome of a single flip is uncertain.

Humans are not very good at understanding risk. Infants in the US (under 1 year old) are twice as likely to die in traffic accidents as drown. We are even worse at dealing with uncertainty. Some people ignore it; others turn uncertainty into risk, assigning probabilities that fit their beliefs to create a familiar sense of security. Nassim Taleb explains how normal folks as well as "experts" — economists, businessmen and traders — repeatedly fail to understand risk and uncertainty in financial markets in his 2001 and 2007 books (*Fooled by Randomness* and *The Black Swan*). Instead of acting with the caution born of ignorance, they assure themselves and others that they know how to invest prudently. Their ignorant confidence has resulted in huge losses for investors and taxpayers.[1]

We have behavioral, financial and physical methods of coping with risk and uncertainty in weather conditions. These mechanisms were developed and refined to fit historical patterns, but these patterns are ending. Climate change means more uncertainty, which implies a decrease in quantified risk and a need for greater behavioral, financial and physical defenses against shocks of unknown size and frequency. Our standard of living will fall as the costs of protection, insurance and risky habits rise. We will be pushed to use more sunscreen, carry bigger umbrellas, change our diet, repel climate refugees at the border, or do something else entirely. That's the problem with uncertainty: you don't know what it looks like until it arrives.

Carbon and climate change

This book is about water, but it cannot ignore the debate on carbon and climate change. First, because water plays a big role in climate; second, because climate change will have dramatic impacts on the supply and demand of water across space and time. Here's my quick take on carbon, climate change, and what to do. I agree that human activities are causing climate change that will be harmful to us. Anthropogenic climate change implies that we can and should do something to mitigate the effect of humans on the climate. Action will require government intervention because the Earth's atmosphere is a global commons where free riders can nullify the impact of one group's GHG reductions by increasing their own emissions. That said, reducing GHGs may be the world's biggest and hardest collective action problem to tackle. (In Chapter 12, I describe one failed experiment that attempted to solve it.)

We must solve this collective action problem if we want to reduce the creation of GHGs. Mitigation can occur via regulations (on light bulb efficiency, for example), some form of cap and trade, and/or fiscal mechanisms such as carbon taxes. Regulations are not likely to have desired effects; cap and trade can be manipulated or weakened in many ways. Carbon credits, offsets and other carbon indulgences are easy to manipulate for fraudulent purposes. Carbon taxes give clear signals of what to do, are easier to implement, and generate revenue. I favor carbon taxes, but I also favor ending existing bad policies such as the tax exemption for jet fuel, subsidies for oil exploration, subsidized energy for farmers, subsidies for kerosene and

---

[1] It's also possible that they counted on a bailout from politicians.

petrol, and subsidies for water consumption (see Chapter 6). That's all I'll say about mitigation; now let's look at how to adapt to climate change.

Robust adaptation with markets and insurance

Most people prefer unexpected good news to sudden tragedy. That's why we spend time and money insulating ourselves against adverse shocks. We insulate against the cold and we shade for the heat. We've learned to not build brick houses in earthquake areas or use wooden roofs in places with wildfires. We've developed informal community networks and markets to protect ourselves against fires, floods, and other troubles. Robust institutions work whether climate change is strong, weak or absent and weather variation is strong, weak or absent. They handle a variety of situations, with costs in proportion to risks. The next few sections describe several ways to adapt.

Robust infrastructure

Climate change promises higher sea levels, greater variation in location and intensity of precipitation, stronger storms, hotter heat waves, deeper freezes, and so on. Seawalls, flood barriers and water storage will need to be strengthened. Transport systems and emergency facilities must cope with greater uncertainty.

Improvements will cost money, but the burden can be lightened by reducing subsidies from taxpayers to users. People live too close to the sea because others pay for their seawalls. A stronger emphasis on user fees will discourage that behavior, reducing the need for and cost of setback defenses. The same holds for protecting land in river floodplains, building on steep hills, maintaining dams for floods, and so on.

Politicians will have a hard time persuading people to pay more now against remote threats. Careful presentation and strong community ties can facilitate agreement: the Dutch — famous for their skills in managing water and knowledgeable of the danger from inaction — are paying for infrastructure improvements to withstand 1-in-10,000 year floods and cope with rising sea levels. Their 100-year program is being implemented with known costs and estimates of benefits based on prior experience with large infrastructure, a preemptive caution towards potential worst-case scenarios from climate change, and a gradual implementation that delays expenses as long as possible while implementing gradual changes while they are cheap (location of new housing, for example). Contrast the Dutch plan with California's relative inaction. Disputes over the existence of climate change, a desire for outside subsidies, lobbying for new housing developments, and delayed maintenance for and improvements to the dikes protecting Sacramento (the state capital) are only a few areas of concern. The dikes around Sacramento are not even certified to 1-in-100 year floods, but 1-in-500-year storms are predicted. Protections in countries like Bangladesh and Myanmar, Indonesia and Iraq are much weaker, and their lack of institutional and financial depth leaves them more vulnerable.

Decentralized solutions

Some people consider the institutions of individual independence a great success. The nuclear family of mother, father and children has displaced the extended family, as child care, education, insurance, elder care, food preparation, cleaning and other services have been outsourced to professionals. But this transition weakens the ties that support us as they weaken the ties that bind us, ties to the extended family and neighbors that are helpful in crisis. Rented support structures may be too weak to handle volatility due to climate change. It's possible to prepare for more self-sufficient coping, but it's also a good idea to rebuild ties with family, friends, neighbors and communities with old-fashioned neighborhood parties and novel activities like community storm drain maintenance.

Businesses can also specialize in emergency services. When Hurricane Katrina hit New Orleans in 2005, people with cars fled the city, but people without cars were stranded. Their communities were not strong enough to evacuate everyone and government services were inadequate, but Walmart was quick to supply food, water, and other emergency equipment to these people. Maybe Walmart made a profit, maybe Walmart improved its reputation, but Walmart definitely helped people.

Insuring against individual bad luck

Insurance will not prevent storms, but it reduces the cost of rebuilding. Insurance price signals (the premium) also indicate when people are taking bigger risks. Car insurance tends to be quite accurate at assessing risks and balancing costs and benefits because of competition in setting rates and selling policies and good data on risks and costs. Insurance for 18 year old male drivers may be more expensive than insurance for 55 year old married women, but that's because the average young man is an inexperienced and aggressive driver who is more likely to get into an accident (I did my part).

The same is true for insurance against floods, crop damage, and so on. Climate change will introduce more volatility into insurance just as it introduces more volatility into the weather. Prices will rise and insured coverage will fall. People will tend to buy less of the more expensive, less comprehensive insurance, which in turn implies that they will lose more from storms.

This situation can be addressed in three ways: do nothing and then resist calls for emergency government relief for victims who lack insurance; require insurance, which may enlarge the market by enough to attract additional supply and lower prices; or provide insurance through the government. This last idea is the worst, because it replaces for-profit insurers that have an incentive to get prices right — and thereby reduce risky behavior. Subsidized government flood insurance in the US is directly responsible for huge flood losses, because it reassures people that it's OK to live in floodplains, too close to the ocean, and so on.

Step back from the margin

Individual actions are easy to take but hard to coordinate. Good infrastructure, detailed weather forecasts and inexpensive building materials have made it easy to live in places with poor weather. People forget about risks or assume that the government will provide. The residents of the Ninth Ward in New Orleans found themselves flooded when poorly designed and maintained levees failed during Hurricane Katrina. The French Quarter was not flooded because it's on high ground. The French who settled there nearly 300 years ago may have wanted good views, but they also knew that they had to carefully choose where to live. The lack of government protection also explains why the Ninth Ward consisted of fishing camps built on floating piers and stilt houses until the 20th century. Residents back then were keenly aware that they lived in a flood zone.

A desire for cheap personal space, spectator profits, and government policies to develop swamplands and floodplains have led to settlement in vulnerable areas, but climate change threatens these communities with tipping into the ocean, flooding by river, or burial by mudslide. It's possible to pull back from the margin, but political leaders need to design policies and allow prices to signal risk.

Bad weather kills poor people

Cherrapunji, a town of about 10,000 people in India's northeast, receives about 11.4 meters (450 in) of rain each year. Cherrapunji is the wettest place on Earth, but erosion and increased runoff caused by deforestation mean that its wells empty during the dry season. Lacking a potable freshwater supply, people buy water from tanker trucks.

Failure is business as usual in Cherrapunji, but climate change will make it worse. Storage will be less adequate, roads will get washed out more often, and the lack of insurance will be even more noticeable. The people of Cherrapunji will live a less-secure, lower-quality life until they can reduce their impact on forest resources and demand for water. Continued inaction may turn the people of Cherrapunji into climate refugees. This is already happening in Africa's Sahel region, where stronger droughts and floods are disrupting food production. According to UNICEF, 225,000 children per year die of malnutrition in the southern Sahelian countries of Burkina Faso, Chad, Mali, Mauritania and Niger. Many people in the region are permanently dependent on emergency food aid. Millions of them will migrate if that short-term aid ends.

People in the developing world lack the resources to deal with climate change or bad weather. The Indian Ocean will probably swallow the Maldives; flooding endangers 160 million Bangladeshis. What will happen? The competent government of the Maldives is making plans to resettle on dry land. The incompetent government of Bangladesh can hardly cope with current conditions. People in the developed world may need to live a bit further back from the beach, in a house on stilts and a better roof, but their biggest problem is going to come from the direct and indirect costs of disruption in the developing world. Supply chains will be disrupted; violence will escalate; food supplies will be stretched or blocked; and desperate people will try to escape their incompetent and corrupt governments.

Good governance results in prosperity and development and determines the difference between coping and panic. Residents of the developed world are going to become experts in governance, whether they like it or not. They need to examine whether their governments are assisting or fighting corruption and incompetence in the developing world. The US supports corrupt governments in Pakistan and (until early 2011) Egypt. The French support corrupt governments in West Africa. The Germans make trade deals with corrupt governments in Iran and Russia. The list goes on. These deals result in strategic and commercial advantages for politicians and business-men, but their cost to citizens — in developed and developing countries — is rising.

We live in interesting times

Climate change is not going to improve life. The weather is going to have more variation, temperatures are going up, and sea levels are rising. We are going to face more problems in more places. Although some people claim money, insurance and machines will solve the problem, everyone agrees that it's not going to be fun. And it may be worse than we expect. What if the levees built to withstand 99 years of storms fail every five years? What if our neighbors who failed to prepare come looking for help? With guns?

We need to change our expectations of weather patterns and strengthen our institutions to adapt to greater variation, unexpected events and emerging weaknesses. Rising risk and uncertainty mean that data-driven models are going to be less accurate; cultural and social institutions are going to be strained in unexpected ways. Adaptation to climate change and higher variation in weather should aim for robustness: better infrastructure, stronger communities, improved insurance and more self-control. The relative costs and benefits of these approaches will determine their shares in the mix of responses, but all of them will work better without government subsidies to risky behavior. Finally, we need to remember that climate change is a global phenomenon. We can prepare for its direct impacts, but we must also prepare for the indirect impacts that we will experience because others are too lazy, poor or corrupt to prepare or cope.

CHAPTER 11

A human right to water

The human right to water is useless when governments are corrupt or incompetent. Turn human rights into property rights; all citizens will benefit from incentives that encourage better water services.

The World Health Organization (WHO) estimates that 2.8 million annual deaths can be attributed to problems with water supply, sanitation and hygiene. Will a human right to water prevent those deaths? Perhaps not. First, 99.96 percent of people already have enough water to live; the other 0.04 percent die from dirty water, not a lack of water. So the right should be for *clean* water. Second, who will pay to deliver these rights? Third, who will enforce a human right to water if corrupt or incompetent governments fail to deliver? After all, the human right to food declared in Article 25, Section 1 of the 1948 Universal Declaration of Human Rights has not kept more than a billion people from living with hunger or prevented 36 million annual deaths from a lack of food.

This chapter addresses these questions and the barriers to getting water to people. It suggests a different solution to the rights-delivery quandary that converts rights from expensive obligations into valuable property rights. Property rights make it possible to use markets to efficiently allocate water among competing uses while generating income for citizen-owners that will allow them to pay the cost of delivering a basic allocation of clean water — and perhaps earn a tidy income.

Rights

Negative rights (such as a right to free speech) provide guarantees that cannot be taken away; positive rights (such as a right to water) create obligations that must be delivered. It costs nothing to allow more people to speak, but the cost of water service rises with pop-

ulation. President Roosevelt's "Four Freedoms" illustrate the differences. In 1941, he proclaimed that Americans should have freedoms
of speech, of religion, from want, and from fear. The first two are
easy to deliver (by not interfering), but it's probably impossible to save
everyone from their subjective, immeasurable wants and fears.

That said, the right to drinking water among nomadic people probably predates the right to land. By tradition, communities that dug
wells and managed them as common property would provide drinking
water to the needy. The tradition of giving water as charity appears in
the Torah and Old Testament. Isaiah 55:1 says:

> Ho, every one that thirsteth, come ye to the waters, and
> he that hath no money; come ye, buy, and eat; yea, come,
> buy wine and milk without money and without price.

While this verse supports the idea that those with thirst should be
able to drink without money, the last words ("buy wine and milk without
money and without price") squares the circle of how it was possible to
give away water or wine or milk. It refers to the tradition of donation
for the benefit of others as a way of giving thanks. There was no free
lunch for the poor; someone paid for the milk that the poor would then
"buy without money."

Alas, the verse omits this accounting, leading modern readers to
claim the existence of free lunches 2,500 years ago justifies them
today. The UN General Assembly seemed to be looking for one in a
July 2010 resolution that:

> Declares the right to safe and clean drinking water and
> sanitation as a human right that is essential for the full
> enjoyment of life and all human rights;

> Calls upon States and international organizations to pro-
> vide financial resources, capacity-building and technol-
> ogy transfer, through international assistance and coop-
> eration, in particular to developing countries, in order to
> scale up efforts to provide safe, clean, accessible and af-
> fordable drinking water and sanitation for all.

Their nonbinding call for financial resources sounds like the rancher
who is "all hat and no cattle" — a great promise that can't be delivered.

But why is the General Assembly making a resolution about water
when it can't even deliver food promised under Article 25? Perhaps

because water services are usually delivered by bureaucratic monopolies that politicians and activists can try to direct. It's much harder to command farmers selling food in markets.

The contrast between food and water is instructive. More people die from a lack of food than water (36 million vs. 2.8 million) but fewer people are hungry (1 billion) than lack access to "improved water and sanitation sources" (884 million and 2.5 billion, respectively). These inputs produce equivalent outputs: the global loss in DALYs (disability-adjusted life years) for diarrhoeal diseases is double the count for all forms of nutritional deficiency. Given the complexity of turning water into food that must be transported, traded and prepared, these numbers show a relative success in addressing hunger. Perhaps more people would get water services if they were delivered in markets the way food is?

Water markets frighten people who conflate the fact that people die without water into a fear that people will die if any water is bought and sold. But does a human right to water conflict with the potential to treat water as a commodity to be bought and sold? Not if we treat some water as a lifeline right but allocate the rest in markets. How much would fall into each category?

According to the WHO, minimum lifeline water is 20 liters per capita per day (lcd) but other estimates claim 135 lcd (approximately 36 gallons per person per day) is necessary for adequate human, economic and social development. Using the higher number, we can separate individual water consumption into a lifeline need of 135 lcd and lifestyle demand for additional quantities. (Note the word pairs, lifeline and lifestyle, need and demand.) What's interesting is that every country in the world has more than 135 lcd of supply. It seems that the access-to-water problem is driven more by inadequate distribution than insufficient supply.

With these ideas in mind, this chapter will explore the dimensions, debates and mechanisms for delivering a human right to water. The next section examines the failure to turn a human right to water into delivered water. The rest of the chapter will explore the potential of using property rights to improve water services to the poor. The basic idea is that citizens with water rights can rent their water flows for money and use that money to pay for their water service. The conventional wisdom is that water flows uphill towards money. Property rights will help the poor pull that money to the top of their hill.

Table 6: Countries with a constitutional right to water, year of enactment of that right, share of the population with access to an improved water supply in the base year and 2006, Human Development Index rank in 2007, and government effectiveness rank in 2008. Countries with "*" do not have complete data for analysis.

	Year of right	Base Access	2006 Access	HDI	Governance
Colombia	1991	89	93	77	85
DR Congo*	2007	45	46	176	210
Ecuador	1998	80	95	80	180
Ethiopia*	1994	13	42	171	128
Gambia	1996	85	86	168	163
Guatemala	1985	79	96	122	133
Iran	1989	92	95	88	160
Kenya	2005	51	57	147	144
Nigeria	1999	50	47	158	184
Panama	1999	92	92	60	84
Philippines	1987	83	93	105	96
South Africa	1996	83	93	129	53
Spain* (regions)	2006	100	100	15	43
Uganda	1995	49	64	157	136
Uruguay*	2004	100	100	50	67
Venezuela*	1999	90	n/a	58	176
Zambia	1996	53	58	164	150

Human rights in water

A meaningful constitutional right to water should have an impact. One way to test for such an impact is to compare statistics for "access to an improved water supply" before the right to water is added to the country's constitution with post-amendment numbers. Table 6 lists countries that guarantee a human right to water, their access to water in a "base year" that varies by country (usually before the right was enacted), and access to water in 2006 (the most recent year for data). After removing countries with data problems (marked with "*"), we have 12 countries where the share of the population with access to an improved water supply increased from 74 percent in the base year to 81 percent in 2006.

That's a positive move, but did it result from a human right or some other factor? It's very hard to use statistics to measure the impact of a change, especially with so few countries, but I tried to do so by comparing these countries with countries at similar levels of economic development (GDP per capita). Base year access in similar countries increased from 77 percent to 82 percent in 2006. The good news is that countries that added rights improved access by 2 percent more;

the bad news is that this difference is probably not due to rights. Indeed, the correlation between access in the base year and access in 2006 is 94 percent in countries that added rights and 97 percent in matched countries that did not, which means access in 2006 basically depends on access in an earlier year — not the absence or existence of human rights to water.

Access to water (let alone access to clean water) requires more than rights; it requires money and a functioning government. Most countries in Table 6 have low ranks in the Human Development Index (HDI) and governance. Countries with low HDI scores have citizens who are unhealthy, uneducated and poor, which makes it hard for them to help themselves. Low ranks in governance mean that their corrupt rulers are unlikely to help them.

Politicians may be making constitutional promises that bureaucrats cannot deliver, because they don't usually deliver much. Transparency International devoted a large portion of its 2008 annual report on governance and corruption to the water sector, giving many examples of provision failure and the disproportionate impact of that failure on the poor. Failure may persist because these bureaucrats and their corrupt bosses can blame outside factors such as the weather, irresponsible customers, lazy engineers, the gods, and so on. But what about the dog that didn't bark? Countries with good HDI and governance values rarely appear in Table 6. Developed countries do not need a human right to water because their citizens already have access to water.

How can we expand access to clean water among residents of developing countries who lack functioning governments? Maybe we can use markets and property rights to deliver water — in the same way that markets deliver bottles of refreshing Coca-Cola pretty much everywhere in the world and mobile phone service to two-thirds of the world's poor. The first step is to give each citizen a property right in his nation's water wealth. The next step is to allow some rights to be traded for cash that can be used to pay the cost of water service. The next section discusses the details.

Property rights

Article 17 of the Universal Declaration of Human Rights states that "Everyone has the right to own property alone as well as in association with others." Note that the Declaration talks about the right to own property (a negative right to be left intact), not the right to property. Property rights are different from human rights in two important ways: property rights can be alienated, but human rights cannot; governments must protect property rights, but they must deliver human rights.

As our discussion shifts from a human right to water to a property right in water, we need to understand whether water can be owned as property and (if so) whether such commodification is harmful to others. For one example in Oregon, the answers are yes and no: property rights and community values combined to produce a suitable reallocation that also resolved a conflict over the Umatilla Indian tribe's right to traditional water flows. The court's recognition of those rights meant farmers had to leave water in the river for salmon. Facing a fight between recent uses and new legal rights, farmers and Indians decided to pursue a middle path, negotiating a sharing agreement to maintain salmon populations while allowing irrigation to continue. Such an outcome would not be possible without the reassignment of property rights (which aided the tribe) and commodity status of water (which aided the farmers). A strict refusal to recognize rights or allow quantitative division of the resource would have left both sides worse off.

Although some argue against the morality of water (or land or labor) being commodified as property, most people embrace the idea of exchanging land or labor for other goods of value, even as they treat land and labor differently. It's ok to rent and sell land, but it's not ok to sell labor: that's slavery.

What about water? If we agree that a property right in water represents a permanent share of renewable water that originates in a location or a temporary quantity of water that can be moved elsewhere, then we can see that people could own water in one place but also rent water flows to others. It's possible to sell rights, of course, but sales can result in mistakes that last a lifetime, reallocations that are too much too fast, or a backlash against the uncertainty or possibility or either. Knowing this, let's start small, with markets for renting annual flows (sometimes called "selling water").

Ownership rights or use rights?

Most people forget the people own water and the state distributes the usufruct rights to use water to maximize its social value (in theory). For most of history, citizen-owners have not paid attention to how their water was used, but increasing scarcity raises the importance of allocation. People in the developed world want to know that water goes to environmental protection or food production; people in the developing world want water for drinking, cooking and cleaning.

The end of abundance means allocations by the state are less likely to match citizen preferences. It also means citizens will be more interested in exercising their ownership rights. But citizens can't just take "their" water; few people directly consume their share of national water wealth. Most citizens will rent their rights (sell the flows) to farmers, fishermen, environmentalists and businessmen who use them to produce value.

Some people worry about selling flows that are necessary for life. This concern can be addressed by dividing ownership into "lifeline rights" that are inalienable, fixed and equal to 135 lcd for every person and alienable "trade rights" that vary with supply and adjust for changes in population. Thus each citizen may get 10,000 lcd of trade rights in year one, 9,800 lcd in year two and 10,500 in year three, depending on precipitation, population and scientific estimates of how much water is free to move around. Trade water is rented, not sold, to protect owners from getting fooled into selling their water too cheaply and communities from drying out. This temporal safety could be augmented by a volumetric ceiling on exports from each watershed that could be relaxed over time, as communities learn about the impacts of exports.[1]

How much water falls into each category? Using the definition and data for "renewable water" supplied by the United Nations Environmental Program, Canadians would get 135 lcd as an inalienable lifeline right and still have 239,265 lcd to allocate as they please. Although that number seems preposterously large, the numbers in water-scarce Israel (with 611 lcd of renewable water) would be 135 lcd for lifeline water and 476 lcd for trade water. Total renewable supplies are 64,100 lcd in Australia, 4,300 lcd in Haiti, 4,200 lcd in Somalia and 27,500 lcd in the US. As mentioned earlier, these volumes would change with precipitation and population.

Property rights in water do not automatically come with a right to delivery. Delivery requires an expensive network that could be regulated as natural monopoly charging a "common carriage" price to everyone. Buyers and sellers of water flows would use the network to complete their trades.

---

[1] Trade water merely refers to water that is traded; it does not refer to the virtual water embedded in traded commodities.

Supply from millions of owners would probably be managed in a fiduciary mechanism similar to the one in the mutual fund (unit trust) industry, where managers are paid to sell water that individuals own but may never see. These managers would not be bureaucrats with job security. They would be competing for business, with their past performance results available to all. This trading system may sound complicated or even impossible to implement in poorer countries, but remember that technology makes mass markets easier to run — residents of these countries already use mobile phones for shopping, banking and money transfers.

Private or public management

Ownership will not mean much without delivery. Private, public and community delivery organizations could buy water on the market; take delivery on site (lake or groundwater) or through a network (surface water); and sell suitably treated water to their customers at prices that reflected the cost of raw water, treatment, transport and service. This trading system is simpler than the current system in which delivery organizations are also responsible for finding water or procuring water rights. Now they would operate their systems; markets would address supplies and prevent shortages. Most customers would pay for their drinking water with income from water sales to industrial, agricultural and environmental interests.

Chapter 4 explored how private or public monopolies can provide poor service. Markets for water will clarify the value of water and increase competition over delivery. This competition will not just take place among existing delivery organizations; the transparency of markets will encourage nontraditional organizations to get into water management, one of the least innovative business sectors. The industry would be transformed from a group of geographical monopolies that source and deliver water to captive customers into an ecosystem of numerous sellers and delivery organizations competing to deliver water to customers using a common-carriage network. This system, already partially established in England, would look familiar — like many stores selling goods that are delivered to consumers by competing shipping companies using the same road system.

Is this just a property grab?

This discussion of human and property rights has so far ignored the rights of current water users. Table 1 shows that most of the "developed" water removed from natural sources and consumed goes to irrigation (the rest is consumed by the municipal and industrial sectors). Although most of these historic users paid (or continue to pay) little or nothing for their rights to divert and consume water, they certainly see their usufruct rights as valuable. The removal or revocation of their rights would mean that most would have to end operations, abandon useless equipment, and sell land at a fraction of its former value as the site of a working farm, operating factory or habitable community.

These facts force us to consider the transition to ownership of water rights by citizens as a gradual process that compensates current users for their loss of usufruct rights while ensuring that the water flows connected with usufruct rights can be purchased or rented. The rights of existing holders could be reduced in 5 or 10 percent increments over a transition of 10–20 years, allowing the share of marketed water to grow as it shifted from "free" to purchased. This gradual regime could also be implemented by selling all water flows and then sharing revenue between old and new owners (old owners receive 90 percent of revenue in year one, 80 percent in year two, and so on) — a variation of all-in-auctions discussed in Chapter 5.

These options are relevant mostly because of the disruption in asset values that would occur in places where land values reflect water rights more than location, soil quality and infrastructure, but disruption will be weaker in places where farmers compete only with each other. Low prices, combined with farmers' access to water delivery infrastructure, means land values will drop by a bit (reflecting the loss of usufruct rights) but not by as much as they would if water supplies were simply cut off. Values for good land that previously had poor water rights may even rise, since those willing to pay could get reliable water in markets. We can predict that some farmers will not be able to compete with environmental, urban or industrial buyers in a market. Although that result would harm their businesses, it would also reflect reallocation of the people's water to higher social and economic priorities and benefit the new owners of water rights — the poor who are more interested in maximizing the value of their water assets and earning income for purchasing reliable water service.

Trading and valuing water

Trade will increase the value of water in use. In most parts of the world, water's price reflects the cost of delivery (wells, pipes, treatment, and so on), not water's value in use. This partial-cost pricing leads to shortage and misallocation. Water prices in a market would reflect value and scarcity and balance demand and supply — eliminating shortages to users with valuable uses.

Recall that this market is for trade water, so we do not have to worry about the poor going thirsty. The allocation of water to high-value urban, agricultural, industrial and environmental uses will not just be good for maximizing the social value of water — it will deliver the greatest income to the poor who are net sellers.

Agricultural interests pay very little for water today because they have usufruct rights or benefit from political favoritism. They will have to pay more (especially if citizens put more water into nature). Such a reallocation may reduce water for food, but it's not as devastating as an environmental drought or bureaucratic order that interrupts supply. Farmers will just treat water as an input to be purchased at prices that reflect real conditions instead of bureaucratic rules.

But what about local demand and supply (im)balances? Let's examine a few scenarios.

A populated dry area will import water from elsewhere. People would have to pay the cost of delivery, but it is assumed that they can sell enough trade water to pay that cost (or move somewhere where they can afford water service). Farmers would have to spend a lot of cash. A place with few people and lots of water will export what's not used locally for production or the environment. Exports will vary with owners' private decisions of how much they value the water in place (protecting an environment that they like) or elsewhere (adding to their cash wealth). Environmentalists can augment these opinions by paying owners to keep water in place. Although some may object to the implication that the environment has no rights to water or the idea that water will be left in the environment only as a result of an owner's choice (compensated or not), this implication is consistent with reality: people already decide how much water stays in the environment.[2]

Location location location

Rights should be administered at a level as close to watershed scale as possible, even if the watershed includes multiple legal, political and cultural boundaries. That said, water rights need to be allocated at the national level, where political and legal tools are strongest. Tradable rights within a country would be allocated within each watershed, perhaps even to specific locations on a river or other source. Owners would then decide if they want to sell their water or leave it in place.

---

[2] It's also possible to exclude minimum environmental flows from trade water rights.

Trading within watersheds would be subject to limitations on infrastructure capacity and damage to neighbors. Trade would also allow farmers and environmentalists to compete over how much water was left in streams or taken out.

Allocation, trading and reallocation could be completely automated, but bureaucrats would need to set total quantities within a basin based on physical and hydrological facts — as they already do for Australia's water markets. Individuals would buy and sell water with simple trading rules. Americans, for example, face the prospect of trading 27 m^3 per day (about 10 million liters per year), so they could use simple rules such as "sell up to 50 percent of my water in protected watersheds when the price exceeds $2 per m^3."

Spatial rights could be automatically redistributed every year to distribute the benefits of ownership (values vary by location) throughout the population. It might make sense to limit rights to the people within a watershed or limit markets to buyers within a watershed. Exports from a watershed would obviously be constrained to the lesser of infrastructure capacity and ecological sustainability.

Although the correct specification and distribution of rights might seem a logistical and hydrological disaster-in-waiting, it's also possible that a transparent process with significant participation by putative owners would produce better outcomes than the current norm of favoring political and economic elites (especially in developing countries). The combination of ownership and management within the citizen incentivizes learning and effort, unlike the current situation where management is delegated to politicians and water managers who can make biased or corrupt allocations without facing punishment for failing to maximize the value of the people's water.

The distribution of rights to many citizens does not just create the basis for a market (because separated owners and users must trade), but the basis for an efficient market. In a market with few buyers and/or sellers, trading volume is lower and transaction costs higher because traders use their market power to distort prices. Prices are accurate and responsive to supply and demand in a mass market. Citizens will allocate water according to their views on how water should be used, taking back the power that they delegated to their representatives. Allocation by price would also favor buyers who could increase their water supply by paying more.

As an example, consider the Colorado River, which passes through seven states on its way to Mexico. Flows on the Colorado vary widely, but let's say that the Colorado's 15 million acre feet (about 18,500 GL) are shared among all 300 million Americans. Each one would allocate his 170 lcd of trade water to in-stream flows, favored users, the market, or a combination of the three. This system would require the same hydrological data as today, a basic web interface for allocation decisions, a reasonable auction and clearing platform, and much less bureaucratic or political input on where water "needed" to go.

Private property helps the poor

Governments everywhere assure citizens (and the poor among them) that bureaucratic and political allocations are in their best interest. Sometimes that's true, but why not let the real owners decide how to allocate their property? Citizens with tradable shares can choose how to allocate their water and turn what economist Hernando de Soto calls "dead capital" into working wealth. Even better, property rights and markets may break an appalling record of poor service to billions of people.

Author and entrepreneur Jamie Workman provides a useful case study of how ownership worked in South Africa. Landless poor non-white laborers were given new water rights; they contributed these rights and sweat equity to a joint venture with local white farmers who contributed land and expertise. Because both parties shared equity and profits in the project, both sides worked harder, and overall profits increased. The nonwhites became wealthier and learned how to farm; whites increased production and profits. Ownership can spur equity and efficiency, empowerment and enrichment.

A market will divert tradable commodity water to its highest and best use, benefitting buyers and sellers but also the poor who suffer disproportionately from corruption and small businesses and farms that do not have political power. In that process of reallocation, a price for water will emerge that will reveal values and reduce waste that grows more costly with scarcity. Prices will make it easy for citizens to push their agent-brokers to maximize the value of their assets; those who fail will be replaced.

Let the people control their water

The best way to deliver a human right to water is to give humans enough money to buy water in a competitive market. The cheapest way to give every citizen money is to allow that citizen to benefit from the value of his share of the national water patrimony. A property rights solution in which citizens and markets replace bureaucrats and politicians in allocating water requires systems to manage data and water trades, but these systems can be scaled — from annual, paper declarations to hourly computerized clearinghouses. More important, it recognizes a human right to water as the combination of an inalienable right to a certain per capita quantity of lifeline water and variable allocation of alienable rights that can be sold for environmental, urban, agricultural or other uses — whatever suits the owner's preferences and pocketbook.

CHAPTER 12

Water wars

Water is hard to capture in conflict. Politicians making subjective allocations of scarce water do not want market allocations. Most water conflicts are about money, not survival.

Does the end of abundance mean the start of water wars? Fights attract onlookers, and few journalists can resist the temptation to drop an old cliché attributed to Mark Twain — "Whiskey is for drinking, and water is for fighting over" — into stories on water scarcity. The truth is that water scarcity doesn't usually lead to conflict. Conflict results when political allocations of water leave winners with abundance and losers with shortage. The problem is not a lack of water as much as a lack of water management.

In Sudan's Darfur, for example, drought may contribute to conflict, but it doesn't cause it. The Sahel (a 5,000 km band between the Sahara and sub-Saharan Africa that includes Darfur) has been in drought for 30 years, but most of the region is at peace. Violence in Darfur results from political and ethnic disputes (perhaps over local oil reserves) as well as local institutions that are too weak to manage access to land and clean water or maintain peace among local tribes with access to cheap weapons. Ironically, conflict can sometimes result when water is abundant. Herdsmen in the Horn of Africa fight more over grazing land when water is abundant and less in drought — rain gives them more food and more time for fighting.

Is conflict over resources inevitable? No. Journalist Thomas Friedman espouses the "Dell Theory of Conflict Prevention," which states that countries that participate in the same global supply chain [for Dell computers] are unlikely to fight one another. This idea restates the conventional wisdom of economics (countries will get richer through trading than fighting), but it doesn't succeed when politicians, generals and war profiteers are happy to sacrifice everyone's trade gains for their own power. That helps us understand why ethnic leaders in Yugoslavia tore their country apart, breaking social, economic and logistical links that tied their republics together for personal glory and power. The same is true for Ethiopia and Eritrea, Thailand and Cambodia, and other country pairs. So Friedman's theory breaks down when leaders sacrifice the majority for their own interests. It also breaks down when conflict offers greater rewards than cooperation (as when the US took Alta California and New Mexico in the Mexican-American War of 1848) or when the passion fueled by nationalism, ideology, revenge, or religious fervor ignores benefit-cost analysis (as with the wars on drugs and terror).

Are we going to have water wars like we have oil wars? No, yes and maybe. The next three sections explain why water wars are not the same as oil wars, why special interests can still cause water wars, and why conflict over water allocation within a country is driven more by political games than water shortages.

It's hard to capture water in a war

"Water wars!" screamed a recent story about an attack on a water tanker in Sudan. The headline was wrong: the gunmen did not want water; they wanted to deny water to refugees. Their tactical assault on a point of vulnerability was part of a strategy to control territory. Fights to capture water are rare — probably because of water's unique properties.

Most water sources are common-pool goods that are owned by none but depleted — in quantity or quality — by all. Common-pool goods can be protected from over-exploitation in three ways. Regulation works when rules and enforcement are effective. Privatization — dividing the commons into exclusive shares that individuals manage according to their preferences — can also work. The commons can also be managed as communal property, using rules and norms to ensure that everyone gets a fair share without over-exploiting the resource.

But these methods can fail. Mismanagement can lead to shortage and conflict over allocations, but conflict is more likely to be settled by compromise than an outright fight. The cost of conflict must be weighed against benefits of controlling a resource that has a low value per unit and is vulnerable to contamination (losers can poison the waters). Conflict isn't necessarily final: it will resume if mismanagement does not balance demand and supply. A long-term solution that prevents scarcity from turning into shortage will deliver sustainability and eliminate conflict.

A fight over oil is different. First, the oil is usually extracted and sold elsewhere, making it easy to convert into cash; water resources are not so easy to distribute or replace with cash. Second, the winners in a conflict over oil can eject losers without fear that they will destroy oil supplies. Saddam Hussein's army tried to destroy Kuwait's oil fields when it retreated in the 1991 Gulf War. Massive fires burned for some time, but production returned within a year. Disputes over transboundary waters (rivers, lakes, aquifers) are more likely to be resolved by peaceful negotiation than arms because it's easy to damage water quality, rendering the water useless for winners and losers.

The lack of hot wars over water resembles the pattern in the Cold War. The US and USSR fought proxy wars and propaganda battles, but they never got into a hot war with nuclear weapons. Many credit this outcome to the danger of mutual assured destruction (MAD) — the combination of a nuclear attack and counterattack that would incinerate both sides in a nuclear fire. Although MAD nearly ended human life on Earth a few times (*Dr. Strangelove* gave one fake example; the Cuban Missile Crisis was an authentic close call), it also worked. MAD prevented a bully from attacking for fear of being vaporized. Perhaps the best part about MAD was its agnostic nature — each side claimed the other was a bully, but both knew that they could not bully without suffering. It's the risk of MAD, a destroyed common water supply, which has created a strong reluctance to fight over water.

Some conflict is not caused by scarcity

But isn't water scarcity at the root of conflict in places like the Middle East? No. Conflict is less about drinking water and survival than irrigation, agricultural production and land values. Israel started the 1967 Six Day War as a preemptive action to avoid invasion by neighboring Arab armies, but it also took the opportunity to seize water sources from Syria, the West Bank, and Gaza. Israel seized Syria's Golan Heights and control over the Sea of Galilee (they call it Kinneret), which now provides a significant share of its water supply. Recent drought has left hundreds of thousands of Syrian farmers without enough water to grow their crops. Shortage is probably the result of poor management, drought, and reduced supplies. Syrian farmers would be growing more if Golan water was still flowing to their farms.

Gaza and the West Bank were harmed through the destruction of existing deep wells and prohibition on drilling replacements. Israeli farmers and settlers face no limits on their wells, so they extract water supplies that are too deep for their Palestinian neighbors. This water apartheid is explicit in its goals and obvious in its results: a transfer of water assets from Palestinians to Israelis.

And that's the pity. The water at the center of Israel's national security strategy isn't for drinking; it's for growing food, much of which is exported. Are children in Gaza dying of thirst while Israelis export bananas and oranges? Not exactly. As I mentioned in Chapter 5, two-thirds of Gaza's water goes to Gazan farmers who pay almost nothing for it. Israeli farmers are also subsidized, but Gaza's problems are (literally) homegrown.

Researchers calculate that it would cost about $10 per person per year to solve water shortages in the region. Ten dollars seems a bargain, so why does conflict persist? Perhaps farmers with a small share of the population and a small part of the economy are driving their countries to fight military, diplomatic and economic battles so they can grow wheat for patriotic pita bread. Or perhaps politicians and nationalists are using water conflict as an excuse to avoid peace that they don't really want. Or perhaps both groups are happy to keep the water wars going.

The bottom line is that the conflict for water in the Levant results from policies that deliver cheap water to farmers, not a life or death struggle.

It's easy to find other claims of greedy neighbors taking water. India and Pakistan routinely accuse each other of stealing water. Downstream nations on the Mekong claim China's water diversions are drying out paddy fields and decimating fisheries. The US and Mexico routinely squabble over flows in the Rio Grande and Colorado rivers. Singapore and Malaysia, Turkey and Syria — the list goes on.

I'm not saying that low flows aren't happening or that there's no harm. I am saying that these outcomes result from politicians saying yes yes yes to domestic water demands and then blaming shortages on foreigners. Better management of local resources would result in less talk of water wars and more talk about sustainability and mutually beneficial exchanges of water, money and expertise. But that would require politicians and bureaucrats to say no to special interests and yes to the interests of most citizens.

Politicians can benefit from conflict over water

Part II began with a description of the principal-agent problem and the importance of the agent's internal desire to work on behalf of the principal. In the water sector, politicians and bureaucrats act as agents making rules and determining water allocations on behalf of citizen-principals. Why? First, because water is often in a common pool, requiring some form of political coordination among various claimants to that pool. Second, because water affects public goods (keeping an environment healthy, for example), which are often coordinated by political forces. Third, water suppliers often have legal and natural monopolies over a local population; some form of political and regulatory oversight is necessary to prevent exploitation.

That doesn't mean that politicians and bureaucrats always deliver efficiency and equity. They can accidentally misallocate water based on incorrect or incomplete knowledge. They must reconcile demands among claimants who prefer opaque political negotiations to transparent market transactions. These claimants are similar in believing they can use a combination of guile, bribery and legal manipulation to their advantage, but they differ in success.

Take the common case of a dispute between farmers and environmentalists. Farmers, for example, may want to increase diversions from a river, while environmentalists want to reduce them. Farmers in the past could argue for more water, but environmental laws and activists now oppose them. The usual outcome is a stalemate that may prolong an unsustainable status quo.

Politicians and bureaucrats can resolve these conflicts, but they hesitate. They may not want to work more for the opportunity to lose popularity, make a decision that relies on a subjective judgment call, or end to lobbying from participants in the conflict. This last option is a reminder that vain or corrupt politicians and bureaucrats tend to favor their own priorities over fairness and efficiency. In the worst case, they will encourage shortage and conflict as a means of increasing their importance, powers of allocation, and access to bribes. Recall from Chapter 7 that these bribes take place in the developing and developed world. In the developing world, bribes may be cash, cars or consultancies. In the developed world, they may be second jobs, special perks or sexy assistants. In either case, politicians abuse their role as guardians of the public trust for personal gain.

It's unfortunate that water users sometimes encourage this behavior. As mentioned earlier, they prefer opaque subjective allocations because they hope to gain some unfair advantage over opponents. The zero-sum nature of political decisions (I win means you lose) feeds their greed, since they think that the right word (or bribe) in the right place can mean they get everything, and their opponents nothing. Unfortunately, their beliefs and behavior are not baseless — history and contemporary events provide many examples of windfall gains from political water allocations. But those examples hide two big problems: the cost of resources that are wasted in the lobbying process and the loss in social welfare that results from an inefficient allocation.

A change from paralysis, conflict and corruption requires better institutions, politicians and regulators. It may be difficult to persuade those in charge to reduce their power, but enough attention from citizens (and customers) makes reform possible. Informed customers may succeed in changing institutions of consensus (a là Ostrom). If they fail, they can try to change the rules to move bulk water allocations to a market where people truck and barter in commodified resources (a là Coase). Markets may be brutal in their logic (money wins), but at least they are simple and transparent. In the long run, they tend to create more benefits for more people because they improve allocation efficiency and flexibility.

The transition from political to market allocation requires that bulk water rights be divided, commodified and distributed. This division can be contentious (perhaps due to historic uses or rights), but it can take place in many ways (two examples are all-in-auctions in Chapter 5 and reallocation to citizens in Chapter 11). Markets reconcile different opinions, set prices that signal value, and allocate goods to highest and best use. These tasks are hard for well-intentioned politicians, but corrupt politicians won't even bother.

A case study in zero-sum behavior

It's important to remember that the possibility of a win-win outcome doesn't mean it's inevitable. This is true in markets (where willing buyers and sellers may not be able to agree on a trade), but it's more common in political venues where it's hard to discover and align values and votes.

In the summer of 2009, I ran an experiment among participants at a workshop on games and climate change at UC Berkeley. Participants were the kinds of people — if not the exact same people — who might serve as technical advisers in high-level climate change negotiations. I began the game with a quick explanation of the differ-ence between game theory and conflict theory. Economists, political scientists and mathematicians use game theory to understand how to win games with rules (like chess or poker). The adherents of conflict theory come from more diverse backgrounds; they are evolutionary scientists, lawyers, military strategists, and so on. Conflict theory is useful when rules do not exist or matter (as when someone brings a gun to a chess match). Negotiations under conflict theory are hard to resolve in the absence of shared institutions because no authority can force an outcome. They work only when countries find some common ground for agreement.

Most participants in the workshop were using game theory to de-scribe and plan for climate change negotiations, but they knew that my experiment (like reality) had no deciding authority. Participants were divided into team A(merica), C(hina), and R(est of the World). Teams A and C were supposed to negotiate a climate change treaty. Poten-tial gains from trade suggested that an agreement could be reached. The real problem would come in dividing those gains. That's why I cre-ated an escape hatch: Team R would choose either A or C's proposal if A and C could not agree. This outside option meant that we would not wait all day, but it also gave A and C the option to circumvent an uncooperative partner by forming a side agreement with outsiders.

Team China proposed a global cap-and-trade system, with emis-sions permits allocated according to population. Team America pro-posed a global carbon tax, with revenues distributed to countries ac-cording to their gross domestic product. C and A were far apart. Af-ter some negotiation, the proposals started to overlap, but the teams couldn't reach an agreement. Team America added one feature to its proposal: it would give Team R "aid" for R's vote. Faced with no bet-ter offer from China, the Rest of the World took the bribe and Team America won.

The moral of the story is that conflicts may not be resolved in favor of the best idea, fairness or efficiency. A corrupt judge might favor his pocketbook over his community. It's important to pay attention to who is voting for what. Does this apply to water? Yes! Politicians can use economic, hydrological and engineering analysis to negotiate water allocations within and among countries, but they may also favor their selfish or biased interests. Fortunately, most water negotiations are local, which makes it easier for the community to participate in the process and influence its outcome.

We're all in it together

This final chapter is about water wars, a term that's inaccurate in the fact that few countries fight over water. Most fights occur inside countries or political jurisdictions, where the end of abundance has brought competing demands into conflict. Politicians and bureaucrats who make allocation decisions over water are key players in these conflicts. They benefit from lobbying by interest groups that spend time and money to get access to scarce water. This process is opaque and wasteful, but most politicians are in no hurry to delegate their power to pick winners to markets, auctions or other transparent mechanisms.

The end of abundance means business as usual cannot continue. Shortages are increasingly costly to people, the economy and the environment. Political and bureaucratic institutions can perhaps be reformed under the influence of community priorities, but they are hard to design and manage effectively. Markets are simpler to design and operate; their prices transparently reflect values, reduce misallocation, and turn conflict into trading opportunities.

We can use markets that treat water as a commodity, or we can use community mechanisms that treat water as a local resource for local benefits. It's not the tool that matters but the outcome. We, the people, want to maximize the benefits of our scarce water to our communities and ourselves.

Afterword: What you can do

Many water problems (shortages, pollution, misallocation, and so on) can be traced directly to out-of-date policies. Fixing them requires five steps. First, understand when and where clean freshwater is scarce. Second, describe and understand local institutions for managing water. Third, identify who wins and loses with the current system for allocating water and costs. Fourth, get to know the folks who manage water, from source to discharge. After making all these steps, you should have a good idea of what doesn't work and why. Then take the fifth step: change rules and practices to pursue management that's fair and efficient — giving everyone an equal opportunity to acquire some portion of scarce water without adverse impacts on others or the environment. The end of abundance will shape this solution but so will a mix of political, economic, social and environmental concerns. Proportions within the mix will reflect local priorities, and those priorities should translate into an a communal pursuit of a sustainable solution. Any solution or change in management institutions should be implemented in stages to make it easier to respond to surprises.

If you're a water manager, politician, regulator or director, you can restore abundance by investigating these ideas, modifying them for local rules, holding public meetings to explain and create new policies, and implementing ideas via pilot programs.

If you are a citizen, businessman, farmer, environmentalist or activist, you need to get the attention of the people who make decisions and persuade them to consider unfamiliar ideas that may involve additional work or risk.

Some of you will be persuasive enough to cause change on your own. Others will need help in understanding the current system and/or getting in front of the people who make decisions. Sometimes a call is all it takes to change policy; other times one must go to meetings, submit petitions, ask for items to be put on the agenda, and so on. This can get frustrating but remember that it's hard to overturn decades of tradition among workers who rarely communicate with customers or face penalties for poor outcomes.

In addition to these actions, you can educate yourself:

- Read your water bill. Does it make sense? Go to a meeting at your water agency. Talk to the managers and staff. Compare your water consumption with your neighbor's. Try to find out how much water is used (and how much it costs) at your work or school. Look at the capital budget. How much money is spent on infrastructure? How many months or years of supply are kept in storage? Get a home water test kit. Compare your tap water with bottled water.

- If you are a farmer, then calculate how much gross revenue and net profit you make per ML (or acre-foot) of water. Check your water table and water quality against historical records. Compare how much you pay for water (including pumping costs) with neighbors.

- If you are in business, then try to understand your water rates. Do those rates come with guarantees on reliability? What plans are in place to limit system demand in your area? How much do your other locations pay for water? Are those supplies reliable too?

- If you are an environmentalist, then pick a watershed and learn about the regulated and unregulated diversions and return flows on the watershed. How do they compare with flows before human intervention? How have regulations improved or failed to change these flows? What other aspects (land use, forestry, animals, recreation) affect the watershed? Who else is interested in clean water flows?

In all cases, it helps to read, write and talk a lot about the people, places and activities that interest you. Record your ideas, impressions and findings in a blog so that others can learn from — and teach — you. Meet with people to compare notes and debate ideas. Talk to local reporters, politicians, water managers, regulators and bureaucrats about the issues that worry them. Remember that problems and solutions are always local; you need to work with locals.

Remember that water issues are complicated. It's easy for one idea to lead to another, crossing political, academic, historic and geographical boundaries. Sometimes these connections (or the failure to recognize them) clarify the source of a problem or the key to fixing it.

For a deeper philosophical background on the incentives and institutions that affect water, check out these books:

- Jared Diamond: *Collapse* (2005)

- Mancur Olson: *The Logic of Collective Action* (1971)

- Elinor Ostrom, Roy Gardner and James Walker: *Rules, Games, and Common-Pool Resources* (1994)

- Marc Reisner: *Cadillac Desert* (1993)

- Thomas C. Schelling: *The Strategy of Conflict* (1960)

- E.F. Schumacher: *Small Is Beautiful: Economics As If People Mattered* (1973)

- James C. Scott: *Seeing Like a State: How Certain Schemes to Improve the Human Condition Have Failed* (1998)

- Nassim Taleb: *The Black Swan: The Impact of the Highly Improbable* (2007)

- James Q. Wilson: *Bureaucracy: What Government Agencies Do and Why They Do It* (1989) and *The Moral Sense* (1993)

- James G. Workman: *Heart of Dryness: How the Last Bushmen Can Help Us Endure the Coming Age of Permanent Drought* (2009)

What about me? I'll continue to blog at www.aguanomics.com and give public talks, but I am also working on projects to gather data on water prices, water use, and water markets, hopefully using wiki-style solutions that facilitate decentralized cooperation.

Visit www.endofabundance.com for updates, corrections and other materials related to this book.

Feel free to contact me at dzetland@gmail.com.

Thanks for reading!

Acknowledgements

My background in the economics of water

I began my PhD at UC Davis in 2002 with the intention of studying the economics of developing countries, a field that concentrates on government failure, corruption and weak institutions. After an ill-fated attempt to study the cultivation of coca (for cocaine) in Peru, I turned to water in California. I got interested in this topic when my adviser Richard Howitt told me about conflict among members of a water cooperative (the Metropolitan Water District of Southern California, or MWD). I was intrigued. Why would members of a cooperative fight instead of cooperate? In my quest for an answer to this question, I went from one "why?" to another "why?" until I had a narrative of events, decisions, and policies that began more than 100 years before the modern conflict. It took me about three years to assemble this narrative into a PhD dissertation, but that process also helped me understand how to apply institutional analysis to the water sector. The major theme of that study (and the central theme here) is how institutions that fail to change with circumstances will not work very well.

I began blogging as a graduate student because I was interested in communicating with non-economists. My aguanomics blog initially focused on problems like those at MWD, but I soon expanded to other problems, places, and institutions, looking for old patterns and new lessons. Some problems could be solved with easy economics (charging higher prices to reduce landscape irrigation); others adopted solutions from my work with MWD (auctions for farmers like auctions at MWD); but some were totally different and difficult to understand. These problems related to human rights, the environment, water quality, aquifer depletion, bottled water, and so on.

In the course of thinking about these problems, suggesting answers and responding to readers, I tried to integrate insights from engineering, politics, religion, ecology, business and sociology. I made mistakes, borrowed good ideas, and flip-flopped my opinions — always searching for better answers.

This book distills that experience, but it also reflects my opinions on how the world is and should be. It's not perfect, but hopefully it will give you what it gave me — a decent answer to a small but powerful question: why?

Getting to press

This book originated with my aguanomics blog. My writing there attracted the attention of several major publishers in late 2008. After many negotiations, I signed a contract with the University of California Press in June 2009. I completed the first draft in May 2010, got a huge amount of feedback (see below), and submitted a second draft to UC Press in October 2010. After several months, outside reviews and committee meetings, it was clear that we disagreed on the tone and audience for this book. After several attempts to find other publishers (and a steadily receding publication date), I decided to self-publish this book via Aguanomics Press. In doing so, I've gone against conventional wisdom in the academic world (again) and lost the opportunity to work with a team on publication. At the same time, I gained speed, flexibility over the materials and marketing, and the opportunity to shape my message. In the balance of things, I decided to take the risk. I hope that you are happy with the result, and I apologize if any errors or typos remain in the text. Hopefully, those few costs will be worth the benefits of a book that arrives eight months earlier and $10 cheaper than it would have with a traditional press.

Everyone who helped

I'd like to thank the editors who spent time on the manuscript and made many useful suggestions on how to develop the text. Jenny Wapner (UC Press), John Byram (U NM Press) and Emily Davis (Island Press) were helpful; Hannah Love (UC Press) deserves a medal for her help on the book and support when I decided to go it alone.

The majority of the credit for this book goes to the 160,000 people who have spent almost 5,000 hours visiting, reading and commenting on my blog since March 2008. Their attention kept me going. Their emails, comments and guest posts kept me learning.

I began this book for those readers, and I have benefited from their presence. Some people commented on the title; others helped with complex ideas or my poor presentation; but the greatest contribution came from the folks who read, proofed and commented on earlier drafts. They are Keith Agoda, Paul Atwood, Candace Au-Yeung, Dan Bena, Joe Berg, Damian Bickett, Philip Bowles, Kirk Boyd, Michael Campana, Lloyd Carter, Ben Casnocha, Kate Cell, Terry Clark, James Cleaver, Gretchen Cummings, Joseph DiGiorgio, Jan Dougall, Elizabeth Dougherty, Eric Fairfield, Timothy Fitzgerald, John Fleck, J. David Foster, Alberto Garrido, Emily Green, David Green, Noah Hall, Claus Haslauer, Laurie Jackson, George J. Janczyn, Shahram Javey, Steve Kasower, Lynne Kiesling, Carolyn Lowry, Wayne Lusvardi, Scott McKenzie, Josue Medellin-Azuara, Cannon Michael, Robert Morrow, Jeff Mosher, Mohamad Mova Al' Afghani, Dennis O'Connor, Karen Piper, Philip Pohl, Franz Raffensperger, J. David Rankin, Amanda Rice, Andy Rosenberg, Debbie Seiler, Taylor Shipman, Terry Spragg, Josh Stark, Michael Strong, James W. Taylor, Brian Thomas, Michael van der Valk, Paul Wagner, Jay Wetmore, and Michelle Wilber. I thank Sheri for super-fast copyediting and Nico for his help on the cover design (and lots of diverting conversations). A special thanks to Katryn Bowe for last minute proofreading (don't blame her for my remaining typos).[1]

In the larger scheme of my so-called career, I thank Richard Howitt for getting me interested in water, Michael Hanemann for the great opportunity at UC Berkeley, and Dave Sunding for his insights into the dirty world of water policy. Rich Sexton has played a big part as my mentor, nudging me away from the sharper objects while allowing me to run into some of the softer ones.

I am grateful for two years of financial support as a Ciriacy-Wantrup postdoctoral fellow at UC Berkeley and a one month Simon Fellowship at the Property and Environment Research Center (PERC).

On a personal level, I want to thank my father for listening to my rants, my girlfriend Anne for her patience with my midnight scribbling, and my friends for tolerating my water obsession.

I dedicate this book to my mother. She brought me to learning, taught me to ask questions, made it safe to accept mistakes, and showed me how to fight for what I believe in.

---

[1] Yes, it's a fragment. Whatever.

Glossary

acequias: In the American Southwest, a communal water management district with semi-formal rules on water allocation and communal maintenance of common infrastructure. The word comes from the Arabic *as-sāqiya*, which means water conduit. *Acequias* were constructed in Spain during Moorish rule, and the term is still used to refer to these aqueducts.

Appropriative rights: The right to divert water from a source for use elsewhere. Often defined by priority ("first in time, first in right"), a quantity ("x units of flow at this diversion point"), and the requirement of continued use ("use it or lose it").

Aquifer: An underground layer of water-bearing porous stone, earth, or gravel that is often recharged by surface percolation or subsurface flows. If they are not being recharged at all, they are called fossil aquifers (the case for aquifers under the Sahara Desert); if they are being drained faster than they are being recharged, then they are being mined (the case of the Ogallala aquifer in the middle of the US). The extent, volume, and flows of aquifers are hard to accurately survey.

Asymmetric information: One person knowing more than another. In **principal-agent** situations, the principal knows less than the agent about the agent's skill and/or effort, problems of adverse selection and moral hazard, respectively. Asymmetric information can be present in many situations, but it is only important when the information is relevant to the transaction. For example, I may not care how much the coffee server makes per hour, but I do care whether the coffee is caffeinated or not.

Baptists and Bootleggers: A slang term for an unholy alliance that combines moral righteousness with selfish greed to stop a reform that would benefit degenerates (according to the Baptists) and/or the competition (according to the Bootleggers). A Baptists and Bootleggers coalition may also support a harmful change; one example is the coalition of environmentalists and corn-processors that supported a requirement that gasoline contain a minimum share of corn ethanol.

Benefit-cost analysis: A process of making choices that identifies potential actions, assigns benefits and costs (in terms of money, time, happiness, and other qualitative and quantitative factors) to each action, and concludes with the choice of the action that gives the greatest net benefit (benefits minus costs) or benefit yield (benefits divided by costs).

Club good: A **non-rival good** that is **excludable** from other people. A fountain in your backyard, for example.

Collective action problem: A small number of people can do a lot of work that benefits everyone. For example, members of Group A could spend a total of 500 hours to save $100 for each person in Group A and Group B. Members of Group B would get $100 in benefits at no time cost. When given the choice of which group to join, most people will join Group B as **free riders**. The results of this collective action are too few people in Group A, no action, and the continuation of a status quo without savings.

Collective good: A good owned by a group. Community norms and institutions determine if it is overexploited (as a **common-pool good**) or not (as a **club good**). Also known as a social good or common property good.

Common carriage: Charging the same price to everyone who uses the network to deliver goods. Common carriage can apply to water, electricity, roads, postal mail, and so on.

Common-pool good: A **rival good** that anyone can use. A public beach, for example, may be overexploited (as an **open-access good** subject to a **Tragedy of the Commons**) or sustainably managed by **institutions** that do not require formal property rights.

Complements: Two goods that often go together, such that an increase in **demand** for one increases demand for the other.

Thus, an increase in demand for pizza (due to a change in tastes) or quantity demanded (due to lower prices for pizza) can lead to an increase in demand for pizza's complement, beer.

Corruption: The abuse of public office for personal gain. Petit (or petty) corruption happens when an official takes a bribe instead of doing his job (to ignore water quality regulations, for example). Grand corruption happens when an official makes policies that benefit his interests over those of the general public (specifying infrastructure contracts go to a certain subset of domestic companies, for example).

Dead zone: An area in the water without oxygen that supports very little life. Dead zones can be natural (as with the Black Sea's deeper anoxic layer that lacks oxygen), but they are frequently associated with human pollution. The most common case occurs when a heavy fertilizer load in water leads to a bloom of algae that use oxygen through respiration or use oxygen as they decompose after death. Other creatures die without oxygen. Anaerobic bacteria can live in a dead zone, since they do not need oxygen.

Decreasing block rates: Volumetric prices that get cheaper per unit, the more you use.

Demand: Our desire for a good, based on our tastes, wealth and the availability of other goods. Given a baseline demand, an increase in the good's price will lower **quantity demanded** for the good, in what is known as the **law of demand**.

Dirty water: Contaminated water contains more than H_2O but may still be safe. **Polluted** water has enough contamination to be unhealthy to humans or inhibit use — the case with polluted water in a wetlands that kills plant and animal life, for example.

Economies of scale: A larger upfront (fixed) cost can reduce ongoing (variable) costs, so that average cost falls with mass production. A larger dam can store water or generate hydropower at a lower cost per unit. A larger water treatment plant can process wastewater or clean drinking water at a lower cost per unit. Note that capacity will limit economies of scale; too much water can overtop a dam or trigger emergency overflows at a wastewater treatment plant; these are diseconomies of scale.

Elasticity: The change in **quantity demanded** for a good in response to a change in its price. If a rise or fall in the price of a good results in a (proportionately) smaller change in quantity demanded, then demand for that good is said to be "inelastic." If quantity demanded changes by a lot, then demand is said to be "elastic." The steeper the slope of a demand curve, the more inelastic is demand. Demand for drinking water is usually inelastic; demand for water to wash the pavement is usually elastic. In technical terms, these relationships are for "own price elasticity," which is shortened to "price elasticity" or just "elasticity." "Cross-price elasticity" refers to the change in quantity demanded for Good B when the price of Good A changes; "income elasticity" refers to the change in demand for Good A when income changes. Both of these elasticities can be positive, zero, or negative, but price elasticity is negative (**law of demand**). Price elasticity between 0.0 and −1.0 is inelastic, meaning that a 1 percent change in price leads to a less than 1 percent change in quantity demanded. A greater-than-one-percent change in quantity demanded means demand is elastic (negative, with values below −1.0). Elasticity of exactly −1.0 is called "unit elastic."

Environmental goods: Valuable goods that cannot be priced in markets because they are not **excludable**, meaning that ownership cannot be made clear. Whales and rivers are environmental goods that can be captured and converted into excludable resources (whale meat and water). Rainbows cannot be captured and converted, so they also cannot be used up.

Evapotranspiration (ET): Evaporation from the ground and transpiration from photosynthesizing plants. ET is the total amount of water that leaves the ground for the air; the rest sits, flows away, or sinks into the ground.

Excludable: The characteristic of a good that a person or organization can possess (**private good** or **club good**) and keep others from using.

Externality: A side effect from an action that affects a bystander, via a third party impact. A negative externality directly or indirectly harms the bystander; a positive one helps her. By definition, actors do not take externalities into account when calculating the costs and benefits of their actions or decisions. Externalities may be reduced through regulations that factor in **third-party impacts** or by entrepreneurs who facilitate negotiations to reach an agreement and exchange of mutual benefit among participants and third parties.

Extrinsic incentive: An outside force that motivates action, such as financial rewards, fame or risk of losing one's job. Salespeople work hard because they are paid commissions based on how many widgets they sell. See also **intrinsic incentive**.

Flow: The change in the quantity of a stock. When I spend $2, my stock of $10 has an outflow of $2.

Fracking: Injecting high-pressure water and other substances underground to fracture rocks to release natural gas trapped in the rocks for recovery and sale. The "process water" that returns to the surface is often polluted.

Free rider: Someone who does not contribute his fair share of money or effort. For example, one person in a group of four paying $1 when all four share a $10 pitcher of beer. See also **collective action problem**.

Gains from trade: The net improvement to a buyer and seller from trade. The buyer pays y for a good whose worth (x) is larger than y; the seller receives y for a good whose worth (z) is lower than y. The gains from trade are the positive number $x - z$.

Goods: Things that we want when their price is zero, as opposed to bads that we will only take if paid to do so. See also **common-pool good**, **club good**, **private good** and **public good**.

Government failure: When an intervention by politicians or regulators worsens a situation, intentionally or not.

Greywater: Water that may be contaminated by soap or dirt that can be used for purposes where purity is not so important. Greywater can be used to irrigate a lawn or field, cool machinery or wash buildings, for example.

Increasing block rates: Volumetric prices that get more expensive per
    unit, the more you use.

Inelastic: See **elasticity**.

Institutions: Formal rules or informal norms that restrain and direct
    our actions. Institutions are more likely to evolve in response
    to changing circumstances than implemented in one go. Insti-
    tutions reflect local conditions and culture instead of one-size-
    fits-all, master-planned design. Institutions evolve and change
    at different rates, which means some institutions can be mod-
    ified while others constrain action.

Intrinsic incentive: An internal force that drives action, such as pride,
    ambition or concern for others. Parents spend hours reading
    baby books with their kids because they love them. They may
    also like the books, but that's another intrinsic incentive. See
    also **extrinsic incentive**.

Investor-owned utilities (IOUs): For-profit companies delivering water
    and/or sewer services. Although often called "private," IOUs
    often have publicly traded shares and generally sell services
    to all comers as a public utility. The term "IOU" is used to clar-
    ify ownership and distinguish IOUs from **municipal utilities**.
    In the US, IOUs are regulated by Public Utility Commissions
    (PUCs) — so-called because of the nature of the service they
    regulate. "Public" or municipal utilities are regulated by elected
    or appointed leaders.

Iron triangle: A three-way alliance of special interests that support
    one another in implementing and protecting programs that
    benefit them at a cost to the majority of the population. For
    example, the iron triangle of politicians, water managers and
    real estate developers that encourage sprawling new housing
    developments.

Knowledge problem: Derived from Hayek's 1945 article "The Use of
    Knowledge in Society," the knowledge problem refers to the
    difficulty of aggregating many pieces of private, subjective in-
    formation from many people. Hayek suggests that markets
    solve the problem using prices that rise when the demand
    from some people exceeds supply from other people. The

knowledge problem gets harder as the number of inter-related allocation decisions increases. Farmers who buy seed, fertilizer, labor, machinery and water in markets will sell their products at prices that are closer to the true cost of production (reflecting **scarcity**, **externalities** and **opportunity costs**) than farmers who do not pay for inputs. The law of unintended consequences, a corollary to the knowledge problem, predicts that a regulation or law designed to produce a given effect may produce an opposite or unexpected effect. For example, regulations that limited outdoor irrigation in Los Angeles to two days a week resulted in a series of burst pipes, as twice-weekly surges in demand strained joints that had operated for years at lower, steadier pressures.

Law of demand: The quantity demanded for a good falls when its price rises. In most cases, this increase in price/cost leads to a search for **substitutes** and/or reduction in consumption. Note that a frenzy to purchase a good that's in short supply (rare art, penthouse apartments, and so on) is not an example of higher prices leading to an increase in quantity demanded as much as higher prices adding to the good's allure. These "positional goods" are valuable for the status they convey, not for their value in use. This analogy may apply to gourmet bottled water. Also see **demand**.

Legal monopoly: See **monopoly**.

Marginal: See **on the margin**.

Market power: When a seller can raise prices and make greater profits because there are no close substitutes for their goods. Competition from similar colas limits Coca-Cola's profits from its "unique" recipe. A **monopoly** has the greatest market power, but some monopolies do not use their market power — either due to regulation, political pressure or self restraint. Note that a company that does not use market power to maximize its long-term profits may be violating explicit contracts and implicit norms directed at maximizing returns to owners and shareholders.

Monopoly: A single seller of a good (a monopsony is a single buyer). Monopolies do not face competition from other sellers because the government has outlawed competition (a legal monopoly like the US Postal Service) or because it's too expensive to enter the market (a natural monopoly like a water agency that already has pipes in the ground). Some companies enjoy monopoly power due to innovation and protection of property rights (like Apple with its iPhone), but this power is diluted by competitors who create similar products or the expiration of patents. Laws or regulations that prevent firms from competing create monopoly power. Monopolies have **market power**, which they can use to increase profits.

Municipal utilities: Utilities that are owned and operated by local government, as opposed to **investor-owned utilities**.

Natural monopoly: See **monopoly**.

Natural resources: Rivalrous goods found in nature that may be managed as a **common-pool good** (fish in the open sea) or **private good** (coal in a mine).

Negative externality: See **externality**.

On the margin: Deciding whether or not to take an additional action, based on the costs and benefits of that action. Costs and benefits change to reflect prior actions. For example, your decision to eat an ice cream will depend on price, your tastes, and whether you have already eaten zero or four ice creams.

Open-access good: A **common-pool good** that may be overused in the absence of institutional restrictions on consumption — as opposed to limits that treat it as a **collective good**.

Opportunity cost: The cost of making one choice, in terms of choices foregone. The opportunity cost of buying a $50 ticket that's worth $200 to you is the value of the other goods that you could buy for $50 cash (say they are worth $70 to you) plus the cost of your time for attending the ticketed event (say $90). The opportunity cost of the ticket is $160 and the benefit is $40 ($200 - $90 - $70).

Other people's money: OPM is a shorthand expression for the political use of one group's money for the benefit of another group. For example, using money from all taxpayers to fund a project that benefits a small group. The opposite of "beneficiary pays," a principle for funding government programs in proportion to the benefits from the program. A group getting 10 percent of the benefits would pay 10 percent of the costs. OPM should not be confused with government transfers that are available on the same terms to all people (but perhaps at different times), such as social security payments or unemployment payments.

Overdrafting: Removing groundwater faster than it recharges; also called **aquifer** mining.

Pollution: See **dirty water**.

Potable water: Water that is suitable for drinking. "Potable" is pronounced like "notable."

Precautionary principle: Any new substance (or process or product) should be prohibited unless evidence shows it to be harmless, now and in the future. The calculation of real or potential harm is often complicated by **uncertainty** and missing data. Note that the Precautionary Principle violates Karl Popper's dictum that a hypothesis is scientific only if it can be falsified. Thus, the precautionary principle is unscientific because it's impossible to prove that a substance is harmless (by showing infinite examples of no harm); it's only possible to *disprove* a claim of harmlessness by showing a single example of harm. Thus we can see how a new substance may never be introduced into use due to its sponsor's inability to "prove" it's harmless.

Price elasticity: See **elasticity**.

Principal-agent: A principal hires an agent to work on the principal's behalf — but does not know if the agent is skilled or exerts effort. As a result of this **asymmetric information**, the principal experiences a lower-than-expected ratio of benefits to costs. A principal-agent-beneficiary relationship divides the principal's costs and benefits. The principal retains the cost of monitoring the agent for performance that creates a benefit for the beneficiary. For example, a politician monitors a manager who delivers service to customers (the politician's constituents).

Private good: A **rival good** which can be **excluded** from others. Swimming goggles, for example.

Public good: A**non-rival good** which cannot be **excluded** from others. A rainbow, for example.

Public trust: The government has a responsibility to make sure that the people's water goes to productive uses but not necessarily to highest and best use.

Quantity demanded: See **law of demand**.

Renewable resource: A **natural resource** that can grow or replace itself, so that harvest from a **stock** is replaced by positive **flows**. An aquifer, fishery or forest is a renewable resource as long as harvesting is slower than re-growth or replacement.

Risk: When an outcome has a known frequency of occurring and a known cost or benefit, then the risk of that outcome is known. For example, since the probability of getting more than 60 heads in one hundred flips of a "fair coin" is known, then the risk of placing a $10 bet on that outcome is also known. **Uncertainty** is different from risk.

Rival good: A good in limited quantity, such that my consumption reduces the quantity available for you to consume.

Scarcity: Scarcity exists when quantity demanded exceeds quantity supplied. Scarcity can results in negative **flows** that reduce a **stock** or a price increase that reduces demand. Scarcity can be sustained as long as stocks are positive. When stocks run out, scarcity turns to **shortage**. For example, gasoline scarcity can turn into a gasoline shortage ("sorry, no gas") if supplies do not arrive on time or if prices are held below the cost of refining and delivering more gasoline.

Shortage: When the **stock** of a good is insufficient to meet demand for it; only some demand can be met. See also **scarcity**.

Social good: See **collective good**.

Some for Free: A way of pricing urban retail water for residential use that gives each person some water for free (or a low price) and additional water at a higher price that restrains demand below supply. Some for Free's structure of **increasing block rates** and rebates of excess revenue make it more progressive than other combinations of fixed and variable service charges.

Stock: See **flow**.

Subsidy: A payment to buyers or sellers of a good or service that lowers its cost but may not lower its price. A $2 subsidy on a good that costs $3 to make can result in a price as low as $1 or as high as the market will bear — $6 for example. Subsidies come from other customers, government funds, and so on. An **opportunity cost** subsidy results when a good is allocated only to favored individuals at a price lower than others are willing to pay. Its value to these privileged individuals (and the cost of misallocation to society) is often unrelated to its price.

Substitutes: Two goods that can meet the same demands, such that an decrease in demand for one increases demand for the other. An increase in the price of bottled water can decrease the **quantity demanded** for bottled water and shift out the **demand** for tap water (more tap water sells at the same price).

Sustainable: The description applied to behavior that can continue indefinitely. Sustainable water use means demand is less than or equal to supply (average **stocks** do not drop) and shortages do not occur.

Tailwater: A shortened version of "agricultural tailwater runoff" from irrigated land; also applies to other "after-use" circumstances (the water flowing downstream from a dam, for example).

Third-party impact: See **externality**.

Tragedy of the Anticommons: When any one person can stop, or veto, a change in rules or an institution that affects many. If any farmer in a group of farmers can object to a rule allowing water trading, then a Tragedy of the Anticommons prevents other farmers from making voluntary trades.

Tragedy of the Commons: When many people with access to a finite resource (a **common-pool good**, for example) over-exploit and destroy it. If many farmers share an aquifer and all race to pump before the water is gone, then a Tragedy of the Commons occurs as the aquifer is destroyed.

Transaction costs: The cost of making a deal or reaching an agreement, whether measured in time, effort, money, or emotional stress. The transaction cost of finding and selecting a book at Amazon.com is lower than buying that book in a store, but some people prefer to pay those costs, because they like shopping in person, dislike computers, and so on.

Uncertainty: As opposed to **risk**, uncertainty refers to a future event whose nature is not predictable, in the sense that the chance of any particular outcome cannot be estimated. The cost or benefit of outcomes can also be uncertain. For example, it may not be possible to quantify either the probability that an underground pipe will leak or the damage from that leak. Thus, a water agency may say that "a pipe burst unexpectedly, causing an unknown amount of damage."

Uniform block rates: Customers pay same price per unit, for each unit they consume.

Usufruct rights: A property right to use something owned by someone else. For example, a farmer's usufruct right to use water owned by the citizens of a country, or a renter's right to use an apartment owned by a landlord.

Utility death spiral: When customers use less water in a system with costs that are mostly fixed and revenues that are mostly variable, then revenues will drop faster than costs and produce losses. The typical response (raising unit prices) reduces demand even further, leading to additional losses, and so on.

Utility: An organization that delivers service (like water or electricity) to anyone who requests it. Utilities are usually **monopolies** with **market power** over consumers, so their service standards and prices are regulated. Economists use "utility" as jargon for happiness (as in "I maximized my utility by eating chocolate ice cream"), but that meaning is not used in this book.

Notes to the text

These notes document statements made in the text. Sources are listed in Works cited, which begins on page 259. Basic concepts and facts that can be looked up via Google or Wikipedia are not documented.

The beginning of the end

3 "...drought year of 2009..." See Lee (2009) and Davis (2009).

5 "The battle to replace..." See Solomon (2010) for a detailed and fascinating global history of the use and management of water.

7 "Institutions can be classified..." See Coase (1998), Williamson (2000), Saleth and Dinar (2004) and Hodgson (2006).

7 "In Spain, irrigators ..." See UNESCO (2008). The lack of market institutions explains, for example, why only 10 percent of water trades predicted in Vaux Jr. and Howitt (1984) have materialized.

10 "Who uses water..." See Elitzak (2004) on agricultural consumption, Zetland (2009c) on use by consumers, and Economist (2010h) on the "virtual water" embedded in products.

11 Table 1: See Kenny et al. (2009), GWI (2010a) and EEA (2009) for US, Mediterranean and EU shares, respectively. The definition of "use" may vary with each of these sources.

12 "In California, for example..." See DWR (2009) on California water policies and Le Quesne et al. (2010) on the description, measurement and value of environmental flows.

13 "...quantity of bottled water demanded..." Economists draw the demand curve with quantity demanded on the x-axis and price on the y-axis, which contradicts the scientific convention of presenting the independent variable (price) on the x-axis. See Zetland et al. (2010) for a discussion of the costs and benefits of this convention but note that the line would still slope down if price was on the x-axis and quantity demanded was on the y-axis.

14 "...Fresno and Clovis..." See Hostetter (2010); Fresno residents are now getting water meters.

14 "...Australians in Brisbane..." See Cart (2009); some of this material comes from conversations with water experts I met in Australia in early 2010.

16 "The price elasticity..." Hildebrand (1984) and MET (1990) show how a water agency flip-flopped from claiming zero to measurable elasticity. See Loaiciga and Renehan (1997), Renwick and Green (2000), Mansur and Olmstead (2007), Nataraj (2007) and Kenney et al. (2008) for case-studies on the elasticity of residential demand.

17 "Only Italians consume..." Bottled water consumption data are from Gleick et al. (2006, Table 13).

Chapter 1: Water from the tap

33 "Dubai has no..." See IDWR (2009).

34 "...52,000 water systems..." See Mehan III (2003) on 52,000 and Kenny et al. (2009) on 86 percent.

35 "Cost-based pricing..." Las Vegas water prices rise to levels higher than San Francisco's but only for customers who use more than 2,500 liters per household per day. See LVVWD (2011) for Vegas prices and SFPUC (2010) for San Francisco prices. See Walton (2010) for head-to-head comparison.

38 "They prefer IBRs..." The combination of fixed costs and any form of block pricing can be regressive. Say, for example, that the fixed charge is $20 per month and variable charges are $1 per unit. That means someone who uses 10 units pays $30, or $3 per unit, while someone who uses 20 units pays $40, or $2 per unit. People disagree whether progressive refers to total price or price per unit.

38 "But IBRs work..." See EBMUD (noyr) and LVVWD (2011).

39 "...first philosophical problem..." One might argue that the upward sloping supply curve for a company or industry resembles an IBR, but companies and industries usually have a single market price for homogenous goods, even when they have different production costs. It's rare to see goods with a lower production cost sold at a lower price than identical goods with higher production costs. Oil produced in Saudi Arabia is sold at the same price (with adjustments against a benchmark for quality) as oil produced in Venezuela, even though Saudi oil is far cheaper to produce.

39 "Some European water..." See Zetland (2011b) for a Belgian example.

42 "...rebates transfer money..." Some people will object to this transfer, but the alternative (prices that reflect cost) can result in shortage. The transfer can also be justified as income to citizens who use less than their proportionate share of national water wealth, an idea is discussed in Chapter 11.

42 "...match our goals..." Young and McColl (2007c) discuss a variation on this theme. They suggest a single price per unit of water (no fixed charge, no change in block rates) that rises in scarcity and falls in abundance. They suggest that price can cover costs and choke demand in droughts (without requiring rebates). Such an idea makes sense in principle, but it's vulnerable to miscalculation and a revenue shortfall.

45 "Unfortunately, intermittent service..." See Foster (2008) on pipe-pressure contamination and Bernstein (2006) on cheap purification chemicals.

45 "...help the poor..." Readers interested in water provision in developing countries should read Segerfeldt (2005), a short and precise argument for increasing the role of for-profit water providers in the developing world. Segerfeldt's main point is that the poor can't do much worse than their current level of zero service from public water providers. See Fernández (2006) on Mexico City.

45 "MDG Target 7C..." See UNDP (2003) on MDGs, UNICEF (2009) on Target 7C, and UNStat (2010) for statistics on access.

46 "...village councils be women..." See Chattopadhyay and Duflo (2004).

47 "After installing meters..." See Kenney et al. (2008) on increased water use with real time meters and NAO (2007) for a discussion of the pros (less consumption) and cons (higher bills) of metered water in the UK.

47 "The format and layout..." See Moskalyuk (2009) and Simon (2010) on psychological means to affect water consumption.

48 "...Santa Barbara, California..." See Loaiciga and Renehan (1997).

48 "...daily use of 140..." See QUU (noyr) on water charges and Cart (2009) on the drop in demand in Brisbane.

Chapter 2: Dirty water

52 "Europeans try to reduce..." See Carson (1962) and Whittington et al. (2008) on pollution and sanitation, respectively. See European Union (2010) on The EU's Water Framework Directive (for protecting water quality at the watershed level) and Breetz et al. (2004) for a survey of water quality trading programs in the US.

52 "...the 2.8 million..." Lewis (2009) updates the discussion of water mortality and morbidity in Prüss-Üstün et al. (2008), which also has DALY data. See Central Intelligence Agency (2010) for global death rate of 8.37 per 1,000 and a population of 6.69 billion.

53 "What are trihalomethanes..." See EPA (noyra) on trihalomethanes and EBMUD (2008) on concentration statistics. For an example of mistaken hysteria over perchlorate contamination in water, see Lusvardi (2005).

53 "...dipped a sterilized cockroach..." See Bennett (2010).

53 "Contaminants of Emerging..." See EPA (noyrb).

55 "...cheaper and better choice..." Matier and Ross (2011) give an example of low flow leading to sewage backups. The solution — more chemical flushing — may be worse for the environment.

55 "Sacramento residents would..." See Joyce (2009) on San Diego (with a service area population of 2.2 million people) and Weiser (2010b) on Sacramento (with 590,000 customers and a population of 1.4 million people).

55 "Sacramento was ordered..." See Weiser (2010a).

56 "The common law..." See Meiners and Yandle (1992).

57 "...set up a mechanism..." See Chakravorty et al. (1995), Weber (2001) and Lankoski et al. (2008) for theoretical proposals addressing spatial and quality dimensions of water markets.

57 "Regulation works best..." See Ciriacy-Wantrup (1961b) on the complications of managing pollution from multiple sources.

59 "These sectors are willing..." See Winpenny et al. (2010) for farmers using reclaimed water in Spain and Mexico.

60 "industrial users facing..." See Thermoenergy (noyr).

60 "...don't always like greywater." See Editorial (2009) on Vegas opposition to greywater and Hedler (2008) on Prescott. Young and McColl (2008b) suggest that wastewater bills should be based on a fixed charge plus volumetric charge calibrated on indoor water use (during winter months when outdoor watering is minimal). They suggest that greywater systems get no discount, since lower volume increase treatment costs per unit.

60 "...living machine..." "Living Machine" is a registered trademark of a company that builds these systems (see www.livingmachines.com), but anyone can use this idea. See Breuer (2011) for an example of using wetlands to clean process water from an oilfield in Oman. Note that a community using ecosystem processing has an incentive to monitor performance, because processing wetlands are their local wetlands.

61 "...half of America's sludge..." For an overview of sludge, see Price (2009); on Los Angeles vs. Kern, see Sahagun (2010). A National Academy of Sciences panel advised further study of the chemicals and pathogens in treated sewage sludge. The panel was cautious in claiming harm but unwilling to say that sludge was harmless (Board on Environmental Studies and Toxicology 2002).

61 "...Indirect Potable Reuse..." See Farrell (2008).

62 "...defecate in the open..." See Eichenseher (2009).

62 "Germs and dirty hands..." See Bakalar (2005) on washing hands, Adams (1999) on women and germs, and Warner (2007) on sponge decontamination.

62 "Poor urban Indians..." See Pepper (2007).

63 "...Argentina's 1990s water privatizations..." See Segerfeldt (2005) on privatization in general and Galiani et al. (2005) on Buenos Aires.

63 "...sell the treated water..." See Weiser (2011a).

Chapter 3: The liquid lifestyle

65 "...more than half..." Hanak and Davis (2006) report that 50–80 percent of California's residential water consumption occurs outdoors; EPA (2008) reports that outdoor use averages 30 percent of total use in the US. To some, this chapter may describe discretionary water use, as opposed to non-discretionary use, but those words imply that we cannot choose how much water to use for showers or cooking. According to the World Health Organization, the daily minimum for health and sanitation is 20 liters per person per day (just under five gallons), which is far lower than the quantity that people in developed (and many developing) countries use (Howard and Bartram 2003). Most of our water use is discretionary.

66 "Consider a green lawn..." One-third acre from Templeton et al. (1998). Water demand statistics range from 113 to 203 cm on Southern California lawns, according to Berg (2010) and Dougall (2010).

69 "...non-price rationing..." Grafton and Ward (2008) calculate that Sydney's watering restrictions reduced household welfare by approximately AUD 150 per year more than price rationing restrictions would. That's equivalent to nearly 20 percent of an average annual water bill. According to an engineer I met at a conference in April 2011, water managers in Riyadh, Saudi Arabia, are only allowed to charge a few cents per cubic meter for water (a subsidy of over 90 percent). With demand far outpacing supply among the 4 million-plus inhabitants of the city, they ration demand by restricting service to one day in four. This method of preventing shortage is harmful for equipment and inconvenient for customers who need to use water tanks during service cuts.

69 "The main problem..." Additional reasons may matter. First, the blocks within the IBR structure may not reflect actual marginal cost. For example, when one block for retail water represents imported water from a wholesale water supplier that sets its price based on average cost. Second, the inclusion of a large share of fixed costs within IBRs results in variable prices that are higher than actual variable costs. For example, delivery of 20 units of water costs $100, with $80 in fixed costs and $20 in variable costs. If fixed charges are set at $20, then variable charges need to cover $20 in variable costs and the other $60 (75 percent) of fixed costs. Monthly charges cover 25 percent of fixed costs; variable charges cover the rest. Although one might assume that this means prices will be high enough to limit demand, the resulting cost-based price may still be too low to reflect scarcity and prevent shortages.

72 "Palm trees are..." See DesertUSA (1997) on palms and OC Almanac (noyr) on palms imported to California.

72 "...palm tree needs..." Water demand for date palms and *Quercus lobata* are from Zaid (2002) and NRCS (noyr), respectively. For lawns as crops, see Lindsey (2005).

73 "...announced an auction..." See CAP (2010) on the auction and McKinnon (2010) on storage; see Holland and Moore (2003) on the CAP's poor benefit-cost ratio.

74 "Sacramento's 1941 Front..." See SUG (noyr) on Sacramento lawn ordinances and UPI (2008) on the $746 ticket.

74 "Other communities defend..." See Sward (2010) on the anti-lawn movement, Romero (2010) on Albuquerque, and Lacy (2011) on spray-painted lawns.

75 "Residential Car washing..." See EPWU (noyr).

77 "...fuel wasters pay..." Although gasoline prices fail to include the cost of negative externalities and drivers benefit from subsidies for cars, driving and oil, retail water prices fail to rise and fall with scarcity and surplus.

78 "In California, golf..." See Zito (2008).

79 "In South Africa..." This complex story can be assembled by reading Visser (2007), Masondo (2008) and Danchin (2010).

Chapter 4: Water for profit

82 "The people of McCloud..." Nestle Waters market share from NWNA (noyr). See Conlin (2008) on the controversy, Zetland (2008i) on price and revenue calculations and Zetland (2008g) on the canceled deal.

83 "...the people of Concord..." See Goodnough (2010).

83 "In 2009, Americans..." See BMC (2010) on bottled water sales in 2009; Nance (2009) and Duhigg (2010) on infrastructure investment; Garrison (2009) on burst pipes and Peterson (2010) on rationing as the cause; LADWP (noyr) reports LADWP's new water conservation ordinance.

84 "...17 million barrels..." Plastic bottles are also used for shampoo, motor oil and other consumer products, but I ignore them here. Interestingly, milk bottles do not often attract deposits or taxes, presumably because the dairy industry has political friends and a cleaner image. See Pacific Institute (2007) on 17 million barrels.

84 "...25 percent of plastic..." Plastic bottles have the highest recycling rate of plastic products. The worldwide recycling rate for bottles is 10 percent and only 1 percent for plastic bags (Oliver 2008). See CDoC (2003) on non-recycling of California bottles, ACC and APR (2008) on recycling rates, Franklin (2006) for more facts on plastics, and Mittelstaedt (2010) on BPA.

85 "...FDA and EPA coordinate..." See Sharfstein (2009).

86 "Fiji Water ran nationwide..." See Internet Broadcasting Systems, Inc. (2006) on Fiji vs. Cleveland and Graff-Zivin et al. (2011) on demand for bottled water.

86 "...law requiring schools..." See Benefield (2010).

86 "...defend their share..." Consider this twist: People used to drink water if they didn't have money and soft drinks when they wanted taste. Bottled water reframed that choice by raising the price of water above free. Now people decide between expensive water and expensive, tasty water. Given equal prices, more people choose tasty soft drinks. Drink companies make money either way.

87 "One study of private..." See Cowen et al. (2005) for the same city study and Pérard (2009) on many water companies.

88 "The mayor of Stockton..." See Zetland (2009e) for my interview with Alan Snitow, who covered the Stockton privatization and re-municipalization for his documentary *Thirst*.

88 "In April 2010..." See Palmeri and Saraiva (2010).

88 "...professional civil servants..." See Wilson (1989) and Schumacher (1973) on professional and local, respectively.

91 "...common carriage charge..." See Ofwat (2002). Cave (2009) says that common carriage has been poorly implemented.

92 "...integrate those lessons..." See Segerfeldt (2005).

95 "...residents of Cochabamba, Bolivia..." AdT appears to have won the no-bid contract because it agreed to build a dam that the World Bank called "uneconomic." Cochabamba didn't need it, but the mayor of Cochabamba wanted it; his friends were going to profit from the dam's construction. That requirement increased AdT's prices and harmed its customers. This material comes from Bonnardeaux (2009), Conant (2009) and Shultz (2009). The quotation is from Conant.

Chapter 5: Food and water

99 "Some people object..." See Polanyi (1944) for an anti-commodity argument and Ciriacy-Wantrup (1956) for conceptions of water rights. I assume that trades take negative externalities into consideration, especially when water moves between watersheds; see Young and McColl (2006) for some general thoughts on the appropriate for managing trades.

100 "...agriculture uses 60–80..." Table 1 of USDA (2007) has statistics on irrigated land (56 million acres), harvested cropland (309 million acres), and land in farms (922 million acres). Irrigated land is 18 percent of harvested cropland. Table 11 shows that 28 percent of harvested cropland (86 million acres) has *some* irrigation and produces 40 percent of farm revenue; so one may claim 18 or 28 percent of harvested cropland produces that 40 percent of total farm revenue. I use 18 percent because it's not clear if the other 10 percent of land is productive, supporting production, or just there. World statistics come from Döll (2002). See Bastiaanssen et al. (2003) for a useful examination of the relations among water application, technology and crop yield in India.

102 "...that area of land..." is quoted from EPA (noyrd).

102 "Storage can be very..." See Young and McColl (2007a) for a discussion of the benefits of storage and how to administer carry-forward; see Famiglietti et al. (2011) and www.waterwatch.nl on measuring aquifer use and recharge (this is just a sample in a vast literature on groundwater hydrology).

102 "...neighbors race to pump..." See Economist (2010f) on groundwater overdrafting, Collier (2011) on Texas, Rodell et al. (2009) on India, and Ciriacy-Wantrup (1961a) on efficient groundwater management.

104 "Regulations can reduce CAFO..." See EPA (noyrc) on 20,000 CAFOs and EPA (2009) on enforcement details.

104 "Crop subsidy programs..." According to Table 35 of Pazdalski (2010), these crops received the most support from the Commodity Credit Corporation in 2009. Payments for dairy and tobacco were also large but connected to different subsidy programs. See Economist (2010d) on the CAP.

105 "A Big Mac has..." See Economist (2010h) on virtual water and the controversy over its calculation; see WFN (noyr) for a detailed beef calculation and Hoekstra et al. (2011) for a guide to water footprinting.

106 "Many arid places use..." See Tarlock (2000) and Schorr (2005) for detailed legal and historical backgrounds.

106 "In the southwestern US..." See Covington (2006) on *acequias*. Indigenous people lived sustainably because there were too few people to put great pressure on resources and the environment, and they lacked the technology to convert more resources into consumption goods. See Diamond (2004) on the consequences of unsustainable activities.

107 "...farmers often use saved..." See Ward and Pulido-Velazquez (2008) and Pfiffer and Lin (2009).

108 "A leading broker..." Visit www.waterfind.com.au for more on Australian water trading.

109 "These third parties..." Sunding et al. (2004) describe and simulate potential third party impacts from Imperial Valley farmers selling water to San Diego. They conclude that the community would benefit from water sales (and requisite fallowing). IID rejected this finding and declared a negative impact; see Yardas and Kusel (2006) for details. Faced with this opposition, San Diego paid additional money (a bribe) to facilitate the water trade (SDCWA 2007).

110 "...the name of public trust..." The definition of "Public Trust," a concept that dates to the Roman era, varies according to local conditions and institutions. In the informal opinion of O'Connor (2011), the public trust doctrine in California (and probably most of the world) requires that the effect of water diversions on public trust resources be considered; it does not require zero impact or that water be put to highest and best use. (The closest approximation to highest and best use is the constitutional prohibition on waste and unreasonable use and the priority of municipal over agricultural uses in shortage.) O'Connor recommends this passage from SCC (1983): "The state has an affirmative duty to take the public trust into account in the planning and allocation of water resources, and to protect public trust uses whenever feasible... As a matter of practical necessity the state may have to approve appropriations despite foreseeable harm to public trust uses. In so doing, however, the state must bear in mind its duty as trustee to consider the effect of the taking on the public trust... and to preserve, so far as consistent with the public interest, the uses protected by the trust."

111 "uncompensated seizure..." Even compensated use is controversial. People still talk about the "rape of Owens Valley" that took place between 1905 and 1930. Los Angeles bought land from some farmers and exported the water that came with that land. The problem with this sale was not so much the transaction, as its effect on others. Los Angeles exported so much water that remaining farmers, the community and the environment dried out. See Libecap (2004) for an economic history of the deal and dispute.

111 "...Palo Verde Irrigation District..." See Haddad (1999) on the origins of the PVID-MWD deal and Zetland (2008c, 2009i) for updates.

111 "This trade also illustrates..." These numbers are illustrative. Actual numbers will depend on MWD's outside options for new water supplies, the relative market power of MWD and PVID, the transaction costs of making a deal, and other unforeseen factors. See Blake (2008) for a snapshot of alfalfa prices and Vargas et al. (2003) for a sample calculation of water how water results in yield and then profit.

112 "In 2007/8..." See GWI (2010b); see NWC (noyr) for detailed information and reports on Australian water markets.

112 "The water temples..." See Lansing (1991).

116 "The tax per mega..." See Ciriacy-Wantrup (1944) on taxing resources for conservation.

116 "Fishermen are similar..." See Gordon (1954) for a Tragedy of the Commons (before it was known by that name) in fisheries.

117 "...endangered bluefin tuna..." See Economist (2010b).

117 "The solution to domestic..." See Martin (2008) for an example of sustainable indigenous fishery management; Zetland (2008j) and EDF (2009) for overviews of fisheries and ITQs; and Economist (2008b) on halibut.

118 "Some entrepreneurs have..." See Zetland (2009f).

119 "Many have overdrafted..." See Economist (2010f) on Indian farmers and Lloyd (2007) and Karam (2008) on Saudi crops and overdrafting.

119 "Farmers in Israel..." See Fisher et al. (2005) for an authoritative overview of water, agriculture and scarcity in the Middle East. For Israeli statistics, see Water Commission (2001) and Rinat (2008).

120 "...Indian farmers are committing..." Lohan (2009) misrepresents a story in *The Independent*, to claim suicides are driven by GMO crops. In a careful analysis, Gruère et al. (2008) do not find a cotton-suicide connection. Economist (2010f) summarizes the challenges faced by Indian farmers. Note that the suicide rate among Indian farmers is about 1.6 per 100,000 people but 10 per 100,000 in the total population.

120 "The US Food Aid..." See Hancock (1989).

Chapter 6: Water for power for water

124 "...nuclear plants shut down..." See AP (2008).

124 "...reflect the real cost..." Tellinghuisen (2011) discusses how energy producers use "too much" water because it's mispriced.

124 "In 2009, 83 percent..." Data are from EIA (noyrb).

125 "...once-through cooling..." See Kenny et al. (2009).

126 "Geothermal energy uses..." See Economist (2010c).

126 "Biofuels are often..." See Service (2009) and Dominguez-Faus et al. (2009) for a comparison of water demands of different biofuels and pollution.

126 "...US corn ethanol..." Although some claim corn ethanol reduces net carbon emissions by 20 percent compared with burning gasoline (Fischer 2010), these estimates fail to include the impact of changing cropping patterns or expansion of land use (Piñeiro et al. 2009). The USDA acknowledges the impact of land use changes but tries to dodge the issue of net carbon impact, claiming that "a comprehensive sustainability analysis would require an assessment of environmental, economic, and social sustainability indicators throughout the biofuel production stream, including lifecycle analyses of carbon and other greenhouse gas emissions," which is, conveniently, the EPA's job (Malcolm et al. 2009, p. 3).

127 "Las Vegas uses..." See DoE (2009) on Las Vegas energy consumption, Krantz (2008) on energy use, and Tavares (2009) on the average at US utilities.

127 "Internalizing that negative externality..." See Elitzak (2004) on 20 percent of cost and Zetland (2009a) on the impact of carbon pricing on water prices.

129 "Carlsbad residents already use..." According to Carlsbad MWD (2005), 81,000 residents use about 22,000 af per year, which is over 900 lcd.

130 "...true for automobile fuel..." Sallee et al. (2011) find that consumers integrate gasoline price signals into their valuation of cars, perhaps making regulations on consumption (such as CAFE in the US) redundant.

131 "...applies in Yemen..." See Evans (2009) on Yemen and ITN (2009) on Venezuela.

Part II: Social water choices

136 "...but when they fail..." Seldon (2005, p. 3) compares the two systems: "'confrontations' in the market are small, and solved by higgling and haggling over price, the peacemaker. In a state economy... decisions are centralized... When [change] takes place it is contrived, jerky, discontinuous, lumpy, convulsive. Disturbance, dislocation, disruption are large-scale."

136 "People call this corruption..." See Transparency International (2008) and Buchanan and Tullock (1962) on corruption in the water sector and public choice, respectively.

Chapter 7: Managers and politicians

142 "A lone individual..." See Berg et al. (1995), Fehr and Schmidt (1999), Fehr and Gächter (2000), Fehr and List (2004), Cosmides and Tooby (2005b), Gürerk et al. (2006), Kroll et al. (2007), Dawes et al. (2007) and Herrmann et al. (2008).

142 "Collective action redefines..." See Axelrod and Hamilton (1981), Axelrod (1984).

143 "...the tit-for-tat..." See Ridley (1997) and Wilson (1993) on virtue and social cooperation; see Tyler (1990) and Kersten (2003), respectively, for legal and satirical views on cooperation.

143 "Evolutionary psychologists claim..." See Tooby and Cosmides (1992), Price et al. (2002) and Cosmides and Tooby (2004, 2005a). See Smith (1759) for an early discussion of how virtue can arise without the threat of punishment in the Afterlife. Quotation from Ridley (1997, p. 193).

144 "Political scientists describe..." See Olson (1971).

146 "...help a special interest group..." See Frampton (1980) and Candee (1989) for a detailed case study of how farmers in the Westlands Water District (the largest irrigation district in the US) were able to circumvent restrictions designed to deliver subsidized irrigation water to small land owners. Farmers on huge properties (many times the 388 hectare limit) only paid 3.3 percent of the cost of water, and they were aided and abetted by politicians and bureaucrats who were supposed to represent the interests of the public and taxpayers.

148 "Many people claim..." See Zetland (2010b) for an extensive discussion of these issues; Economist (2011a) on selfish public employees; and Wilson (1989) and Akerlof and Kranton (2000) on professional pride and identity.

149 "I tested these..." See Zetland (2008a).

149 "MWD is self-regulated..." The state Legislature has formal authority over MWD but has not been exercised for 50 years (Zetland 2008a).

150 "Does this result..." Water managers are motivated by a mixture of forces. Managers are more likely to pursue customer interests in strong communities and less likely where individualism dominates; see Henrich et al. (2001) and Herrmann et al. (2008) for comparisons of trust, cooperation and punishment in different cultures. Bouma (2007) concludes that it's difficult to maintain cooperation when many Indian villages share the same watershed.

151 "...members of Group A punish..." Long ago in Holland, people were given the death penalty for damaging dikes; today, they do not face capital punishment (Ayar 2005).

152 "...coal-ash-laden water..." See Moore (2009) for details on the spill and management coverup and Zetland (2009d) for a longer discussion of how to change managers' incentives.

152 "...compare different agencies..." See www.ib-net.org for comparative data on 2,000 utilities in 85 countries.

154 "...a prediction market..." Similar to markets used to predict the winner of an election; see, for example www.tippie.uiowa.edu/iem.

155 "Many take the easy road..." See Zetland (2010b) for a discussion on aid failure in developing countries. Aid programs to deliver wells fail in two big ways. They often drill wells and install pumps without ensuring that the community has a way to regulate withdrawals from the well or keep the pumps working. The developing world is littered with dry wells and broken pumps. The second problem comes from failure to secure quality water, either because of contamination from sewage or pollutants or because the well water is unsafe (as was the case with arsenic-polluted wells in Bangladesh). See Zetland (2008l,f) on poor installations and Ee Lyn (2009) on arsenic in Bangladesh.

155 "These problems can..." See Segerfeldt (2005) on private water and Pommerehne and Feld (1994), Barr et al. (2003), Dietz et al. (2003) and Bjorkman and Svensson (2009) on community resource management.

155 "WaterHealth International..." See www.waterhealth.com on the company, which has over 450 facilities operating in India, Philippines, Ghana and Bangladesh. Bhatnagar (2011) told me and other conference attendees the cholera story, which is documented in local-language newspapers.

156 "...pursuit of a big pie...Newspapers regularly cover the debate over inequality (Economist (2011c), for example). See Smith (1759), Wilson (1993) and Ridley (1997) for deeper inquiries into the relation between self and others.

251

Chapter 8: Dams, pipes and pumps

159 "...farmers could not earn..." Coman (1911, pp. 40, 44, 45) observes that the best irrigation projects (in Southern California, for example) were developed prior to the Reclamation law. She concludes with "...much of the reclamation work remaining to be done is beyond the scope of private enterprise. The federal government alone...can afford to wait decades for returns on capital invested, water right charges can be gauged by what the settler can afford to pay, and considerable leeway allowed before cancelation of entry. A private company would be ruined by so generous a policy." In other words, only the government would fund, build and give away uneconomic projects; Powell (2009) explains how that happened.

159 "Reclamation Act of 1902..." See Reisner (1993) for much of this history and Arax and Wartzman (2003) for a case study of the Boswell family's quest to circumvent acreage limitations — often with the support of politicians, the Bureau of Reclamation, and US Army Corps of Engineers.

160 "...benefit/cost ratios were falling..." See Ciriacy-Wantrup (1955) on the pros and cons of benefit-cost in government decision making.

160 "...The environmentalists behind RHH..." See Zetland (2008b) for statistics and references. San Francisco is currently spending $4.6 billion on infrastructure improvements, mostly unrelated to Hetch Hetchy. California's population was 36,960,000 in July 2009 — but see the dispute over that number on page 253.

162 "...All American Canal..." See NASA (2009) on the AAC, and Clifford (2008) on the impact of lining on Mexicans. The canal is called "All American" because it runs just north of the Mexican border and replaced the Alamo Canal, an American-owned canal inside Mexico that brought water to California. Irrigators wanted to replace the Alamo because its operation was subject to Mexican laws and customs. The Bureau of Reclamation built the AAC in the 1930s for the benefit of Imperial Irrigation District using typical OPM subsidies.

165 "...society pays the subsidy..." See Frampton (1980) and Candee (1989) on the games that politicians, bureaucrats and special interests play to control and capture subsidies "for the public good."

165 "...farmers in vacant lands..." Native Americans lived in these areas. Some tribes had hunter-gatherer lifestyles, but others diverted water for irrigation. Their traditional uses of water are sometimes codified as Winters Rights, which were created by a 1908 Supreme Court decision that recognized that Native Americans had the right to receive adequate water, whether or not they were on reservations. By my understanding, Winters Rights are often senior to other prior appropriation rights, which means than a fully allocated water supply can go to over-allocated at the stroke of a pen.

165 "Las Vegas is..." This analysis originally appeared in Zetland (2008k); historical populations are from Census (2010); economic activity provided to the author in April 2010 by Applied Analysis of Las Vegas, which stated that 80% of Nevada's $130 billion in economic activity takes place in Clark County.

166 "Since its construction..." Quotation from Reid Staffer (2009). As of 4 Apr 2011, the Hoover Power Allocation Act of 2010 (HR 4349) has not been passed. See USBR (2009) for each contractor's exact allocation of Hoover power.

166 "The wholesale value..." According to Thomas (2010), Hoover power is sold at a cost of $18 per MWh or 1.8 cents per kWh. Total Hoover generation from USBR (2009); wholesale market prices from CAISO (2010). Tetreault (2011) reports a strong political backlash against recent proposals to allocate cheap Hoover power to other groups.

167 "In 1840. . ." See Beeson et al. (2001).

167 "Politicians direct managers. . ." Many people remember the 1974 movie *Chinatown* for the water-growth subplot in which a land speculator arranges to bring water to his dry lands, dramatically increasing their value. See Ciriacy-Wantrup (1969) on the relationship between natural resources and economic growth. Read Zetland (2009g) for more on the "iron triangle" and Piper (2011) for a personal view on dewatering, dust, and poor human health.

167 "Low fees made it. . ." See Walton (2010) on monthly charges and SNWA (2010a) on Total Operating Revenues and Connection Charges. At the opposite extreme, consider Bolinas, a little town north of San Francisco that prefers slow growth. Bolinas has not increased the number of meters above 580 since 1971; one changed hands in 2005 for $310,000 (Bernstein 2010).

168 "The global real estate. . ." See Zetland (2009h) on housing prices and SNWA (2010b) on connection charges.

168 "New building returned. . ." See Streitfeld (2010).

168 "Average cost pricing. . ." See Mullin (2009) for a discussion of special districts for managing water, and how their structure affects growth, sustainability and relations between neighboring areas.

168 ". . . postage-stamp pricing. . ." See Zetland (2008a) on Southern California; see Zetland (2010d) and Foley and Maywald (2008) on PSPs and water prices, respectively, in South Australia.

169 ". . . driven by imported water. . ." See Zetland (2009g) on sprawl in Southern California and Zetland (2009j) on options for the Delta.

170 "I looked at. . ." I wrote in favor of Lund et al. (2008), in Zetland (2008m) and reversed my opinion at Zetland (2008h).

170 "Growth patterns would. . ." See Zetland (2008d) for outdoor use, Zetland (2008a) for per capita use in Southern California, and Zetland (2010c) on consumption in Australia.

171 ". . . power and water shortages. . ." See ITN (2009) on water shortages and UPI (2010) on the end of the drought.

171 "International development aid. . ." See Zetland (2010b). Donations for wells free up money for military hardware (fungibility), provide a concentrated target for corruption, and encourage government failure by breaking the connection between taxes, votes and spending.

172 ". . . many big aid agencies. . ." See Blanchfield (2009) on water aid and Hancock (1989) & Perkins (2004) on aid that fails or misguides, respectively.

172 "When asked to choose. . ." See Rijsberman (2004) and Whittington et al. (2008) on electricity, sanitation and scale.

172 ". . . communal management of groundwater. . ." See Technical Support Team (2008), World Bank (2010) and Economist (2010f).

Chapter 9: Water and the environment

175 "The Aral Sea..." See New Scientist (1989) and Adler (2002) on the Aral and Cuyahoga, respectively.

177 "Some people believe..." Jains and pagans also have a spiritual relation with nature (Economist 2009a); see Ciriacy-Wantrup (1971) on safety-first environmental policies.

177 "Perhaps Nigeria..." See EIA (noyra, 2011) on Nigeria and Economist (2010g) for 40 years of spills.

179 "Ostrom wrote her..." I am the "intellectual grandchild" of the Ostroms: I started with a dissertation on MWD and used institutional methods to understand systems, their origins and their potential for change. See Ostrom (1953), Ostrom (1965), and Ostrom et al. (1994), respectively, on MWD, groundwater management, and managing the commons.

179 "...sunk cost fallacy..." The fallacy arises from the idea of saving past spending. The choice after buying a movie ticket, for example, is between spending time at the movie or spending that time elsewhere. Instead of thinking this way, many people go to the movie to "get their money's worth," but the ticket money is gone, whether or not they go. It's more accurate to say that they want to go to the movie to get "their time's worth." Some people support sunk cost arguments because they are the beneficiaries of the decision to throw good money after bad (OPM). Höffler (2008) presents an evolutionary defense of sunk cost behavior, arguing that additional (wasted) investment enhances learning and reduces the chance of a repeat.

180 "...the life of the fishery..." See Zetland (2008e) on how American Indians managed their fish and river for 10,000 years, Economist (1997) on value-subtraction, and Bernstam (1995) on Soviet waste.

180 "...productive sugarcane fields..." See Haley (2011, Tables 3a, 4, 49) on sugar prices and consumption; Alvarez and Polopolus (2008) on history; and Young (2009) for data by district.

181 "...zero net tax..." The idea for ZNT came from Candace A, a student in my class at UC Berkeley. I had asked students to "explain how a leader can promote an environmental program that will benefit the average person — but not special interest groups — and still get re-elected." I hoped that their unfamiliarity with collective action problems would make it easier for them to come up with creative, useful answers. This was one.

182 "...38 million people..." Believe it or not, the US Census and State of California do not agree on the state's population. USCB (2010) puts it at 36,961,664 in 2009; CADoF (2010) claims 38,476,724.

182 "...640 desalination plants..." Capital costs averaged from GWI (2009b), which gives an average cost of $4,000 per m^3 per day of capacity and GWI (2009a), which states that the cost of a plant producing 62,700 acre-feet per year is $700 million ($3,300 per m^3 per day of capacity). Using the average of $3,650 per m^3 per day of capacity, it's about $490 billion for the state.

182 "...billion in agricultural output..." Gross state product is about $1.8 trillion. According to CDFA (2010), California farmers export $13 billion in crops to other countries. That leaves $23 billion to be consumed in the US. Assuming Californians consume double the per capita average, in-state consumption would be only $6 billion, or 16 percent of production.

183 "...level of urban Israelis..." A 60 percent reduction in municipal and industrial demand (currently 20 percent of 49,000 GL) implies a new per capita consumption of about 280 lcd for Californians, which is close to the 274 lcd that Israelis use (Water Commission 2001).

184 "...implemented in Michigan..." See www.miwwat.org for more on the Michigan program.

185 "...baseline water flows..." Young and McColl (2008a) reverse the normal idea (given x units in the river, how much should be diverted?) to one based on outcomes: given y inflows to the river and z desired at its mouth, how do we divide $y - z$?

186 "The activists who protest..." See Batty (2009), Kwok (2010), Sun (2009) and Essential Action (noyr), respectively.

186 "...farmers in arid Rajasthan..." See Sebastian (2010).

186 "The people of Kenya..." See Zetland (2010a).

Chapter 10: Weather and climate change

189 "Atmospheric and hydrological cycles..." See Syed et al. (2010) and visit www.ucchm.org.

190 "...compare eight dead..." See CNN Wire (2010) and Bryant (2011), respectively.

191 "These changes will be inconvenient..." See Syed et al. (2010).

190 "Perhaps 75 percent..." The connection between these GHGs and climate change is not one-for-one, meaning that water vapor is not necessarily responsible for three-fourths of climate change; it's probably responsible for less; see Schmidt et al. (2010) for estimates and explanations.

191 "...risk and uncertainty..." See Knight (1921) for an early treatment and Taleb (2001, 2007) for applications to political and financial mismanagement.

191 "Infants in the US..." See Xu et al. (2010, Table 11). Some of these losses resulted from moral hazard (the knowledge that the government would cover losing bets) or heads I win, tails you lose incentives.

192 "...harmful to us..." Some people believe that climate change will be useful because it warms in colder places. This optimism ignores increases in variation that will bring bigger storms, spillover effects from other parts of the world, and disrupted ecosystems that cannot cope with permanently higher temperatures (Syed et al. 2010). See Stern (2007) and NIC (2008) for discussions of the global adverse impacts of climate change on people, societies and security.

192 "...easy to manipulate..." See Economist (2009b) and Hansen (2011) on carbon credit fraud and theft, respectively.

193 "Most people prefer unexpected..." See Kahneman and Tversky (1979), Tversky and Kahneman (1986) and Kahneman et al. (1990) on risk, loss aversion and the cost of insulating against loss, respectively.

193 "the Dutch..." See Deltacommissie (2008) on Dutch flood preparations, Eisler (2009) on Sacramento levees, and Weiser (2011b) on 500-year storms.

194 "...Walmart was quick..." See Worthen (2005) on Walmart and Katrina. Populist anti-price-gouging laws do nothing to increase supply and everything to produce "Sorry. No gas" signs. In emergency situations, it's important to ration essential items (gasoline, water, food, batteries, and so on), and higher prices are effective at reducing panic purchases so that everyone gets the chance to buy a share of the scarce goods.

194 "...Insurance will not..." Insurance works by weighing the risks of individual actions against the cost that might result from those actions and pooling risks so that the average insurance policy produces a profit. Some policies receive payouts that are larger than cumulative premiums but not the average policy.

195 "The lack of government..." For a detailed critique of failures by the US Army Corps of Engineers in and around New Orleans, see references described in Zetland (2009b). See Lehrer (2009) and Spangler (2011), respectively, on federal "crowding out" of private flood insurers and cross subsidies to people who do not pay the right price for insurance or act to limit their damages.

196 "Cherrapunji is the wettest..." See Bhaumik (2003).

196 "...Africa's Sahel region..." See Economist (2010e).

196 "...swallow the Maldives..." See Economist (2008a) on Bangladesh and the Maldives.

Chapter 11: A human right to water

199 "...World Health Organization..." Prüss-Üstün et al. (2008) give WHO numbers (updated by Lewis (2009)) and discuss the adverse impacts of dirty water; Whittington et al. (2008) discuss the history of water supply and sanitation. Food and starvation statistics are from FAO (2009) and Squires (2009).

199 "It costs nothing..." Some argue that negative rights do cost money. The Fifteenth Amendment of the US Constitution ("The right of citizens of the United States to vote shall not be denied or abridged by the United States or by any State on account of race, color, or previous condition of servitude") is defined in the negative, but elections cost money. True, but those costs are mostly fixed. The cost of positive rights rises with each person. The utopian laundry list of positive "shoulds" associated with a right to water in CESCR (2002), for example, would strain any treasury.

200 "While this verse..." See Salzman (2006) on drinking water and Verdicchio (2009) on "buy without money."

200 "...July 2010 resolution..." See United Nations General Assembly (2010).

201 "...the global loss in DALYs..." See Table A2 in WHO (2008) for figures of 72.8 million and 38.7 million DALYs, respectively. The figure for diarrhoeal DALYs is lower here than Prüss-Üstün et al. (2008) (see notes for Chapter 2) — probably due to different counting methods or periods.

201 "...success in addressing hunger..." There are many examples of political interference in food markets that have contributed to hunger and starvation. See Sen (1999) for that discussion and the famous observation that "famines do not occur in democracies."

201 "...minimum lifeline water..." Minimums of 20 and 135 lcd come from Howard and Bartram (2003) and Chenoweth (2008), respectively. BAWSCA (2009) and Zetland (2008a) report municipal and industrial consumption that ranges from 200–1,200 lcd in California, with a median consumption of about 300 lcd.

202 "...access to an improved..." Recall from Chapter 1 that Millennium Development Goal 7 aims at "access to an improved water supply." Some countries may indirectly promote a human right to water as a derivation of another right or international agreement (some claim United Nations General Assembly (2010) creates national obligations for all UN members). Since these variations are impossible to accurately quantify , I ignore them.

202 Table 6: Data come from International Environmental Law Research Centre (2009), Kaufmann et al. (2009), UNDP (2008) and UNICEF (2009). Spain and Uruguay are dropped because they had 100 percent access to water when their constitutional right was enacted. Ethiopia and Venezuela are dropped because the former had no pair-country (too poor) and the latter has no data on access to water after 1995. DR Congo is dropped because its human right is too recent for comparative data.

203 "...correlation between access..." A simple OLS regression fails to reject the hypothesis that rights make no difference. (In lay terms, this can be interpreted as rights do not improve access) The regression of 2006 share of population with access to water on base year share of population with access, 2006 GDP(PPP) per capita, base year GDP(PPP) per capita, and a dummy for rights shows a statistically significant coefficient for base year access but not the other variables (R^2 = 0.85; Prob > F = 0.000). Although this regression could use more variables and data, it does not contradict the bivariate pairwise comparison in the text.

203 "Transparency International devoted..." See Transparency International (2008). Also see Zetland (2011a), which shows the 2008 correlation between World Bank governance indicators and access to water for 170 countries is 0.66. Correlation does not prove causality, but it makes sense that better governance contributes to better water supplies. For a longer analysis, see Krause (2003), a study of 69 developing countries that concludes: "higher levels of democratic participation have a positive effect on coverage with WS [water and sanitation] services... the qualitative comparison of the four Colombian cities finds some evidence that a higher quality of local governance (strong civil society and business organisations, better control of corruption and lower levels of non-state armed groups' activities) has a positive effect on the internal efficiency of providers and on the coverage with WS services" [p. 6].

203 "...citizens already have access..." The provision of water to the "water poor" of France and the UK is mainly though subsidies to water bills, "social tariffs" (increasing block rates) and outright cash transfers to increase income. All of these programs face opposition from taxpayers. For example, "only 39% [of UK customers] would consider a £2 cross subsidy between customers acceptable" (Tsanga Tabi 2011, p. 22).

203 "...mobile phone service..." See Economist (2011b).

204 "...farmers and Indians decided..." See Hiers (2011).

205 "...renewable water..." According to UNEP (2009), "total actual renewable water resources (TARWR) are equal to the sum of internal renewable water resources and incoming flow originating outside the country. The computation of TARWR takes into account upstream abstraction and quantity of flows reserved to upstream and downstream countries through formal or informal agreements or treaties. It is a measure of the maximum theoretical amount of water actually available for the country."

206 "...common-carriage network..." See Fagan (2000) on some of the early complications of common carriage for water and Ofwat (2010, noyr) for recent developments, applications and guidance.

207 "...land values reflect..." In places where land and water titles are separated (such as Australia and Chile), the impact on land values would be small. The impact on land values with attached water will be small where water is abundant (rights do not change the cost of delivery) and large where water is scarce.

209 "...subject to limitations..." See Gould (1988) and Murphy et al. (2000) on how to calibrate and implement these constraints.

209 "... set total quantities..." See Young and McColl (2007d) for a proposal for cap and trade among urban water users in Australia. They emphasize that people could sell excess rights to reduce their delivery costs. See Young and McColl (2007b) on how to create and manage a register of property rights in water.

210 "... break an appalling record..." See Holden and Thobani (1996) on how tradable water rights can improve failing administrative systems.

210 "... spur equity and efficiency..." See De Soto (2000) and Workman (2003), respectively.

Chapter 12: Water wars

213 "... doesn't usually lead..." Wolf (1997) claims that only 7 of 412 international crises that took place between 1918 and 1994 were linked to water; one was the Arab-Israeli war of 1967. See Wolf (noyr) for a list of transboundary conflicts and Gleick (2009) for a larger set of conflicts over water that uses an "imprecise" definition and includes more than just transboundary conflicts. See Barraqué (2011) for a discussion of urban water conflicts resulting from inefficient management.

213 "In Sudan's Darfur..." See Economist (2010a) on water in Darfur and the Sahel and Kevane and Gray (2008) for the research behind it. I also rely on the opinions of two experts in the area, Hoffmann (2011) and Schwennesen (2010).

213 "Thomas Friedman espouses..." See Friedman (2005).

214 "... water tanker in Sudan." See AP (2010).

214 "... dividing the commons..." See Bricker (2011) for an interesting discussion and application of these methods to water management in Oregon.

215 "... mutual assured destruction..." See Schelling (1992) on the use of focal points as a means of coordinating and avoiding MAD; see Allison (1969) on the Missile Crisis. Campana (2005) and Gleick (2006) discuss water terrorism, but such terror is not going to displace traditional methods until people are more afraid of tap water than being blown up in planes, trains or restaurants.

216 "... children in Gaza..." Fisher et al. (2005), written by experts from Israel, Jordan and Palestine, offers a thorough accounting and analysis of water use in the region.

218 "... gain some unfair advantage..." See Arax and Wartzman (2003) on political lobbying for access to water and Mehlum and Moene (2002) on value destruction in conflict.

218 "... requires better institutions..." See Buchanan and Tullock (1962) on the design of long-run institutions and Ciriacy-Wantrup (1967) on changing institutions for allocating water.

218 "In the summer of 2009..." See Zetland (2009k) for a description and video of this session. It turns out that this scenario (one country getting its way with a bribe) was different from what actually happened during climate change negotiations later that year in Copenhagen: China and the US joined forces to prevent any agreement (Traufetter 2010).

Works cited

ACC and APR (2008). United States National Post-Consumer Plastics Bottle Recycling Report 19, Plastics Division of the American Chemistry Council and the Association of Postconsumer Plastic Recyclers, Washington, DC.

Adams, C. (1999). Does flushing the toilet cause dirty water to be spewed around the bathroom? *The Straight Dope*, 16 Apr.

Adler, J. H. (2002). Fables of the Cuyahoga: Reconstructing a History of Environmental Protection. *Fordham Environmental Law Journal*, 14:89–146.

Akerlof, G. A. and Kranton, R. E. (2000). Economics and Identity. *Quarterly Journal of Economics*, 115(3):715–53.

Allison, G. T. (1969). Conceptual Models and the Cuban Missile Crisis. *American Political Science Review*, 63:689–718.

Alvarez, J. and Polopolus, L. C. (2008). The History of US Sugar Protection. *EDIS document*, SC 019.

AP (2008). Drought could shut down nuclear power plants. *Associated Press*, 23 Jan.

AP (2010). Gunmen kill 2 peacekeepers in Sudan's south Darfur. *Seattle Times*, 7 May.

Arax, M. and Wartzman, R. (2003). *The King of California: J. G. Boswell and the Making of a Secret American Empire*. PublicAffairs, Cambridge, MA.

Axelrod, R. (1984). *The Evolution of Cooperation*. Basic Books, New York.

Axelrod, R. and Hamilton, W. D. (1981). The Evolution of Cooperation. *Science*, 211(4489):1390–1396.

Ayar, B. (2005). Hoogheemraden van Rijnland waren streng maar rechtvaardig. *hetWATERschap*, 30 Sep:17.

Bakalar, N. (2005). Many don't wash hands after using the bathroom. *New York Times*, 27 Sep.

Barr, A., Lindelow, M., and Serneels, P. (2003). To Serve the Community or Oneself: The Public Servant's Dilemma. *Center for Study of African Economies Working Paper*, 11.

Barraqué, B. (2011). *Urban Water Conflicts: UNESCO-IHP*. Taylor & Francis, Oxford, UK.

Bastiaanssen, W., van Dam, J., and Droogers, P. (2003). Introduction. In van Dam, J. and Malik, R., editors, *Water productivity of irrigated crops in Sirsa district, India: Integration of remote sensing, crop and soil models and geographical information systems*, pages 11–20. WATPRO, Wageningen, NL.

Batty, D. (2009). Brazilian faces retrial over murder of environmental activist nun in Amazon. *The Guardian*, 8 Apr.

BAWSCA (2009). Annual Survey FY 2007-08, Bay Area Water Supply and Conservation Agency, San Mateo.

Beeson, P. E., DeJong, D. N., and Troesken, W. (2001). Population Growth in US Counties, 1840-1990. *Regional Science and Urban Economics*, 31(6):669–699.

Benefield, K. (2010). Schools must offer water with lunch. *Press Democrat*, 18 Dec.

Bennett, D. (2010). Ewwwwwwwww! The surprising moral force of disgust. *Boston Globe*, 15 Aug.

Berg, J. (2010). Personal Communication. 7 May. Berg is a landscape expert at Municipal Water District of Orange County.

Berg, J., Dickhaut, J., and McCabe, K. (1995). Trust, Reciprocity, and Social History. *Games and Economic Behavior*, 10(1):122–142.

Bernstam, M. S. (1995). Comparative trends in resource use and pollution in market and socialist economies. In Simon, J. L., editor, *The State of Humanity*, pages 503–522. Blackwell Publishers Ltd., Cambridge, MA.

Bernstein, F. A. (2010). The price for building a home in this town: $300,000 water meter. *New York Times*, 14 Apr.

Bernstein, M. (2006). Tiny water purification packet helps save lives worldwide. *Innovations Report*, 30 Mar.

Bhatnagar, S. (2011). Personal Communication. 20 Apr. Bhatnagar is CEO of WaterHealth International.

Bhaumik, S. (2003). World's wettest area dries up. *BBC World News*, 28 Apr.

Bjorkman, M. and Svensson, J. (2009). Power to the People: Evidence from a Randomized Field Experiment of a Community-Based Monitoring Project in Uganda. *Quarterly Journal of Economics*, 124(2):735–769.

Blake, C. (2008). Good times roll for Arizona alfalfa hay growers. *Western Farm Press*, 10 Mar.

Blanchfield, M. (2009). Canada's foreign aid to be more accountable not larger: minister. *National Post*, 9 May.

BMC (2010). Bottled water confronts persistent challenges. Press release, Beverage Marketing Corporation.

Board on Environmental Studies and Toxicology (2002). *Biosolids Applied to Land: Advancing Standards and Practices*. National Academy Press, Washington, DC.

Bonnardeaux, D. (2009). The Cochabamba "water war": An anti-privatisation poster child? *International Policy Network Report*, 16 Mar.

Bouma, J. A. (2007). *Voluntary cooperation in the provision of a semi-public good: Community-based soil and water conservation in semi-arid India*. PhD thesis, Universiteit van Tilburg (Environmental Economics).

Breetz, H. L., Fisher-Vanden, K., Garzon, L., Jacobs, H., Kroetz, K., and Terry, R. (2004). Water Quality Trading and Offset Initiatives in the US: A Comprehensive Survey. *Dartmouth College Working Paper*.

Breuer, R. (2011). Commercial scale produced water treatment using wetlands — reducing the environmental impact of oilfield operations. *Bauer working paper*.

Bricker, J. L. (2011). Entitlement, Water Resources, and the Common Good. *Working Paper*. Posted at http://www.kysq.org/docs/Bricker.pdf.

Bryant, N. (2011). Australia floods: 72 missing and at least eight dead. *BBC News*, 10 Jan.

Buchanan, J. M. and Tullock, G. (1999/1962). *The Calculus of Consent*. Liberty Fund, Indianapolis.

CADoF (2010). California County Population Estimates and Components of Change by Year, July 1, 2000-2010. December, State of California, Department of Finance, Sacramento.

CAISO (2010). 2009 Market Issues and Performance – Special Revised Executive Summary, Department of Market Monitoring, California Independent System Operator Corporation, Sacramento.

Campana, M. E. (2005). Terrorists and ground water: Is weaponization possible? *Ground Water News and Views*, Spring.

Candee, H. (1989). The Broken Promise of Reclamation Reform. *Hastings Law Journal*, 40:657–685.

CAP (2010). CAP Staff Add Water Program Proposal, Central Arizona Project, Phoenix.

Carlsbad MWD (2005). Urban Water Management Plan, Carlsbad.

Carson, R. (1962). *Silent Spring*. Houghton Mifflin, New York.

Cart, J. (2009). Brisbane writes a case study on saving water. *Los Angeles Times*, 24 Nov.

Cave, M. (2009). *Independent Review of Competition and Innovation in Water Markets: Final report.* Ofwat, London.

CDFA (2010). California Agricultural Highlights 2010, California Department of Food and Agriculture, Sacramento.

CDoC (2003). Plastic water bottles not being recycled. California Department of Conservation website. Retrieved 6 Jan 2011 from http://tinyurl.com/2793zx.

Census (2010). State & county quickfacts. US Census Bureau website. Retrieved 4 Feb 2011 from http://quickfacts.census.gov/qfd/states/32/32003.html.

Central Intelligence Agency (2010). The World Fact Book. People tab on WFB website. Retrieved 6 Jan 2011 from https://www.cia.gov/library/publications/the-world-factbook/geos/xx.html.

CESCR (2002). Substantive Issues Arising in The Implementation of The International Covenant on Economic, Social and Cultural Rights. The right to water (arts. 11 and 12 of the International Covenant on Economic, Social and Cultural Rights). General Comment 15, United Nations Committee on Economic, Social and Cultural Rights, Geneva.

Chakravorty, U., Hochman, E., and Zilberman, D. (1995). A Spacial Model of Optimal Water Conveyance. *Journal of Environmental Economics and Management*, 29:25–41.

Chattopadhyay, R. and Duflo, E. (2004). Women as Policy Makers: Evidence from a Randomized Policy Experiment in India. *Econometrica*, 72(5):1409–1443.

Chenoweth, J. (2008). Minimum Water Requirement for Social and Economic Development. *Desalination*, 229:245–256.

Ciriacy-Wantrup, S. V. (1944). Taxation and the Conservation of Resources. *Quarterly Journal of Economics*, 58(2):157–195.

Ciriacy-Wantrup, S. V. (1955). Benefit-Cost Analysis and Public Resource Development. *Journal of Farm Economics*, 37(4):676–689.

Ciriacy-Wantrup, S. V. (1956). Concepts Used as Economic Criteria for a System of Water Rights. *Land Economics*, 32(4):295–312.

Ciriacy-Wantrup, S. V. (1961a). Projections of Water Requirements in the Economics of Water Policy. *Journal of Farm Economics*, 43(2):197–214.

Ciriacy-Wantrup, S. V. (1961b). Water Quality, a Problem for the Economist. *Journal of Farm Economics*, 43(5):1133–1144.

Ciriacy-Wantrup, S. V. (1967). Water Policy and Economic Optimizing: Some Conceptual Problems in Water Research. *American Economic Review*, 57(2):179–189.

Ciriacy-Wantrup, S. V. (1969). Natural Resources in Economic Growth: The Role of Institutions and Policies. *American Journal of Agricultural Economics*, 51(5):1314–1324.

Ciriacy-Wantrup, S. V. (1971). The Economics of Environmental Policy. *Land Economics*, 47(1):36–45.

Clifford, F. (2008). Troubled waters; The increasingly meager flow of the Colorado River into Mexico imperils the millions who depend on it. *Los Angeles Times*, 25 May.

CNN Wire (2010). Urgent cry for help as death toll rises from Pakistan flooding. *CNN News*, 16 Aug.

Coase, R. (1998). The New Institutional Economics. *American Economic Review*, 88(2):72–74.

Coase, R. H. (1960). The Problem of Social Cost. *Journal of Law and Economics*, 3(1):1–44.

Collier, K. (2011). Bills address water issues. *San Angelo Standard Times*, 25 Mar.

Coman, K. (1911). Some Unsettled Problems of Irrigation. *American Economic Review*, 1(1):1–19. Republished in Vol 101 of the 2011 AER, pp. 36-48.

Conant, J. (2009). Defeating the multinationals is just the start of the problem for anti-globalization movements. *AlterNet*, 9 Jan.

Conlin, M. (2008). A town torn apart by Nestlé. *Businessweek*, 16 Apr.

Cosmides, L. and Tooby, J. (2004). Knowing Thyself: Evolutionary Psychology of Moral Reasoning and Moral Sentiments. *Business, Science and Ethics*, pages 91–127.

Cosmides, L. and Tooby, J. (2005a). Evolutionary Psychology, Moral Heuristics, and the Law. In *Heuristics and the Law*. MIT press, Cambridge, MA.

Cosmides, L. and Tooby, J. (2005b). Neurocognitive adaptations designed for social exchange. In Buss, D. M., editor, *Evolutionary Psychology Handbook*, chapter 20, pages 584–627. Wiley, New York.

Covington, R. (2006). The Art and Science of Water. *Saudi Aramco World*, May/Jun:14–23.

Cowen, C., Mescher, A., Miller, J., Pettway, K., and Pink, B. (2005). A Framework for Evaluating Water System Ownership and Management Alternatives. Group Master's Thesis, UC Santa Barbara (Environmental Science and Management).

Danchin, P. (2010). A human right to water? The South African Constitutional Court's decision in the Mazibuko case. *EJIL: Talk!*, 13 Jan.

Davis, R. (2009). San Diego's plan hits water savers, hogs evenly. *voiceofsandiego.org*, 13 Feb.

Dawes, C. T., Fowler, J. H., Johnson, T., McElreath, R., and Smirnov, O. (2007). Egalitarian Motives in Humans. *Nature*, 446(7137):794–796.

De Soto, H. (2000). *The Mystery of Capital: Why Capitalism Triumphs in the West and Fails Everywhere Else*. Basic Books, New York.

Deltacommissie (2008). Working Together with Water: A Living Land Builds for Its Future. Report of Findings, Delta Commissie, Haarlem, NL.

DesertUSA (1997). California Fan Palm. DesertUSA website. Retrieved 6 Jan 2011 from `http://www.desertusa.com/magnov97/nov_pap/du_nov_fanpalm.html`.

Diamond, J. (1997). *Guns, Germs, and Steel: The Fates of Human Societies*. W.W. Norton, New York.

Diamond, J. (2004). *Collapse: How Societies Choose to Fail or Succeed*. Viking Adult, New York.

Dietz, T., Ostrom, E., and Stern, P. C. (2003). The Struggle to Govern the Commons. *Science*, 302(5652):1907–1912.

DoE (2009). Energy savings and environmental impact. Department of Energy, L-Prize. Retrieved 3 Jan 2011 from `http://www.lightingprize.org/about_ssl.stm`.

Döll, P. (2002). Impact of Climate Change and Variability on Irrigation Requirements: A Global Perspective. *Climatic Change*, 54:269–293.

Dominguez-Faus, R., Powers, S. E., Burken, J. G., and Alvarez, P. J. (2009). The Water Footprint of Biofuels: A Drink or Drive Issue? *Environmental Science & Technology*, 43(9):3005–3010.

Dougall, J. (2010). Personal Communication. 7 May. Dougall is a landscape expert at Las Virgenes Municipal Water District.

Duhigg, C. (2010). Saving US water and sewer systems would be costly. *New York Times*, 14 Mar.

DWR (2009). Highlights: California Water Plan Update 2009, California Department of Water Resources, Sacramento.

EBMUD (2008). Annual Water Quality Report, East Bay Municipal Utility District, Oakland.

EBMUD (noyr). Water rates & service charges. East Bay Municipal Utility District website. Retrieved 6 Jan 2011 from `http://www.ebmud.com/for-customers/account-information/water-rates-service-charges`.

Economist (1997). Democracy at a price. *The Economist*, 18 Sep.

Economist (2008a). Adapt or die. *The Economist*, 11 Sep.

Economist (2008b). Economies of scales. *The Economist*, 18 Sept.

Economist (2009a). A matter of faith. *The Economist*, 9 Nov.

Economist (2009b). Money grows on trees. *The Economist*, 6 Jun.

Economist (2010a). Climate wars. *The Economist*, 8 Jul.

Economist (2010b). Fin times. *The Economist*, 18 Mar.

Economist (2010c). Hot rocks and high hopes. *The Economist*, 2 Sep.

Economist (2010d). If the CAP doesn't fit. *The Economist*, Apr.

Economist (2010e). It's getting harder all the time: climatic extremes, from drought to flood, threaten survival. *The Economist*, 2 Dec.

Economist (2010f). Making farmers matter: and monitor, budget, manage — and prosper. *The Economist*, 20 May.

Economist (2010g). The politics of disaster. *The Economist*, 6 May.

Economist (2010h). Trade and Conserve. *The Economist*, 20 May.

Economist (2011a). (Government) workers of the world unite! *The Economist*, 6 Jan.

Economist (2011b). Not just talk. *The Economist*, 27 Jan.

Economist (2011c). The few. *The Economist*, 20 Jan.

EDF (2009). Unique opportunity to restore oceans. Environmental Defense Fund website. Retrieved 10 Jan 2011 from http://www.edf.org/article.cfm?contentID=8765.

Editorial (2009). A murky plan for graywater. *Las Vegas Sun*, 15 Apr.

Ee Lyn, T. (2009). Man-made ponds linked to arsenic in Bangladesh water. *Reuters*, 15 Nov.

EEA (2009). Water resources across Europe — confronting water scarcity and drought, European Environment Agency, Copenhagen.

EIA (2011). Crude oil and total petroleum imports top 15 countries. US Energy Information Administration website. Retrieved 11 Feb 2011 from http://www.eia.doe.gov/pub/oil_gas/petroleum/data_publications/company_level_imports/current/import.html.

EIA (noyra). Nigeria: Analysis. US Energy Information Administration website. Retrieved 11 Feb 2011 from http://www.eia.gov/countries/cab.cfm?fips=NI.

EIA (noyrb). Primary energy consumption by source, 1949-2009. US Energy Information Administration website. Retrieved 3 Jan 2011 from http://www.eia.doe.gov/emeu/aer/txt/ptb0103.html.

Eichenseher, T. (2009). Lack of toilets "One of the biggest scandals in the last 50 years". *Nat Geo News Watch*, 18 Mar.

Eisler, P. (2009). Army corps cracks down on flunking levees. *USA Today*, 24 Feb.

Elitzak, H. (2004). Behind the Data: Calculating the Food Marketing Bill. *Amber Waves*, Feb:43.

EPA (2008). Outdoor Water Use in the United States. *Water Sense*, Aug.

EPA (2009). EPA Targets Clean Water Act Violations at Livestock Feeding Operations. *EPA Enforcement Alert*, 10(2).

EPA (noyra). Basic information about disinfection byproducts in drinking water: Total Trihalomethanes, Haloacetic Acids, Bromate, and Chlorite. US Environmental Protection Agency, Office of Water. Retrieved 3 Apr 2011 from http://water.epa.gov/drink/contaminants/basicinformation/disinfectionbyproducts.cfm

EPA (noyrb). Contaminants of emerging concern. US Environmental Protection Agency website. Retrieved 6 Jan 2011 from http://www.epa.gov/waterscience/criteria/aqlife/cec.html.

EPA (noyrc). Cwa national enforcement initiatives. US Environmental Protection Agency, Civil Enforcement website. Retrieved 8 Jan 2011 from http://www.epa.gov/oecaerth/civil/cwa/cwaenfpriority.html.

EPA (noyrd). What is a watershed? US Environmental Protection Agency, Office of Water. Retrieved 3 Jan 2011 from http://water.epa.gov/type/watersheds/whatis.cfm

EPWU (noyr). Conservation ordinance. El Paso Water Utilities website. Retrieved 6 Jan 2011 from http://www.epwu.org/conservation/ordinance.html.

Essential Action (noyr). Shell in Nigeria: What are the issues? Essential Action website. Retrieved 8 Feb 2011 from http://www.essentialaction.org/shell/issues.html.

European Union (2010). Water protection and management (Water Framework Directive). Europa summaries of EU legislation website. Retrieved 23 Mar 2011 from http://europa.eu/legislation_summaries/agriculture/environment/l28002b_en.htm

Evans, J. (2009). Yemen could become first nation to run out of water. *The Sunday Times*, 21 Oct.

Fagan, M. (2000). Thames heads north with Heinz contract. *The Telegraph*, 27 Aug.

Famiglietti, J. S., Lo, M., Ho, S. L., Bethune, J., Anderson, K. J., Syed, T. H., Swenson, S. C., de Linage, C. R., and Rodell, M. (2011). Satellites measure recent rates of groundwater depletion in California's Central Valley. *Geophys. Res. Lett.*, 38(3):L03403–.

FAO (2009). The State of Food Insecurity in the World. Progress Report, Food and Agriculture Organization of the United Nations, Rome.

Farrell, M. B. (2008). Water's odyssey from sewer to cup. *The Christian Science Monitor*, 3 Jul.

Fehr, E. and Gächter, S. (2000). Cooperation and Punishment in Public Goods Experiments. *American Economic Review*, 90(4):980–994.

Fehr, E. and List, J. A. (2004). The Hidden Costs and Returns of Incentives: Trust and Trustworthiness among CEOs. *Journal of the European Economic Association*, 2(5):743–771.

Fehr, E. and Schmidt, K. M. (1999). A Theory of Fairness, Competition, and Cooperation. *Quarterly Journal of Economics*, 114(3):817–868.

Fernández, E. (2006). Water most expensive for city's poorest. *El Universal*, 24 Apr.

Fischer, D. (2010). Ethanol's contrasting carbon footprints. The Daily Climate website. Retrieved 3 Jan 2011 from http://wwwp.dailyclimate.org/tdc-newsroom/2010/02/ethanols-contrasting-carbon-footprints.

Fisher, F. M., Huber-Lee, A., Amir, I., Arlosoroff, S., Eckstein, Z., Jarrar, A., Jayyousi, A., Shamir, U., Wesseling, H., Haddadin, M. J., and Hamat, S. G. (2005). *Liquid Assets: An Economic Approach for Water Management and Conflict Resolution in the Middle East and Beyond*. RFF Press, Washington, DC.

Foley, K. and Maywald, K. (2008). New Water Prices For 2009-2010. Press release, Government of South Australia.

Foster, J. D. (2008). Personal Communication. 10 Sep. Foster is resident adviser to the Energy, Environment and Urban Governance Division of the Administrative Staff College of India (Hyderabad).

Frampton, M. L. (1980). The Enforcement of Federal Reclamation Law in the Westlands Water District: A Broken Promise. *UC Davis Law Review*, 13:89–122.

Franklin, P. (2006). Down the drain: Plastic water bottles should no longer be a wasted resource. Container Recycling Institute website. Retrieved 6 Jan 2011 from http://www.container-recycling.org/media/newsarticles/plastic/2006/5-WMW-DownDrain.htm.

Friedman, T. (2005). *The World Is Flat: A Brief History of the Twenty-First Century*. Farrar, Straus and Giroux, New York.

Galiani, S., Gertler, P., and Schargrodsky, E. (2005). Water for Life: The Impact of the Privatization of Water Services on Child Mortality. *Journal of Political Economy*, 113(1):83–120.

Garrison, J. (2009). Two more L.A. water mains burst overnight, bringing more questions. *LA Times Blog*, 16 Sep.

Gleick, P. (2009). Water conflict chronology. World's Water website. Retrieved 4 Apr 2011 from http://www.worldwater.org/conflict.html.

Gleick, P., Cooley, H., Katz, D., Lee, E., Morrison, J., Palaniappan, M., Samulon, A., and Wolff, G. (2006). *The World's Water: 2006-2007: The Biennial Report on Freshwater Resources*. Island Press, Oakland.

265

Gleick, P. H. (2006). Water and Terrorism. *Water Policy*, 8:481–503.

Goodnough, A. (2010). Bottled water ban vexes Concord vendors. *NYT Green Blog*, 23 Jun.

Gordon, H. S. (1954). The Economic Theory of a Common-Property Resource: The Fishery. *Journal of Political Economy*, 62(2):124–142.

Gould, G. A. (1988). Water Rights Transfers and Third-Party Effects. *Land and Water Law Review*, 23(1):1–41.

Graff-Zivin, J., Neidell, M., and Schlenker, W. (2011). Water Quality Violations and Avoidance Behavior: Evidence from Bottled Water Consumption. *NBER Working Paper*, 16695.

Grafton, R. Q. and Ward, M. B. (2008). Prices versus Rationing: Marshallian Surplus and Mandatory Water Restrictions. *The Economic Record*, 84:S57–S65.

Gruère, G. P., Mehta-Bhatt, P., and Sengupta, D. (2008). Bt Cotton and Farmer Suicides in India: Reviewing the Evidence. *IFPRI Discussion Paper*, 808.

Gürerk, O., Irlenbusch, B., and Rockenbach, B. (2006). The Competitive Advantage of Sanctioning Institutions. *Science*, 312(5770):108–111.

GWI (2009a). California versus capitalism. *Global Water Intelligence*, 5 Nov.

GWI (2009b). Capital costs of Australian desalination plants are rising. *Global Water Intelligence*, 10(9).

GWI (2010a). Ministers from 43 Euro-Mediterranean countries have failed to reach agreement on the proposed Strategy for Water in the Mediterranean. *Global Water Intelligence*, 11(4).

GWI (2010b). Would water rights trading work for Saudi Arabia? *Global Water Intelligence*, 19 Aug.

Haddad, B. M. (1999). *Rivers of Gold: Designing Markets To Allocate Water In California*. Island Press, Washington DC.

Haley, S. (2011). Sugar and sweeteners: Recommended data. Briefing Room, United States Department of Agriculture, Economic Research Service.

Hanak, E. and Davis, M. (2006). Lawns and Water Demand in California. *California Economic Policy*, 2(2):1–22.

Hancock, G. (1989). *Lords of Poverty: The Power, Prestige, and Corruption of the International Aid Business*. MacMillan, London.

Hansen, F. E. (2011). Europe grapples with stolen carbon credits. *Wall Street Journal*, 31 Jan.

Hardin, G. (1968). The Tragedy of the Commons. *Science*, 162(3859):1243–1248.

Hedler, K. (2008). Buyer of PV effluent credits sells 200 acre-feet. *The Daily Courier*, 1 Nov.

Henrich, J. et al. (2001). In Search of Homo Economicus: Behavioral Experiments in 15 Small-Scale Societies. *American Economic Review*, 91(2):73–78.

Herrmann, B., Thoni, C., and Gachter, S. (2008). Antisocial Punishment Across Societies. *Science*, 319(5868):1362–1367.

Hiers, R. H. (2011). Water: A Human Right or Human Responsibility? *Willamette Law Review*, 47.

Hildebrand, C. E. (1984). The Relationship between Urban Water Demand and the Price of Water. Consultant Report, Metropolitan Water District of Southern California, Los Angeles.

Hodgson, G. M. (2006). What Are Institutions? *Journal of Economic Issues*, 40(1):1–25.

Hoekstra, A. Y., Chapagain, A. K., Aldaya, M. M., and Mekonnen, M. M. (2011). *The Water Footprint Assessment Manual: Setting the Global Standard*. Earthscan, London.

Höffler, F. (2008). Why Humans Care about Sunk Costs While (Lower) Animals Don't. An Evolutionary Explanation. *MPI Working Paper*.

Hoffmann, C. (2011). Personal communication. Hoffman works on water conflicts and climate change in Sudan.

Holden, P. and Thobani, M. (1996). Tradable Water Rights: A Property Rights Approach to Resolving Water Shortages and Promoting Investment. *World Bank Policy Research Working*

Paper, 1627.

Holland, S. P. and Moore, M. R. (2003). Cadillac Desert Revisited: Property Rights, Public Policy, and Water-Resource Depletion. *Journal of Environmental Economics and Management*, 46:131–155.

Hostetter, G. H. (2010). Fresno turns page on new water-meter chapter. *The Fresno Bee*, 12 Jul.

Howard, G. and Bartram, J. (2003). Domestic Water Quantity, Service, Level and Health. Technical report, World Health Organization, Geneva.

IDWR (2009). Dubai demand increase outstrips desalination supply. International Desalination & Water Reuse Quarterly website. Retrieved 5 Jan 2011 from http://www.desalination.biz/news/news_story.asp?id=4806.

International Environmental Law Research Centre (2009). Human right to water: Constitutional provisions. webpage accessed 12 Dec. http://www.ielrc.org/water/doc_hr.htm.

Internet Broadcasting Systems, Inc. (2006). Drink company pulls ad mocking Cleveland. *KTVU*, 28 Jul.

ITN (2009). Chavez asks Venezuelans to stop singing in the shower to save water. *ITN Source*, 24 Oct.

Joyce, E. (2009). San Diego gets pollution waiver for Point Loma plant. *KPBS*, 7 Oct.

Kahneman, D., Knetsch, J. L., and Thaler, R. H. (1990). Experimental Tests of the Endowment Effect and the Coase Theorem. *Journal of Political Economy*, 98(6):1325–48.

Kahneman, D. and Tversky, A. (1979). Prospect Theory: An Analysis of Decision under Risk. *Econometrica*, 47(2):263–91.

Karam, S. (2008). Saudi Arabia scraps wheat growing to save water. *Reuters*, 8 Jan.

Kaufmann, D., Kraay, A., and Mastruzzi, M. (2009). Governance Matters VIII: Aggregate and Individual Governance Indicators, 1996-2008. *World Bank Policy Research Working Paper*, 4978.

Kenney, D. S., Goemans, C., Klein, R., Lowrey, J., and Reidy, K. (2008). Residential Water Demand Management: Lessons from Aurora, Colorado. *Journal of the American Water Resources Association*, 44(1):192–207. http://www.kysq.org/docs/Kenney.pdf.

Kenny, J. F., Barber, N. L., Hutson, S. S., Linsey, K. S., Lovelace, J. K., and Maupin, M. A. (2009). Estimated Use of Water in the United States in 2005. Circular 1344, US Geological Survey.

Kersten, E. (2003). *The Art of Demotivation*. Despair Ink, Austin.

Kevane, M. and Gray, L. (2008). Darfur: Rainfall and Conflict. *Environmental Resource Letters*, 3(034006):1–10.

Knight, F. (1921). *Risk, Uncertainty, and Profit*. Hart, Schaffner & Marx, Boston.

Krantz, S. P. (2008). 2008 Integrated Resource Plan Annual Status Report. Letter from Southern Nevada Water Authority to Colorado River Commission of Nevada. Retrieved 3 Jan 2011 from http://tinyurl.com/36urh9n.

Krause, M. (2003). *The political economy of water and sanitation in developing countries: Cross-country evidence and a case study on Colombia*. PhD thesis, Justus-Liebig-University (Economics).

Kroll, S., Cherry, T. L., and Shogren, J. F. (2007). Voting, Punishment, and Public Goods. *Economic Inquiry*, 45(3):557–570.

Kwok, A. (2010). Groups slams death of environmental activists. *Inquirer.net*, 3 Mar.

Lacy, M. (2011). Spraying to make yards green ... but with paint, not water. *New York Times*, 9 Apr.

LADWP (noyr). Water conservation ordinance. Los Angeles Department of Water and Power website. Retrieved 6 Jan 2011 from http://www.ladwp.com/ladwp/cms/ladwp001257.jsp.

Lankoski, J., Lichtenberg, E., and Ollikainen, M. (2008). Point/Nonpoint Effluent Trading with Spatial Heterogeneity. *American Journal of Agricultural Economics*, 90(4):1044–1058.

Lansing, J. S. (1991). *Priests and Programmers: Technologies of Power in the Engineered Landscape of Bali*. Princeton University Press, Princeton.

Le Quesne, T., Kendy, E., and Weston, D. (2010). *The Implementation Challenge: Taking stock of government policies to protect and restore environmental flows*. WWF and The Nature Conservancy, Washington, DC.

Lee, M. (2009). Residents question officials on water rationing plans. *San Diego Union-Tribune*, 10 Feb.

Lehrer, E. (2009). How the Federal Government Obstructed the Development of Private Flood Insurance. Insurance Choices policy report, Independent Institute.

Lewis, S. (2009). Diarrhoea kills over a million over-fives each year. *SciNet News*, 30 Oct.

Libecap, G. D. (2004). Transaction Costs: Valuation Disputes, Bi-Lateral Monopoly Bargaining and Third-Party Effects in Water Rights Exchanges. The Owens Valley Transfer to Los Angeles. *NBER Working Paper*, 10801.

Lindsey, R. (2005). More lawns than irrigated corn. *Earth Observatory*, 8 Nov.

Lloyd, J. (2007). The difficulties of regional groundwater resources assessments in arid areas. *Arabian Journal for Science and Engineering*, 32(1C).

Loaiciga, H. A. and Renehan, S. (1997). Municipal Water Use and Water Rates Driven by Severe Drought: A Case Study. *Journal of the American Water Resources Association*, 33(6):1313–1326.

Lohan, T. (2009). 1,500 Indian farmers commit mass suicide: Why we are complicit in these deaths. *AlterNet*, 16 Apr.

Lund, J., Hanak, E., Fleenor, W., Bennett, W., Howitt, R., Mount, J., and Moyle, P. (2008). Comparing Futures for the Sacramento-San Joaquin Delta. Report, Public Policy Institute of California, San Francisco.

Lusvardi, W. (2005). News Coverage of Perchlorate Issue is Thirty Miles Wide, But Only One Inch Deep. *10News.com*, 5 May.

LVVWD (2011). Rates and usage thresholds. Las Vegas Valley Water District website. Retrieved 5 Jan 2011 from http://www.lvvwd.com/custserv/billing_rates_thresholds.html.

Malcolm, S. A., Aillery, M., and Weinberg, M. (2009). Ethanol and a Changing Agricultural Landscape. *Economic Research Report*, 86.

Mansur, E. T. and Olmstead, S. M. (2007). The Value of Scarce Water: Measuring the Inefficiency of Municipal Regulations. *NBER Working Paper*, 13513.

Martin, G. (2008). Battling Upstream: The tribes on the Klamath know that as the river goes, so go the salmon. *San Francisco Chronicle*, 13 Apr.

Masondo, A. (2008). Statement by the Executive Mayor of Johannesburg: Judgement of the Phiri case. *City of Johannesburg website*, 14 May.

Matier, P. and Ross, A. (2011). Low-flow toilets cause a stink in SF. *San Francisco Chronicle*, 28 Feb.

McKenzie, R. B. (2008). *Why Popcorn Costs So Much at the Movies: And Other Pricing Puzzles*. Springer, New York.

McKinnon, S. (2010). Arizona drought prompts unusual water proposal. *The Arizona Republic*, 28 Dec.

Mehan III, G. T. (2003). EPA announces significant progress toward protecting nation's drinking water sources. *WaterNews*, 3 Jun.

Mehlum, H. and Moene, K. (2002). Battlefields and Marketplaces. *Defence and Peace Economics*, 13(6):485–496.

Meiners, R. E. and Yandle, B. (1992). The Common Law Solution to Water Pollution: The Path

Not Taken. PERC Reports, PERC, Bozeman.

MET (1990). Water Conservation Pricing Approaches of the Metropolitan Water District, Metropolitan Water District of Southern California, Los Angeles.

Mittelstaedt, M. (2010). Bpa widespread in ocean water and sand. *The Globe and Mail*, 1 Apr.

Moore, R. W. (2009). Hearing on The Tennessee Valley Authority's Kingston Ash Slide: Evaluation of Potential Causes and Update on Cleanup Efforts, Inspector General, TVA, Knoxville.

Moskalyuk, A. (2009). Yes! 50 scientifically proven ways to be persuasive. Alex Moskalyuk blog. Retrieved 6 Jan 2011 from http://www.moskalyuk.com/blog/yes-50-scientifically-proven-ways-to-be-persuasive.

Mullin, M. (2009). *Governing the Tap: Special District Governance and the New Local Politics of Water*. The MIT Press, Cambridge, MA.

Murphy, J. J., Dinar, A., Howitt, R. E., Rassenti, S. J., and Smith, V. L. (2000). The Design of "Smart" Water Market Institutions Using Laboratory Experiments. *Environmental and Resource Economics*, 17(4):375–394.

Nance, S. (2009). New drinking water infrastructure reports = BIG $ needs. *AWWA Streamlines*, 1(7).

NAO (2007). Ofwat – Meeting the demand for water 2006-2007. Value for Money Report 150, National Audit Office.

NASA (2009). All-American Canal, California-Mexico border. NASA Earth Observatory website. Retrieved 4 Feb 2011 from http://earthobservatory.nasa.gov/IOTD/view.php?id=37078.

Nataraj, S. (2007). Do Residential Water Consumers React to Price Increases? Evidence from a Natural Experiment in Santa Cruz. *ARE Update*, 10(3):9–11.

New Scientist (1989). Soviet cotton threatens a region's sea — and its children. *New Scientist*, 18 Nov(1691).

NIC (2008). *Global Trends 2025: A Transformed World*. Office of the Director of National Intelligence, Washington DC.

NRCS (noyr). Conservation plant characteristics for Quercus lobata. Natural Resources Conservation Service (USDA) website. Retrieved 6 Jan 2011 from http://plants.usda.gov/java/charProfile?symbol=QULO.

NWC (noyr). Water markets. National Water Commission website. Retrieved 15 May 2011 from http://www.nwc.gov.au/www/html/248-introduction-water-markets.asp.

NWNA (noyr). Nestle Waters North America share of category. Nestle Waters North America website. Retrieved 6 Jan 2011 from http://www.nestle-watersna.com/OurBusiness.htm.

OC Almanac (noyr). Are Palm trees native to southern California? OC Almanac website. Retrieved 6 Jan 2011 from http://www.ocalmanac.com/Environment/ev19a.htm.

O'Connor, D. (2011). Personal Communication. 25 Apr. O'Connor is the principal consultant to the California Senate's Natural Resources & Water Committee.

Ofwat (2002). Access Codes for Common Carriage: Guidance, Office of Water Services, Birmingham, UK.

Ofwat (2010). Introducing a water supply licensing operational code and common contract – a consultation on guidance changes. Consultation, Markets and Economics Division Business Support, Ofwat, London.

Ofwat (noyr). Water supply licensing. Ofwat website. Retrieved 1 Mar 2011 from http://www.ofwat.gov.uk/competition/wsl/.

Oliver, R. (2008). All about: Recycling plastics. *CNN*, 7 Apr.

Olson, M. (1971). *The Logic of Collective Action*. Harvard University Press, Cambridge, MA.

Ostrom, E. (1965). *Public Entrepreneurship: A Case Study in Ground Water Basin Management*. PhD thesis, UCLA (Political Science).

Ostrom, E., Gardner, R., and Walker, J. (1994). *Rules, Games, and Common-Pool Resources.* Ann Arbor Books, Ann Arbor.

Ostrom, V. (1953). *Water Supply*, volume VIII of *Metropolitan Los Angeles: a Study in Integration.* Haynes Foundation, Los Angeles.

Pacific Institute (2007). Bottled water and energy. *A Fact Sheet*, 20 Aug.

Palmeri, C. and Saraiva, C. (2010). Los Angeles credit rating on $3.2 billion in bonds cut to Aa3 by Moody's. *Bloomberg News*, 8 Apr.

Pazdalski, R. (2010). Agricultural outlook: Statistical indicators. USDA ERS website. Retrieved 8 Jan 2011 from http://www.ers.usda.gov/Publications/AgOutlook/AOTables/.

Pepper, D. (2007). India's rivers are drowning in pollution. *Fortune*, 4 Jun.

Pérard, E. (2009). Water Supply: Public or Private? An Approach Based on Cost of Funds, Transaction Costs, Efficiency and Political Costs. *Policy and Society*, 27(3):193–219.

Perkins, J. (2004). *Confessions of an Economic Hit Man.* Berrett-Koehler Publishers Inc., San Francisco.

Peterson, M. (2010). LA's water rationing blamed in water main blowouts last summer, consultant says. *KPCC*, 13 Apr.

Pfiffer, L. and Lin, C.-Y. C. (2009). Incentive-Based Groundwater Conservation Programs: Perverse Consequences? *ARE Update*, 12(6):1–4.

Piñeiro, G., Jobbágy, E. G., Baker, J., Murray, B. C., and Jackson, R. B. (2009). Set-asides Can Be Better Climate Investment than Corn Ethanol. *Ecological Applications*, 19(2):277–282.

Piper, K. (2011). Dreams, Dust and Birds: The Trashing of Owens Lake. *Design Observer*, 24 Jan.

Polanyi, K. (2001/1944). *The Great Transformation: The Political and Economic Origins of Our Time.* Beacon Press, Boston.

Pommerehne, W. W. and Feld, L. P. (1994). Voluntary Provision of a Public Good: Results from a Real World Experiment. *Kyklos*, 47(4):505–517.

Powell, J. L. (2009). *Dead Pool: Lake Powell, Global Warming, and the Future of Water in the West.* University of California Press, Berkeley.

Price, C. (2009). Sludge, farmer's friend or toxic slime? *Grist*, 4 May.

Price, M., Cosmides, L., and Tooby, J. (2002). Punitive Sentiment as an Anti-Free Rider Psychological Device. *Evolution and Human Behavior*, 23:203–231.

Prüss-Üstün, A., Bos, R., Gore, F., and Bartram, J. (2008). Safer Water, Better Health: Costs, Benefits and Sustainability of Interventions to Protect and Promote Health. MDG Comprehensive Overview, World Health Organization, Geneva.

QUU (noyr). Residential water and sewerage charges. Queensland Urban Utilities website. Retrieved 6 Jan 2011 from http://www.urbanutilities.com.au/Residents/Account_information/Residential_water_and_sewerage_charges/.

Reid Staffer (2009). Nevada Delegation Introduces Hoover Power Allocation Act. Press release, Press Release from the Office of Senator Harry Reid (D-NV).

Reisner, M. (1993). *Cadillac Desert.* Penguin Books, New York.

Renwick, M. E. and Green, R. D. (2000). Do Residential Water Demand Side Policies Measure Up? An Analysis of Eight California Cities. *Journal of Environmental Economics and Management*, 40:37–55.

Ridley, M. (1997). *The Origins of Virtue: Human Instincts and the Evolution of Cooperation.* Viking Adult, New York.

Rijsberman, F. (2004). The Water Challenge. In *Copenhagen Consensus 2004.* Environmental Assessment Institute, Copenhagen.

Rinat, Z. (2008). Israel's water demand will hugely outweigh supply during 2008. *Haaretz*, 16 Apr.

Rodell, M., Velicogna, I., and Famiglietti, J. S. (2009). Satellite-based estimates of groundwater depletion in India. *Nature*, 460(7258):999–1002.

Romero, D. (2010). Council says no to xeriscape proposal. *KRQE News 13*, 3 Aug.

Sahagun, L. (2010). Counties ask high court to rule on Kern County's human waste ban. *Los Angeles Times*, 18 Mar.

Saleth, R. M. and Dinar, A. (2004). *The Institutional Economics of Water: A Cross-Country Analysis of Institutions and Performance*. World Bank, Washington DC.

Sallee, J., West, S., and Fan, W. (2011). Do Consumers Recognize the Value of Fuel Economy? Evidence from Used Car Prices and Gasoline Price Fluctuations. *University of Chicago Working Paper*.

Salzman, J. (2006). Thirst: A Short History of Drinking Water. *Duke Law Faculty Scholarship. Paper*, 1261.

SCC (1983). NATIONAL AUDUBON SOCIETY et al., Petitioners, v. THE SUPERIOR COURT OF ALPINE COUNTY, Respondent; DEPARTMENT OF WATER AND POWER OF THE CITY OF LOS ANGELES et al., Real Parties in Interest. S.f. no. 24368, Supreme Court of California. 33 Cal. 3d 419; 658 P.2d 709; 189 Cal. Rptr. 346; 1983 Cal. LEXIS 152; 21 ERC (BNA) 1490; 13 ELR 20272.

Schelling, T. C. (1960). *The Strategy of Conflict*. Harvard University Press, Cambridge, MA.

Schelling, T. C. (1992). Some Economics of Global Warming. *American Economic Review*, 82(1):1–14.

Schmidt, G., Ruedy, R., Miller, R., and Lacis, A. (2010). The Attribution of the Present-Day Total Greenhouse Effect. *Journal of Geophysical Research*, 115(D20106).

Schorr, D. B. (2005). Appropriation as Agrarianism: Distributive Justice in the Creation of Property Rights. *Ecology Law Quarterly*, 32(2).

Schumacher, E. F. (1973). *Small Is Beautiful: Economics As If People Mattered*. Blond & Briggs, London.

Schwennesen, E. (2010). Personal communication. Schwennesen worked on land management among pastoral peoples in Africa for many years; he told me about oil prospecting in the Darfur region.

Scott, J. C. (1998). *Seeing like a State: How Certain Schemes to Improve the Human Condition Have Failed*. Yale University press, New Haven.

SDCWA (2007). Water Authority and Imperial Irrigation District settle arbitration over socioeconomic impacts from water transfer. San Diego County Water Authority website. Retrieved 20 Mar 2011 from http://tinyurl.com/sdcwa.

Sebastian, S. (2010). Parched Keoladeo National Park gets a new lease of life. *The Hindu*, 6 Sep.

Segerfeldt, F. (2005). *Water For Sale: How Business and the Market Can Resolve the World's Water Crisis*. CATO Institute, Washington, DC.

Seldon, A. (2005). Change by Degree or by Convulsion. In *Government Failure and Over-Government*, volume 5 of *The Collected Works of Arthur Seldon*, pages 3–19. Liberty Fund, Indianapolis.

Sen, A. (1999). *Development as Freedom*. Alfred A. Knopf, New York.

Service, R. F. (2009). Another Biofuels Drawback: The Demand for Irrigation. *Science*, 326(5952):516–517.

SFPUC (2010). Rate schedules for water service and wastewater service. San Francisco Public Utilities Commission website. Retrieved 5 Jan 2011 from http://sfwater.org/detail.cfm/MC_ID/21/MSC_ID/156/C_ID/4621.

Sharfstein, J. M. (2009). Regulation of Bottled Water: Statement of Principal Deputy Commissioner of Food and Drugs Food and Drug Administration Department of Health and Human Services before the Subcommittee on Oversight and Investigations House Committee on Energy and Commerce. FDA website. Retrieved 25 Apr, 2011 from http://www.fda.gov/NewsEvents/Testimony/ucm170932.htm.

Shultz, J. (2009). The Cochabamba Water Revolt and Its Aftermath. In Shultz, J. and Draper, M. C., editors, *Dignity and Defiance, Stories from Bolivia's Challenge to Globalization*. University of California Press, Berkeley.

Simon, S. (2010). The secret to turning consumers green. *Wall Street Journal*, 18 Oct.

Smith, A. (2000/1759). *The Theory of Moral Sentiments*. Prometheus Books, Amherst, NY.

SNWA (2010a). Basic Financial Statements, Southern Nevada Water Authority, Las Vegas.

SNWA (2010b). Statistical section (unaudited financial statements), Southern Nevada Water Authority, Las Vegas.

Solomon, S. (2010). *Water: The Epic Struggle for Wealth, Power, and Civilization*. Harper, New York.

Spangler, T. (2011). US Rep. Candice Miller's bill would end flood insurance program in '13. *Detroit Free Press*, 18 Feb.

Squires, N. (2009). At UN food summit, Ban Ki-Moon warns of rise in child hunger deaths. *The Christian Science Monitor*, 16 Nov.

Stern, N. (2007). *The Economics of Climate Change: The Stern Review*. Cambridge University Press, Cambridge, UK.

Streitfeld, D. (2010). Building is booming in a city of empty houses. *New York Times*, 15 May.

SUG (noyr). Sacramento's front yard landscape ordinance. Sustainable Urban Gardens website. Retrieved 6 Jan 2011 from http://www.sacgardens.org/aboutCode.html.

Sun, S. (2009). Activist's murder raises controversy for Canadian mining firm. *Digital Journal*, 15 Dec.

Sunding, D., Kubota, G. H., and Mitchell, D. (2004). Third-Party Impacts of Land Fallowing Associated with IID-SDCWA Water Transfer: 2003 and 2004. Consultant Report, Local Entity and San Diego County Water Authority.

Sward, S. (2010). Water conservation could limit suburban lawns. *New York Times*, 9 Jan.

Syed, T. H., Famiglietti, J. S., Chambers, D. P., Willis, J. K., and Hilburn, K. (2010). Satellite-based global-ocean mass balance estimates of interannual variability and emerging trends in continental freshwater discharge. *Proceedings of the National Academy of Sciences*, 107(42):17916–17921.

Taleb, N. N. (2001). *Fooled by Randomness: The Hidden Role of Chance in the Markets and in Life*. Random House, New York.

Taleb, N. N. (2007). *The Black Swan: The Impact of the Highly Improbable*. Random House, New York.

Tarlock, A. D. (2000). Prior Appropriation: Rule, Principle, Or Rhetoric? *North Dakota Law Review*, 76:881–910.

Tavares, S. (2009). Water usage, treatment brings increased power consumption. *Las Vegas Sun*, 20 Oct.

Technical Support Team (2008). Andhra Pradesh Farmer Managed Groundwater Systems Project. Completion Report, The Officers of the Andhra Pradesh State Ground Water Department and Government of Andhra Pradesh, India.

Tellinghuisen, S. (2011). Every Drop Counts: Valuing the Water Used to Generate Electricity, Western Resource Advocates, Boulder.

Templeton, S., Zilberman, D., and Yoo, S. (1998). An Economic Perspective on Outdoor Residential Pesticide Use. *Environmental Science & Technology*, 2:416–423.

Tetreault, S. (2011). Agency backs down on changes in Hoover Dam rules. *Las Vegas Review Journal*, 20 May.

Thermoenergy (noyr). The changing economics of process water use and disposal. Thermoenergy website. Retrieved 6 Jan 2011 from http://www.castion.com/IndustrialSolutions/effluent-water-treatment.aspx.

Thomas, B. G. (2010). Personal communication. 12 May. Thomas is the CFO of the Metropolitan

Water District of Southern California.

Tooby, J. and Cosmides, L. (1992). The Psychological Foundations of Culture. In *The Adopted Mind: Evolutionary Psychology and the Generation of Culture*. Oxford University Press, Oxford, UK.

Transparency International (2008). *Global Corruption Report 2008: Corruption in the Water Sector*. Cambridge University Press, Cambridge, UK.

Traufetter, G. (2010). The US and China joined forces against Europe. *Der Spiegel*, 8 Dec.

Tsanga Tabi, M. (2011). Implementing Human Right to Water in Europe: Lessons from French and British Experiences. *CEMACREF working paper*.

Tversky, A. and Kahneman, D. (1986). Rational Choice and the Framing of Decisions. *Journal of Business*, 59(4):S251–S278.

Tyler, T. R. (1990). *Why People Obey the Law*. Princeton University Press, Princeton.

UNDP (2003). Millennium Development Goals: A Compact among Nations to End Human Poverty. In *Human Development Report*. United Nations Development Program, New York.

UNDP (2008). *Human Development Report*. United Nations Development Program, New York.

UNEP (2009). Water resources - total renewable (actual) – 2008. The GEO Data Portal, as Compiled from FAO, AQUASTAT FAO's Information System on Water in Agriculture, United Nations Environment Program.

UNESCO (2008). Irrigators' tribunals of the Spanish Mediterranean coast. UNESCO website. Retrieved 25 Apr, 2011 from `http://www.unesco.org/archives/multimedia/?s=films_details&id_page=33&id_film=371`.

UNICEF (2009). MDG Indicators: 7.8 Proportion of population using an improved drinking water source. webpage accessed 12 Dec. `http://mdgs.un.org/unsd/mdg/Metadata.aspx?IndicatorId=0&SeriesId=665`.

United Nations General Assembly (2010). The human right to water and sanitation. 26 July Resolution A/64/L.63/Rev.1*, United Nations Sixty-fourth Session.

UNStat (2010). Statistical Annex: Millennium Development Goals, Targets and Indicators, Development Indicators Unit, Statistics Division, United Nations.

UPI (2008). Dead lawn could yield $746 fine. *UPI News*, 2 Jul.

UPI (2010). Venezuela rain eases opposition pressure on embattled Chavez. *United Press International*, 25 May.

USBR (2009). How is the firm energy generated at Hoover Dam allocated? Bureau of Reclamation – Lower Colorado Region website. Retrieved 22 Nov 2010 from `http://www.usbr.gov/lc/hooverdam/faqs/powerfaq.html`.

USBR (2009). Hydropower at Hoover Dam. Bureau of Reclamation – Lower Colorado Region website. Retrieved 4 Feb 2011 from `http://www.usbr.gov/lc/hooverdam/faqs/powerfaq.html`.

USCB (2010). State and county QuickFacts. US Census Bureau website. Retrieved 11 Feb 2011 from `http://quickfacts.census.gov/qfd/states/06000.html`.

USDA (2007). Census of Agriculture. Five-yearly Report, US Department of Agriculture.

Vargas, R. N. et al. (2003). Sample Costs to Establish and Produce Alfalfa. Alfalfa cost and return study, University of California Cooperative Extension, Davis.

Vaux Jr., H. J. and Howitt, R. E. (1984). Managing Water Scarcity: An Evaluation of Interregional Transfers. *Water Resources Research*, 20(7):785–792.

Verdicchio, M. (2009). Buy without money? Confidence and Joy blog. Retrieved 1 Mar 2011 from `http://confidenceandjoy.com/buy-without-money/`.

Visser, E. (2007). Closing the tap on water leakages. *City of Johannesburg website*, 24 Oct.

Walton, B. (2010). The price of water: A comparison of water rates, usage in 30 us cities. *Circle of Blue*, 26 Apr.

Ward, F. A. and Pulido-Velazquez, M. (2008). Water Conservation in Irrigation Can Increase

Water Use. *Proceedings of the National Academy of Sciences*, 105(47):18215–18220.

Warner, J. (2007). Microwave kills germs in sponges. *WebMD Health News*, 24 Jan. Accessed 22 Nov 2010.

Water Commission (2001). Water in Israel — Consumption and Production 3rd Edition, Demand Management Division, Ministry of National Infrastructures, Tel Aviv.

Weber, M. L. (2001). Markets for Water Rights under Environmental Constraints. *Journal of Environmental Economics and Management*, 42(1):53 – 64.

Weiser, M. (2010a). Sewage plant upgrade ordered. *Sacramento Bee*, 9 Dec.

Weiser, M. (2010b). State board wants Sacramento to reduce sewage in river. *Sacramento Bee*, 4 Sep.

Weiser, M. (2011a). Assembly OKs bill on sale of Sacramento's treated wastewater. *Sacramento Bee*, 26 May.

Weiser, M. (2011b). The "Big One" might be a flood. *Sacramento Bee*, 14 Jan.

WFN (noyr). Beef. Water Footprint Network website. Retrieved 8 Jan 2011 from http://www.waterfootprint.org/?page=files/productgallery&product=beef.

Whittington, D., Hanemann, W. M., Sadoff, C., and Jeuland, M. (2008). Sanitation and Water. In *Copenhagen Consensus 2008*. Environmental Assessment Institute, Copenhagen.

WHO (2008). *The Global Burden of Disease: 2004 Update*. World Health Organization, Geneva.

Williamson, O. E. (2000). The New Institutional Economics: Taking Stock, Looking Ahead. *Journal of Economic Literature*, 38(3):595–613.

Wilson, J. Q. (1989). *Bureaucracy: What Government Agencies Do and Why They Do It*. Basic Books, New York.

Wilson, J. Q. (1993). *The Moral Sense*. Free Press, New York.

Winpenny, J., Heinz, I., Koo-Oshima, S., Salgot, M., Collado, J., Hernandez, F., and Torricelli, R. (2010). The Wealth of Waste: The Economics of Wastewater Use in Agriculture. FAO Water Reports 35, FAO Land and Water Division, Rome.

Wolf, A. T. (1997). "Water Wars" and Water Reality: Conflict and Cooperation along International Waterways. In Lonergan, S., editor, *Environmental Change, Adaption, and Security*, pages 251–265. Kluwer, Boston.

Wolf, A. T. e. a. (noyr). The transboundary freshwater dispute database. The Program in Water Conflict Management and Transformation website. Retrieved 15 Apr 2011 from http://www.transboundarywaters.orst.edu/database/.

Workman, J. G. (2003). The Grapes of Mirth: Fresh Water Becomes Fresh Leverage Behind Race-Based Farmland Reform. *ICWA Letters*, JGW-13.

Workman, J. G. (2009). *Heart of Dryness: How the Last Bushmen Can Help Us Endure the Coming Age of Permanent Drought*. Walker & Company, New York.

World Bank (2010). Deep Wells and Prudence: Towards Pragmatic Action for Addressing Groundwater Overexploitation in India, The World Bank, Washington, DC.

Worthen, B. (2005). How Wal-Mart beat Feds to New Orleans. *CIO*, 1 Nov.

Xu, J. et al. (2010). Deaths: Final data for 2007. *National Vital Statistics Reports*, 58(19).

Yandle, B. (1983). Bootleggers and Baptists: The Education of a Regulatory Economist. *Regulation*, 7(3):12.

Yardas, D. and Kusel, J. (2006). The Local Entity 2003-2005: A Progress Report on Socioeconomic Mitigation Efforts Under the IID-SDCWA Water Conservation and Transfer Agreement, Environmental Justice Coalition for Water, Santa Monica.

Young, K. (2009). Agriculture census data now available by congressional district. USDA website. Retrieved 8 Feb 2011 from http://www.agcensus.usda.gov/Newsroom/2009/05_08_2009.asp.

Young, M. and McColl, J. (2006). Governance of Large Water Bodies. *Droplets*, 4.

Young, M. and McColl, J. (2007a). Irrigation Water: Use It or Lose It Because You Can't Save It! *Droplets*, 6.

Young, M. and McColl, J. (2007b). New Water for Old: Speeding up the Reform Process. *Droplets*, 9.

Young, M. and McColl, J. (2007c). Pricing Your Water: Is There a Smart Way to Do It? *Droplets*, 10.

Young, M. and McColl, J. (2007d). Urban Water Pricing: How Might an Urban Water Trading Scheme Work? *Droplets*, 5.

Young, M. and McColl, J. (2008a). A Sustainable Cap: What Might It Look Like? *Droplets*, 12.

Young, M. and McColl, J. (2008b). Yucky Business: Paying for What We Put Down the Drain. *Droplets*, 14.

Zaid, A. (2002). Date Palm Cultivation. FAO Plant Production and Protection Paper 156, Food and Agricultural Organization, Rome.

Zetland, D. (2008a). *Conflict and Cooperation Within an Organization: A Case Study of the Metropolitan Water District of Southern California.* PhD thesis, UC Davis (Agricultural and Resource Economics).

Zetland, D. (2008b). Cost and benefit of dams. Aguanomics blog. Retrieved 4 Feb 2011 from `http://www.aguanomics.com/2008/04/cost-and-benefit-of-dams.html`.

Zetland, D. (2008c). From farms to cities. Aguanomics blog. Retrieved 10 Jan 2011 from `http://www.aguanomics.com/2008/04/from-farms-to-cities.html`.

Zetland, D. (2008d). Household uses of water. Aguanomics blog. Retrieved 4 Feb 2011 from `http://www.aguanomics.com/2008/07/household-uses-of-water.html`.

Zetland, D. (2008e). How to manage a river. Aguanomics blog. Retrieved 8 Feb 2011 from `http://www.aguanomics.com/2008/04/how-to-manage-river.html`.

Zetland, D. (2008f). It's complicated. Aguanomics blog. Retrieved 25 Apr 2011 from `http://www.aguanomics.com/2008/09/its-complicated.html`.

Zetland, D. (2008g). Nestle blinks. Aguanomics blog. Retrieved 6 Jan 2011 from `http://www.aguanomics.com/2008/05/nestle-blinks.html`.

Zetland, D. (2008h). Reconsidering the Peripheral Canal. Aguanomics blog. Retrieved 4 Feb 2011 from `http://aguanomics.com/2008/12/reconsidering-peripheral-canal.html`.

Zetland, D. (2008i). Regional oped: nicely Nestle? *YubaNet*, 11 Apr.

Zetland, D. (2008j). Sustainable fisheries. Aguanomics blog. Retrieved 10 Jan 2011 from `http://www.aguanomics.com/2008/09/sustainable-fisheries.html`.

Zetland, D. (2008k). Vegas versus Imperial. Aguanomics blog. Retrieved 4 Feb 2011 from `http://www.aguanomics.com/2008/03/vegas-versus-imperial.html`.

Zetland, D. (2008l). Wateraid. Aguanomics blog. Retrieved 25 Apr 2011 from `http://www.aguanomics.com/2008/05/wateraid.html`.

Zetland, D. (2008m). Yes on the Peripheral Canal. Aguanomics blog. Retrieved 4 Feb 2011 from `http://www.aguanomics.com/2008/08/yes-on-peripheral-canal.html`.

Zetland, D. (2009a). Carbonated water. Aguanomics blog. Retrieved 3 Jan 2011 from `http://aguanomics.com/2009/09/carbonated-water.html`.

Zetland, D. (2009b). Engineers doing it right. Aguanomics blog. Retrieved 20 Feb 2011 from `http://www.aguanomics.com/2009/03/engineers-doing-it-right.html`.

Zetland, D. (2009c). Farmers don't use much water. Aguanomics blog. Retrieved 5 Jan 2011 from `http://www.aguanomics.com/2009/01/farmers-dont-use-much-water.html`.

Zetland, D. (2009d). Fixing monopolistic utilities. Aguanomics blog. Retrieved 31 Jan 2011 from `http://www.aguanomics.com/2009/01/fixing-monopolistic-utilities.html`.

Zetland, D. (2009e). Stockton update. Aguanomics blog. Retrieved 6 Jan 2011 from `http:`

//www.aguanomics.com/2009/06/stockton-update.html.

Zetland, D. (2009f). Sustainable tuna. Aguanomics blog. Retrieved 10 Jan 2011 from http://www.aguanomics.com/2009/05/sustainable-tuna.html.

Zetland, D. (2009g). The End of Abundance: How Water Bureaucrats Created and Destroyed the Southern California Oasis. *Water Alternatives*, 2(3):350–369.

Zetland, D. (2009h). Vegas hits the wall. Aguanomics blog. Retrieved 4 Feb 2011 from http://www.aguanomics.com/2009/03/vegas-hits-wall.html.

Zetland, D. (2009i). Water chats – Smith of PVID. Aguanomics blog. Retrieved 10 Jan 2011 from http://www.aguanomics.com/2009/03/water-chats-smith-of-pvid.html.

Zetland, D. (2009j). Water Reallocation in California: A Broken Hub Will Not Wheel. *Journal of Contemporary Water Research and Education*, 144:18–28.

Zetland, D. (2009k). What's happening in Copenhagen. Aguanomics blog. Retrieved 3 Mar 2011 from http://www.aguanomics.com/2009/12/whats-happening-in-copenhagen.html.

Zetland, D. (2010a). Floral externalities. Aguanomics blog. Retrieved 8 Feb 2011 from http://www.aguanomics.com/2010/04/floral-externalities.html.

Zetland, D. (2010b). Save the Poor, Shoot Some Bankers. *Public Choice*, 145:331–337. 10.1007/s11127-010-9708-4.

Zetland, D. (2010c). Self-interest and community. Aguanomics blog. Retrieved 8 Feb 2011 from http://www.aguanomics.com/2010/03/self-interest-and-community.html.

Zetland, D. (2010d). Water chat with Mike Young. Aguanomics blog. Retrieved 4 Feb 2011 from http://www.aguanomics.com/2010/03/water-chat-with-mike-young.html.

Zetland, D. (2011a). Getting water to the poor. Aguanomics blog. Retrieved 5 May 2011 from http://www.aguanomics.com/2011/04/getting-water-to-poor.html.

Zetland, D. (2011b). Utilities DO charge per person. Aguanomics blog. Retrieved 3 Mar 2011 from http://www.aguanomics.com/2011/02/utilities-do-charge-per-person.html.

Zetland, D., Russo, C., and Yavapolkul, N. (2010). Teaching Economic Principles: Algebra, Graph or Both? *The American Economist*, 55(1):123–131.

Zito, K. (2008). Golf courses try to play through drought. *San Francisco Chronicle*, 6 Aug.

Index

Made in the USA
Lexington, KY
07 March 2012